GRIM REAPER

Someone had to go back into the stagnant, hip-high water to search for the other two boys' bodies.

Officer Bryn Ridge volunteered. He stepped into the water several yards away from the place little Michael Moore's nude body was found, kicked his feet out behind him to assume a belly-down position, and reached down until he could feel the mushy bottom.

Slowly he started upstream, feeling for evidence in the muck with his hands. Piece by piece it came: a Cub Scout hat; three small pairs of pants; two shirts; a pair of child's underwear.

Then suddenly, he stopped. He felt something clammy pushed down hard into the mud. He took hold of it and carefully pulled the naked body of little Stevie Branch to the surface. The eight-year-old boy had been lying facedown at the bottom of the stream, hog-tied, his body brutally beaten, the left side of his face ripped open.

A few feet away, Ridge found Chris Byers. Like the others, his little body was naked, beaten, hog-tied. But when Ridge lifted him out of the water, he discovered an even greater horror.

Chris Byers had been viciously castrated as well.

BOOK YOUR PLACE ON OUR WEBSITE AND MAKE THE READING CONNECTION!

We've created a customized website just for our very special readers, where you can get the inside scoop on everything that's going on with Zebra, Pinnacle and Kensington books.

When you come online, you'll have the exciting opportunity to:

- View covers of upcoming books
- Read sample chapters
- Learn about our future publishing schedule (listed by publication month *and author*)
- Find out when your favorite authors will be visiting a city near you
- Search for and order backlist books from our online catalog
- Check out author bios and background information
- Send e-mail to your favorite authors
- Meet the Kensington staff online
- Join us in weekly chats with authors, readers and other guests
- Get writing guidelines
- AND MUCH MORE!

**Visit our website at
http://www.kensingtonbooks.com**

THE BLOOD OF INNOCENTS

GUY REEL
MARC PERRUSQUIA
BARTHOLOMEW SULLIVAN

PINNACLE BOOKS
KENSINGTON PUBLISHING CORP.

The names of some individuals in this true story have been changed to protect their privacy.

PINNACLE BOOKS are published by

Kensington Publishing Corp.
850 Third Avenue
New York, NY 10022

Copyright © 1995 by Guy Reel, Marc Perrusquia, and Bartholomew Sullivan

All rights reserved. No part of this book may be reproduced in any form or by any means without the prior written consent of the Publisher, excepting brief quotes used in reviews.

If you purchased this book without a cover, you should be aware that this book is stolen property. It was reported as "unsold and destroyed" to the Publisher and neither the Author nor the Publisher has received any payment for this "stripped book."

Pinnacle and the P logo Reg. U.S. Pat. & TM Off.

First Printing: September, 1995

Printed in the United States of America

10 9 8 7

Acknowledgments

The authors would like to acknowledge the cooperation and assistance of The Commercial Appeal, the circuit court clerks of Clay, Craighead, and Mississippi counties in Arkansas, defense attorney Daniel T. Stidham and circuit judge John N. Fogleman, and our literary agent, Janet Manus. Technical support was provided by Dewitt Reel.

For the life of the flesh is in the blood, and I have given it to you upon the altar to make atonement for your souls; for it is the blood that makes atonement for the soul.

Therefore I said to the children of Israel, "No one among you shall eat blood, nor shall any stranger who sojourns among you eat blood."

— Leviticus 17:11-12

Holy Michael, Archangel, defend us in the battle; be our protection against the wickedness and snares of the Devil. Rebuke him, O God, we humbly beseech thee, and do thou, O Prince of the heavenly host, by the power of God, thrust into hell Satan and the other evil spirits who wander through the world seeking the ruin of souls.

— An old Roman Catholic prayer

Preface

The evening light of the muggy May afternoon slowly softened over the neighborhood around Robin Hood Hills, where the shouts of children blended with the nearby whine of interstate traffic. A pearl-white full moon was about to rise.

It was May 5, 1993, a Wednesday night in West Memphis, Arkansas. It was church night and, out of respect, the Arkansas General Assembly had ordered that the local dog track be closed on both Wednesdays and Sundays. The usual flow of local traffic across the river from Memphis had abated for the day, but the eighteen-wheelers kept rolling. Interstate 40 was jammed with travelers and the huge truck stops and cheap motels were busy with the usual weary truckers and motorists crossing the Mississippi River at America's midsection.

On May 5, West Memphis's Holiday Gardens subdivision, shielded from the highway by a four-acre, creek-carved patch of woods, was abuzz with the typical activities of a late spring evening. In the neighborhood of modest homes and well-trimmed lawns just south of the woods, children were furiously completing their day's play. It was a neighborhood of families and dogs, filled with people tending gardens, working on their cars, or just socializing with neighbors.

Three eight-year-old boys were playing together that day, riding their bicycles and hanging out.

These neighborhood boys— Steve Branch, Christopher Byers, and James Michael Moore— were in the habit, as second-graders and Cub Scouts often are, of exploring their local woods. And Robin Hood Hills was a perfect escape. Boggy and bayoued and riddled with poison ivy, mosquitos, and snakes, it was just the place to have adventures.

They'd gotten out of Weaver Elementary School at 2:45 P.M. It took Michael less than a minute to walk home. His backyard backed up to the school yard. Christopher lived across the street from Michael; Stevie lived a few blocks away. They were close friends.

On their bikes that afternoon they cut across yards and around fire hydrants, and they sped into the woods.

Later, a man driving through the area told police he saw a fourth boy with them, another eight-year-old. The fourth boy would later say he saw what happened to his friends in the woods. He would emerge from the woods, but his friends would not.

The police file begun that day would eventually total thousands of pages containing photographs, depositions, false leads, interviews with psychics, claims of Satanism, macabre artwork, dark poetry, and even incantations for curing cramps or attracting a lover. It would lead to dozens of unanswered questions and would prompt speculation about a modern age of senseless violence, teenage alienation, and even the nature of good and evil.

Steve Branch, Chris Byers, and Michael Moore were all eight years old, all from working-class families, all still relatively carefree little boys. One was quiet but mischievous, another was a studious leader, another was fiercely playful and not always obedient.

Their story began with a bicycle ride and ended in the dank forest of Robin Hood Hills, just off the highway behind the Blue Beacon truck wash. It was there, neighbors later learned, that a day of child's play turned into a tale of torture, mutilation, and murder.

One

Speaking in Spanish

The tall, heavyset man stood over the cowering young boy and swung his leather belt. The stinging blow struck the child on his blue-jeaned buttocks, and he yowled.

John Mark Byers needed to show his stepson the consequences of riding a skateboard down the middle of the street. The belt cracked again as little Christopher hung on tight to the bar in the family living room. He hit him just twice, maybe three times, Byers would later tell the police, shaking his head to show his regret. If only he could take it back. A million times he'd take it back. But when he thought it over, he would console himself. There was no way he could have known then he'd never see Chris alive again.

Byers had caught his stepson rolling down Fourteenth Street, flat on his stomach, spread-eagle across the skateboard. It was no small matter either that Chris was riding south, straight into a mostly black neighborhood. That was open defiance of one of his stepdad's rules.

And when it came to race, Byers had very clear rules. A self-employed jeweler and pawn dealer with shoulder-length blond hair that he was fond of wearing in a ponytail, Byers was no more tolerant than the rural Arkansas Delta that had spawned him. He was a mix of seeming incongruities: A cigarette-smoking Baptist and gun-toting family man, both Freemason and free spirit. He had friends on the police force. Some folks might call him a "good ol' boy," albeit a fashionable one, in the style of a Duane Allman or some other great Southern rocker.

"I didn't want him riding his bike, skateboard, or anything, any direction down Fourteenth," Byers would explain. "And the reason for it was that there was so many black kids that walked this way."

Byers took no guff from his two stepsons. Still, eight-year-old Chris had been a lot of trouble.

First, there was the slingshot. Chris's errant missiles raised a furor, and his mother had to take the weapon from him and hide it. Chris played with matches, too. The previous fall, he had started a couple of small fires. Then came the muddy clothes and the evasive explanations.

As spring arrived, Chris began disappearing for a few hours at a time. He'd return a mess, mud caked on his shoes, socks, and pants. Carefully, he'd hide the soiled garments under his bed to escape his mother's wrath. But eventually she'd catch him and interrogate him. She suspected Chris was sneaking off to Robin Hood Hills. But when she confronted him, Chris would deny it.

Melissa Byers began to worry deeply about her son.

Frail from a premature birth, the sandy-haired boy had developed dark circles under his eyes. Mrs. Byers couldn't lay her finger on the problem, but she became worried that someone could have been molesting her boy. She consulted the guidance counselor at Chris's school. She even sat Chris down and asked him point-blank, "Has anyone touched you?"

No, Chris answered, no one.

Chris was diagnosed as hyperactive. At times, his condition could tickle his parents. Chris could never stay still for long, and he squirmed around like a worm. That earned Chris an affectionate nickname: "Wormer"—"the Worm" for short. Chris kept his parents busy, always chatting, always asking a thousand questions, always asking why. Sometimes it was hard to listen to him.

One day about three months before the skateboard incident, Chris ran up to his mom with some news. A strange man dressed in black had pulled into the driveway in a green car, then popped out of the car door with a camera in his hand. The man snapped a photograph of Chris as he stood in the yard. Chris ran into the house, and the man quickly drove off. Melissa Byers didn't think much of Chris's tale at the time, but the image would haunt her for months. The strange man, dressed entirely in black. Black hair. Black coat. Black shirt. Black pants and shoes. At the time, she shrugged it off as perhaps someone from the mortgage company checking the condition of the house. Besides, her son was always up to something.

The boy's high energy often led to spankings such as the one this day, his six-foot-five stepdad hulking over him, long hair flopping as he laid down the law. Byers was annoyed by his stepson's disregard for his orders. He needed to get his message across. *Don't ride your skateboard down the middle of the street. Don't go where the black kids are. If you want to play, go north toward Goodwin Street.*

When the whipping was over, Byers ordered Chris outside to pick up litter in the yard.

Byers had a lot on his mind. He'd recently declared bankruptcy, and he was fighting to hold on to the middle-class lifestyle he'd carved out for his wife and her two sons, Chris and Ryan, age fourteen. He'd lost his pawnshop. He blamed that on a shady business partner. Now his health was failing, too. At thirty-six, he suffered curious dizzy spells, even blacking out at times.

Despite their struggles, they lived well. Their house, a comfortable two-story home with three bathrooms and an in-ground swimming pool, sat on a large corner lot kept trimmed by a John Deere riding lawn mower. They'd moved in four years earlier, buying the house for a good price in this pocket of well-kept homes surrounded by the rough-and-tumble neighborhoods that dot the east side of West Memphis, Arkansas.

Friendly and outgoing, he and his wife threw large pool parties and barbecues that often churned late into the night. The music was loud, and their guests didn't always have room to park on the street, at times pulling their cars onto a neighbor's yard, stirring disharmony in the community.

The flow of people in and out of the Byers home was a curious sight. Many guests were lawmen. Police, sheriff's deputies, and law-enforcement officers from around the area counted Byers as a friend. Other guests looked more like Byers— long-haired men with tattoos and weathered faces. Everyone agreed that Byers knew how to host great parties.

Byers walked out to the carport and watched Chris pick up bits of litter. The large man's temper had cooled, but he remained stern. Walking to his car, he told Chris he'd better still be here working when he returned. Byers had an errand to run.

It was May 5, 1993, and Byers was headed to a

THE BLOOD OF INNOCENTS

court appointment. His other stepson, Ryan, was testifying as a witness in a hit-and-run case.

As Byers sped off to pick up Ryan, Chris remained in the carport, doing his work. The sun was tilting toward the horizon, but the late afternoon remained warm and sticky. In a while, Christopher came back inside to ask his mother for a snack and a drink. She obliged. It was easy to forgive her shy, inquisitive son, who could crawl into anyone's lap and melt his heart.

It was nearly 6 P.M.

West Memphis hugs the Mississippi River across from Memphis, Tennessee, a relationship that has always defined the small east Arkansas city as little more than a rest stop along the way to someplace else. The Mississippi flows a mile wide past downtown Memphis before taking one of hundreds of meandering jogs on its way south to New Orleans. On one side stands the Memphis skyline, its skyscrapers and distinctive Pyramid basketball arena rising from the bluffs on the river's east bank. On the other there is no apparent development, just wild woods and the flat, broad cotton fields stretching for miles into Arkansas. Almost invisible, the city of West Memphis is a little downstream.

The river has been both a blessing and a curse to West Memphis. Flooding was so frequent, so devastating in the past century that the original city was uprooted and moved back behind a levee, a fortified wall of earth. The city of 28,258— ninth largest in Arkansas— is by far the biggest in rural Crittenden County, a 599-square-mile section of river bottomland. Layered in thick, rich alluvium deposits, the result of thousands of years of flooding, the Delta soil is among the most fertile farmland on Earth.

In Mark Twain's day, Crittenden County provided a mental warning post for riverboat pilots respectful of the power of the mighty Mississippi. Here, the Devil's Elbow, a notoriously violent bend in the river, claimed many a vessel. And it was here in 1865 that more than 1,600 men perished in the greatest maritime disaster in United States history when the riverboat *Sultana* sank while carrying just-released Yankee prisoners of war upstream from Vicksburg to freedom.

Today, Devil's Elbow is dead, cut off from the channel. The shifting river found new paths over its years of flooding, leaving remnants of itself— oxbow lakes— along the way. Now, a sturdy levee system and management by the U.S. Army Corps of Engineers has stifled the flooding and shifting currents.

These days a new river flows through West Memphis, one of concrete and asphalt, securing the city's reputation as a way station.

Motorists know, and typically forget, West Memphis as the confluence of Interstates 40 and 55, which merge for about seven miles here, then split again at the river. Sweeping south from St. Louis, I-55 breaks east at West Memphis, crosses the river into Memphis, then turns south again through Mississippi on the way to New Orleans. Originating near Los Angeles in the west, I-40 makes a straight shot east across the lower plains of Oklahoma, passing through Little Rock and then West Memphis before crossing the Mississippi River, rounding downtown Memphis, and shooting east on its long, hilly trek toward Nashville, Raleigh, and the East Coast.

Interstate travelers usually stop in West Memphis only to get gas or to buy a sandwich in a plastic box.

The city has become an oasis for long-haul truckers, with several freight terminals and two massive truck-stop complexes catering to their needs. The ribbons of highway envisioned by President Eisenhower in the 1950s have had a phenomenal impact on West Memphis. For one, the interstate helped fuel rampant growth. The city's population has more than tripled since 1950, when it had just 9,112 residents. But with the growth, troubles have come. Memphis and West Memphis trumpet their claim as America's distribution center, a title tied to the shipment of Nike tennis shoes, food products, and Federal Express overnight packages, yet it may apply just as appropriately to the underworld trade of drugs, child pornography, and prostitution.

The deals that go down in motel rooms along the interstate in West Memphis are the subject of widespread gossip and local legend, but you won't find them advertised in Chamber of Commerce brochures.

West Memphis's growth also has been fueled by the general prosperity of Memphis, a link that has long been the East Arkansas city's lifeline. In the very early 1920s the still-unincorporated settlement had just a few hundred residents who received mail at a post office called Hopefield. The community incorporated in 1923 and took the name West Memphis, supposedly at the urging of local lumber mill owner Zachary Taylor Bragg, who figured he could sell his products at a higher price if he had the name Memphis listed as the source.

Today, West Memphis and adjacent Marion, the Crittenden County seat, have in part become bedroom communities for professionals and others who live there but work in Memphis. Enjoying inexpensive housing and a lower cost of living, West Memphis commuters face a quick ten-minute jaunt to downtown Memphis.

People in Crittenden County shop in Memphis, visit doctors in its huge complex of teaching hospitals and medical centers, and head for evenings out at sporting events, movie theaters (there are none in West Memphis), or music venues, like those on world-renowned Beale Street, the home of the blues. Memphis, by far the largest city in the region, has a strange, attractive quality of disappointment about it. It is a vibrant place of contrasts, with neighborhoods of stately mansions and dilapidated public housing projects, fine restaurants and hole-in-the-wall barbecue joints. H.L. Mencken called Memphis the "buckle" of the Bible Belt, and the city remains a center of staunch conservatism, despite recent efforts to redefine itself.

Tennessee's largest city, Memphis is a place of escape and opportunity, home to FedEx and a regional hub for Northwest Airlines. Yet it still plays second fiddle to Nashville, the state's geographic heart, political center, and country-music mecca. Memphis has long attempted to declare itself a major city, vying in vain for a National Football League franchise, courting industries that never came, even changing the name of the local college from Memphis State University to the more important-sounding University of Memphis. But in the end, it has been the world that has defined Memphis.

Thousands still return each year to pay their respects to Elvis, the King of rock 'n' roll, who remained largely unaccepted by city leaders until he died in 1977 at his beloved Graceland mansion.

While Graceland has become a symbol of hero worship and decadent opulence, another city landmark, the Lorraine Motel, stands as a mournful icon of the Civil Rights movement. It was there, in the city's definitive moment of disgrace, that the Reverend Martin Luther King, Jr., was shot through the tie knot by an assassin in April 1968. King had come to Memphis amid open hatred and ridicule to help in a garbage workers' strike against City Hall, and many people believe the local white power structure had a hand in the Civil Rights leader's murder.

But times change, even in Memphis. The Lorraine Motel, once a second-rate downtown inn, is now the National Civil Rights Museum, a first-rate interpretative center in the heart of downtown regentrification. Tourism can be a healing salve. The city that once worked so hard to hide and deny its African American heritage now celebrates it. It built a shrine to the man it once vilified. It promotes Beale Street, once the city's black Main Street. Finally, in death, it has embraced Elvis, who borrowed the black man's music and gave it to the world.

And in 1991, Memphis elected its first black mayor.

A trip across the river into Crittenden County, in a way, is like a trip back in time. There are two bridges, the Hernando DeSoto, which is modern and expansive with a sweeping M-shaped steel support structure towering above; and an older one, the "Mississippi bridge," as Chuck Berry called it in his composition "Memphis," the song popularized by rockabilly singer Johnny Rivers in 1964. Opened in 1949, the Memphis-Arkansas Bridge consists of a flat, dull-silver overhead support structure and a narrow span with four cramped lanes carrying Interstate 55 traffic. The bridge's eastern abutment sits high along the bluffs in south Memphis, then descends across the river onto the low, flat bottomland in Arkansas.

Three miles to the west, an I-55 exit leads onto

Broadway Boulevard, the main drag running seven miles through the length of West Memphis. Once proclaimed one of the longest main streets in America, Broadway was a dirt road as late as 1920 when it was known as the Broadway Trail.

Today, Broadway slices a cross section of life in West Memphis, where Old South and New South coincide, each oblivious to the other, both thriving.

East Broadway starts as a wide, curbless four-lane street lined with boarded-up gas stations and vacant motels, dark taverns, car dealerships, mobile-home parks, auto repair shops, and trash-strewn open lots, leading down to the city's core, with its pawn and resale shops, convenience stores, and hole-in-the-wall restaurants offering chitlin plates or hot tamales, a Delta delicacy. There is a feel of grunginess here in West Memphis, the feel of a working-class city fallen on hard times. The city fathers threw some money at the problem a few years back by installing some decorative streetlamps, angled parking spaces, flowered landscaping and transplanted trees for a couple blocks at the core of downtown. Decorative lights hung in the trees all year round.

The interstates accelerated downtown's decay, stealing business with fast-food restaurants, new motels, gas stations, and a small shopping mall. But Broadway remains at the town's heart, stretching past the city government offices, banks, and tidy retail shops on the city's west end, where a sign outside West Memphis High School honors boys' state basketball championships in 1980 and 1991, proudly proclaiming the school Home of the Blue Devils.

The city's west side is a part of town travelers rarely see. There, mostly clustered in all-white communities, lie stately homes on sprawling estates and tidy, well-kept middle-class neighborhoods with a feel of suburbia about them. The contrast between east and west is sharp and clear. Out here on the west side are the main public library, the municipal airport, and the exclusive Meadowbrook Country Club, with an eighteen-hole golf course, swimming pool, and tennis courts.

Unlike Memphis, which is majority black, Crittenden County is majority white, and blacks hold few positions of power.

A subordinate caste of blacks and whites remains entrenched here, fifty years after the dissolution of the sharecropper system. Because of mechanization and migration to urban areas, less than five percent of the county's residents still find jobs in farming, and more than a fourth of the residents live in poverty. Many poor whites congregate in trailer parks north of town and on West Memphis's east side. Like a slice of Appalachia, alcoholism and indifference to education often pose problems in these communities. West Memphis always has been a rough place, sprouting gambling dens and illegal betting tracks years back, when one strip through the black community on the city's south side became known as "Little Chicago," rivaling Beale Street for its wild nightlife. But on Tuesdays, there is a night curfew for minors that is strictly enforced.

It was in this world of black and white, rich and poor, have and have not, where little Christopher Byers and his two classmates started growing up.

And it was here that the families of these three boys struggled.

The Moores lived across the street from Christopher and his family on another spacious corner lot. The family owned a handsome white two-story house with green shutters, a two-car garage and a privacy fence around the backyard. Todd Moore was a truck driver and leader of a Cub Scout pack. His wife, Diane, tended house. The Moores were conservative and reserved, and they kept mostly to themselves. They didn't particularly care for Mark and Melissa Byers. Those loud parties, with the guests parking on the grass, had put a deep wedge between the two clans.

Down the street, ice cream delivery man Terry Hobbs lived with his wife, Pam, in a comfortable ranch house. Pam worked evenings as a waitress to make ends meet. Pam's ex-husband had been convicted of armed robbery, and the couple had endured a rocky marriage until it finally ended. After Pam met Terry, she got back on her feet. They were trying to make it.

While the adults weren't close, the boys of these three families were fast friends.

Steve Branch, Pam Hobbs's son, liked to pretend he was a Teenage Mutant Ninja Turtle. Friends and family smiled and held their breath as little Stevie flipped forward and backward and karate-kicked until he fell down exhausted. Stevie loved to sing, and his mother called him her little Elvis. But to his four-year-old sister, Amanda, Stevie was simply "Bubba," the best big brother a girl could hope for. Their house had log reindeer in the front yard and Stevie's chow, King, in the back. Stevie had his mom's blond hair, which bleached nearly white in the summer. His eyes were crystal blue. For a kid, he was built pretty solid. Already, he was a ladies' man. He was "courting" a pal's ten-year-old sister, an older woman, his stepdad joked. To prove his love, Stevie had bought her a birthstone ring at Wal-Mart.

Michael Moore was the leader, the popular one. He was the sheriff. Sheriff Mike. He had a little

THE BLOOD OF INNOCENTS

badge to prove it, one his dad had bought for him. Michael worked hard to please his daddy. He was a Cub Scout in Todd Moore's pack. Michael played T-ball, too. His dad took his picture, a photo of Michael at bat, and the boy proudly carried it in his little billfold. Michael was a cute kid, with mischievous blue eyes and dark hair.

He was fascinated with gadgets. One of his teachers recalled he constantly smuggled his treasures to school— video game controls, flashlights, pocket knives, and "other little distractors" that she would confiscate and return at the end of the day. Michael wasn't known as a troublemaker, but he was known to make trouble at times. One day after school, he and Chris Byers rooted through the dumpster behind Weaver Elementary School, throwing trash onto the school playground. The janitor threatened to call the police until the youngsters courteously put the garbage back. They then resumed what they did best— riding their bikes in wide loops around the playground.

The boys were in second grade together, and they were in the same Cub Scout pack at Holy Cross Episcopal Church. All had passed the rank of Wolf Cub.

Pam Hobbs took Stevie out of school early that day, that last day. She had a lot to do. Stevie and Amanda grew anxious as their mother raced through household chores, then on the run, slipped on her blue-and-white waitress outfit. Mrs. Hobbs would be working the evening shift down at Catfish Island, a family-owned restaurant along the interstate. Her husband, Terry, wasn't due home yet for another hour.

Suddenly, little Michael Moore was there at the door. "Can Stevie come out and play?" he asked in his soft, polite voice. Pam Hobbs frowned. She didn't need this now. But Michael persisted. "We'll just be gone an hour," he pleaded. Michael was on his green bike, Pam would recall later. And there sat poor Stevie, so eager to hop on his spanking new red Renegade dirt bike that his grandad had just bought him. She gave in.

"Okay, just for an hour." But she warned him, "If you're not home by four-thirty, you'll be grounded."

Down the street, Michael and Stevie found Chris outside his house where his stepdad had left him. Suddenly, Chris forgot about the earlier backside admonition. Several neighbors recalled seeing two bikes heading north up Fourteenth Street, Michael on one, Chris riding double on the back with Steve. At least Chris was obeying half of his stepdad's orders: He wasn't going south down Fourteenth Street.

They seemed to be heading up to Robin Hood Hills, the woods along the interstate. Chris's mother didn't want him in the woods, and for good reason. Drifters from the interstate often were spotted there, and it was widely rumored that drug deals went down there. The Blue Beacon, a truck wash on the interstate service road, bordered the woods on the north. On the other side sat the Mayfair Apartments, a rough, low-income housing development.

But the boys were in the habit of going into the woods and setting up fort there. It was simply too much to resist. Unlike the surrounding flat landscape, the area had deep ravines, one called the Devil's Den, and bushy knolls, such as Turtle Hill. A murky stream called Ten-Mile Bayou ran down the center, and cottonwood puffs hung in the air.

There was plenty of legend here. Some kids claimed an ax-murderer lived in the woods. But Michael, Steve, and Chris had their own fascination. On at least two or three occasions, a playmate would later claim, the boys had hidden while strange men with painted faces sat in a circle and recited incantations in what the boys took for Spanish. They smoked funny-smelling cigarettes and did "nasty" things with their bodies. Neighbors would later report that a satanic cult met in the patch of boggy woods. One couple whose house backed up to the woods once came home to see their water bed in tatters and their dog slaughtered on the floor.

Robin Hood provided a world of fascination and wonder, an escape from school and discipline, punishment at the hands of stepfathers, and the hard intolerance that permeates West Memphis.

Aaron Hutcheson was another eight-year-old boy, another Weaver Elementary School second-grader. He had only recently left his friends' more comfortable neighborhood, moving into one of those gloomy trailer parks not far away. When school let out that day, Michael and Chris had begged Aaron to come along with them.

Aaron's mother told the boy's friends no, he wouldn't be able to go. But later— Aaron would tell many different stories about what happened that day— he would say that he did in fact find them and accompany them into the woods.

Robin Hood Hills was ringing with the laughter of at least three men— two drinking beer, one well into a pint of cheap bourbon— as the boys walked their bikes along a narrow trail in the underbrush. The giant trees hung over them, hiding the sky. It was growing dark.

Aaron said he climbed a tree and was in a tree house when something happened. There was a boy struggling. Shouting and crying. The thud of fists. This wasn't play.

Out on the interstate, the traffic roared by, drowning out the screams.

Two

"Help me look for my boy."

John Mark Byers returned with his stepson Ryan about 6:30 that evening, swinging his dull-silver 1985 Isuzu into the driveway and under the carport.

Chris wasn't there, despite his stepdad's orders. Byers's temper flipped on. Once again, Chris was in trouble.

Byers went inside and asked his wife where her son was. Melissa Byers, on the phone with a friend, said Chris had been in and out a couple times, but she hadn't seen him for a while.

Byers went out to the backyard. He looked around the pool area, then poked his head over the six-foot wood privacy fence and yelled into a neighbor's yard. There was no answer. Byers told Ryan to get on his skateboard and check with some neighbor girls down the street, but the teen returned without his brother.

Now Byers was genuinely upset. The family was supposed to eat at a nearby Shoney's, but Chris was spoiling the plans. Byers summoned Melissa and Ryan into the Isuzu, and they began driving around. They rode eight blocks east down Barton Avenue, past the familiar mix of clipped and overgrown lawns and repetitious brick facades decorating house after house. All heads turned left when they stopped at the intersection of Ingram Boulevard, looking toward the Flash Market convenience store, where little Chris often bought soda and candy, and the adjacent laundry where the family washed clothes. They gazed across the street toward a school playground.

There was no sign of the boy.

The family swung north toward the interstate, looping west down Goodwin Avenue, past the entrances to Robin Hood Hills, where neighbors later said they had last seen the boys heading into the thick underbrush. But the Byerses saw nothing. They turned south again, going another mile down to Broadway Boulevard, the city's decaying central business district.

By now it was 7:30 P.M. The sun hung low in the sky. The Byerses had been looking for an hour, circling the neighborhood in a wide loop of some four or five miles. Frustrated, Byers turned into the lot at the General Dollar Store, and pulled up alongside a parked police car to ask for help.

"Why don't you give it till around eight o'clock?" the cop said. "If you don't find him, call the police station."

The family headed for home, scouting the neighborhood along the way. Children completed their play as overhead streetlights began warming up, flickering dimly. Slowly, the sun slipped below the horizon at eleven minutes before eight. Shadows deepened. Children left the streets. Byers was angry—and worried, too.

Once home, he made the first of several phone calls to the Crittenden County Sheriff's Office. Mark and Melissa had not seen their son for two and a half hours. That was reason for concern, no question, but John Mark Byers seemed to sense something ominous. He demanded police action. Two weeks later he would tell police detectives he called the sheriff's office early that night because he knew the county had a search-and-rescue squad that could help find the boys.

"I was starting to get, you know, worried 'cause my son has never gone off anywhere," he said.

But the calls didn't do much good, and later, there would be threats of a lawsuit over the slow police action. A sheriff's deputy on the other end of the line told Byers to call West Memphis police—it was the city's jurisdiction, not the county sheriff's. Byers hung up and placed the call.

A few minutes later, West Memphis patrolman Regina Meek knocked at the front door. Meek, a heavyset, businesslike officer, pulled out a pen and started taking a report.

Christopher Byers. Four feet four inches tall. Fifty pounds. Light brown hair, brown eyes. Last seen about 5:30 P.M. cleaning the yard. He was wearing blue jeans, dark shoes, and a white, long-sleeve shirt. "The victim is on Ritalin for hyperactivity, but on this date has not taken his medication," the report noted.

As Meek turned to leave, there was another knock on the door. It was Diane Moore, Michael's mom from across the street.

"Have y'all found Christopher?" she asked. The question took them by surprise. How would she know Chris was missing? The two families were neighbors, but they were not close. Todd Moore, Diane's husband, had called the police on more than one occasion when the pool party guests parked on their lawn.

But Byers had a different explanation for the feuding. He claimed to police that he stopped inviting the Moores because they just didn't fit in with the rest of the guests.

Mrs. Moore explained that she had been walking her dog around the block and had seen Michael and Steve Branch riding their bicycles together. Christopher was riding double on the back of Steve's bike, she said. Diane Moore, a short, pale woman with long, wavy reddish-orange hair— a petite woman quite in contrast to the towering Byers— pointed down the street. She said it looked like Chris's skateboard was lying there. Byers walked down to check it out. Sure enough, it was Chris's board.

"That's the first time that my wife and I knew that he was with anybody else," Byers later told detectives. "We figured he was just alone."

Now Officer Meek was taking a second report. Michael Moore, four feet tall, sixty pounds. Brown hair. Blue eyes. He was last seen wearing blue pants, a blue Cub Scouts of America shirt, a Cub Scout hat, and tennis shoes.

"Complainant stated she observed the victim (her son) riding bicycles with his friends, Steve Branch and Christopher Byers. When she lost sight of them, she sent her daughter to find them. The boys could not be found," the report said.

That image would later haunt the Moores. Diane Moore would describe in great detail how her ten-year-old daughter Dawn ran down the street to call Michael home for supper, spotting him and his friends a couple blocks away. But when Dawn yelled at Michael to come home, he had slipped out of earshot, then from sight. Michael often would venture through the neighborhood, but, under orders from his mom, he generally came home before the streetlights turned on for the night.

Diane Moore and Mark and Melissa Byers were alarmed but pacified by the belief that Chris, Michael, and Steve had just sneaked off for some fun.

"We're thinking, well, they're around the neighborhood here," Byers said. "All three of them together."

Soon, under the full moon, small search parties began to mobilize throughout the neighborhood.

The search had quickly converged on Robin Hood. There had been plenty of places to look— the schoolgrounds near Michael's house, a creek behind Steve Branch's home, the railroad tracks that ran through wooded areas throughout town. But Robin Hood, just a half-mile north of the corner where Chris and Michael lived, was an obvious hiding place.

It became even more obvious when, after Diane Moore had pointed out Chris's skateboard in the street, Byers said he and other family members began going door-to-door to question neighbors. Several doors down, a boy and girl said they had seen Chris, Michael, and Steve about 6:30 P.M. as the boys were going into the woods near Fourteenth Street. One witness later testified he saw four boys— not three— entering the woods there.

For neighborhood kids like twelve-year-old Brit Smith, Robin Hood was the natural place to look. When his friend Ryan Clark called about 8:30 P.M. and said his brother and his friends were missing, Brit and some other boys immediately headed for the woods. Kids on bikes in this part of town usually meant one thing: a trip to Robin Hood to test the steep inclines and meandering dirt trails. There they would zip under the dense canopies of cottonwood, elm, and maple, past wild berries and patches of bramble.

Brit rode over to the area with an older friend, Robbie Young, and his older sister's boyfriend, Ritchey Masters.

Ritchey, Robbie, and Brit shared a mixed sense of nostalgia and respect for the woods. There was the "halfpipe"—two steep hills side by side near the center of the woods where kids on bicycles built up speed before dropping suddenly downward, then up, soaring in outrageous stunts. There also was the tale of One-Eyed Pete, an ax-wielding man who supposedly lived in the woods. Ritchey and Robbie started the story of One-Eyed Pete, but many children believed it: Bums and drifters from the interstate were commonly spotted in Robin Hood. That night, as Ritchey and Brit pulled onto the dead-end of Fourteenth Street—a short patch of asphalt north of Goodwin that local kids considered the main entrance to Robin Hood—all these myths and legends lay in the backs of their minds. Before them was the viny underbrush, under the yellowish glow of the full moon.

Other searchers soon showed up. Byers arrived with Ryan. Ritchey and Robbie told Brit to wait in the car until his mother arrived, then the older pair started walking down a trail into the woods. But Brit got out of the car anyway.

Byers, dressed in shorts and flip-flops and unprepared for a search of deep woods, left for home to change. Terry Hobbs, Steve Branch's stepfather, decided to look on the west edge of the undergrowth.

Not wanting to be left out, Brit and Ryan walked

into the woods, making their way through the darkness to the drainage canal called Ten-Mile Bayou. On pleasant afternoons they had fished here for gar, crappie, and brim. Now on the brushy bank, they could hardly see their hands before their faces. It had rained several days the week before and again over the weekend, and the ground was boggy and thick with mud. It was hot, the temperature in the eighties, the mosquitos thick. Brit tried to navigate with a flashlight. He was shining it through the blackness when he and Ryan spotted a familiar landmark, a tree with a rope hanging from a limb where kids often played. The two boys stood on the bank atop two broken concrete slabs for several minutes, shouting Chris's name into the woods.

A loud splash crashed in the water below them.

Brit, darting his dark eyes about, thought it sounded like someone had thrown a big slab of rock into the water. Ryan later likened the splashing to the sounds of someone wrestling in the water. Startled, the boys cried louder for Chris. There was another splash.

"Chris, if that's you, it's not a funny game," Ryan called out into the dark. Ryan and Brit kept silent and still, so tense they could hear themselves breathing.

Then came another loud splash. This time Brit, dipping his flashlight, could see waves rippling toward the bank.

"Chris! Chris!" they yelled again. But now they were truly frightened.

"If there's another splash, let's turn around and start walking out of here," Ryan told Brit, "and when we get across this little ditch, start running."

Another forceful splash crashed below them. This time, the boys turned and walked away. According to plan, they took off running. They raced out of the woods, through stickers, briers and vines, out onto Goodwin, covering a half-mile before they finally stopped. There, they met up with another party of searchers on the west edge of the woods.

Trouble, it seemed, was breaking out all over.

At 8:42 P.M., police received a call from the Bojangles fast-food chicken house at 1551 North Missouri Street. A black man, apparently dazed and covered in blood and mud, had staggered into the restaurant. He went into the ladies' rest room, where he stayed the better part of an hour as the evening-shift workers prepared to close down for the night. The man had blood on his face and blood dripping from his forearm, and, generally, was "disarrayed," the youngish restaurant manager Marty King recalled. Wearing a blue nylon jogging suit and a cast on one arm, he also had thick mud caked on his shoes, "like he'd been through a field," King said. Water was soaked into his pants up to his knees.

King grew concerned as the man stayed in the rest room about thirty to forty-five minutes. At one point, King poked his head in the door. Excrement covered the floor, and it was on the man, too. The man, propping himself up, had also smeared blood on the walls.

King asked if he was all right.

"Yeah," he grunted.

When he finally walked out, he left a pair of sunglasses in the toilet bowl.

King watched as the man, about five-feet nine and 180 pounds, stumbled toward the back parking lot, reversed himself, then headed south down Missouri Street, out of sight.

Officer Meek arrived a few minutes after King's call to police. She pulled her cruiser up to the drive-through window and asked what the problem was. King told her the man had left. Meek didn't hang around. She had just received another call; someone had egged a house. She never got out of her car.

After Meek left Bojangles, restaurant employees mopped up the bathroom.

King found the incident chilling. From the site where the boys were found, Bojangles was less than a mile west along Ten-Mile Bayou, the main storm drain for West Memphis. King later said of the bloodied man, "The next day, when you find out the boys had been murdered, it's kind of eerie."

Over at Catfish Island, Pam Hobbs was clearing tables when her husband Terry pulled up. Pam still had little idea what was going on. She had bought two twenty-five-cent sourballs— one for daughter Amanda, and one for little Stevie.

"Where's Stevie?" Pam asked as she walked out to the waiting car.

"We can't find him, Momma," little Amanda answered.

Terry explained what was going on. Pam felt a shudder go through her. At times like these, she was a pessimist. Her mind jumped ahead. *He's dead. I'll never see him again,* she thought. No one worries like a worried mother. Already, the words were haunting her: *We'll only be gone an hour. Just an hour.*

The Hobbses called the police and made it official: Stevie was missing. There, at Catfish Island, officers took a third report: Steve Branch. Four feet two inches tall. Sixty pounds. Blond hair and blue eyes. He was last seen wearing blue jeans and a white T-shirt. He was riding his new Renegade bicycle.

Back in the woods, it was Ritchey Masters's turn for a scare. After leaving Brit, Ritchey and Robert Young started walking the winding trails. Armed with flashlights, they followed what they believed to be the tracks of two bicycles in the mud. Suddenly the tracks stopped—and there was nothing.

Ricthey and Robert continued on, walking deeper into the woods. They heard a sharp crack, what sounded like a shot from a small-caliber gun. They paused. It could have been a car backfiring, they thought. They were near enough to the interstate to hear it.

On they went, through stickers and bramble patches, down a deep gully and back up a hill. They came to a fat steel sewage pipe that juts out of a steep bank on one side of Ten-Mile Bayou and enters the bank on the other side, spanning the broad drainage creek like a footbridge. In fact, the pipe and two accompanying iron side rails are used as a bridge by workers who live in the residential area south of Robin Hood but earn a living at the truck washes, convenience stores, and truck stops along the interstate. It's also a bridge for the more gutsy bikers willing to risk a ten-foot fall into Ten-Mile Bayou.

Ritchey and Robbie walked halfway across the pipe, suspiciously shining their flashlights into the murky water below. They crossed, then followed a trail through tall weeds on the drainage ditch's north bank, calling for Chris again. They were starting to get spooked.

"We need to turn around and get out of here," Robert told Ritchey.

The telephone rang about 9:30 that night at Narlene Hollingsworth's trailer home north of town.

Dixie Hubbard, a distant relative by marriage, needed a ride home from work. Narlene was happy to oblige. But she'd already had a fender bender earlier that day, and a bit shaky, she wasn't about to travel alone. Her husband, Ricky, two sons, two daughters, and a family friend all piled into her 1982 red Ford Escort station wagon and Narlene spun off down a gravel road in the Lakeshore Estates trailer park.

Their destination was four miles ahead at the Flash Market laundry at the corner of Barton and Ingram, the one the Byers clan had passed three hours earlier. Dixie manned the laundry desk there from two to ten P.M. Tonight she had no way home until Narlene had volunteered to come get her. It was a trip Narlene Virginia Hollingsworth would not forget.

At forty-two, Narlene, a tiny brunette, had lived most of her life in rural Arkansas. Born thirty miles up the Delta in Joiner, she dropped out of school in the eighth grade, married young, and when that marriage failed, wed her ex-husband's brother, Ricky.

But things never were smooth for her and her family. For instance, her son, Anthony, had been convicted of carnal knowledge with an underage girl. But if Narlene ever dreamed of escape through adventure and public attention, her chance was about to come as she and her tribe sputtered down the service road along the interstate.

Two shadowy figures appeared on the south shoulder of the access road ahead, walking toward the Hollingsworth car. They looked familiar. The pair was walking away from Robin Hood Hills, some five hundred yards to the east. As they neared, Narlene flashed her headlights to high beam.

It was Damien Echols, a quiet teenage boy from a trailer park on the east side of West Memphis, who spent much of his time at Lakeshore. As usual, he was dressed head-to-toe in black. Walking beside him was his pregnant red-haired girlfriend, Domini Teer, age sixteen.

"They were dirty and muddy," Narlene later said in a statement to police. As the car passed, Domini grabbed a yellow road construction sign jutting from a plastic barrel and pointed it toward the Hollingsworths. Narlene turned to her husband sitting next to her and asked him why Damien and Domini were out so late. Ricky told her to stop worrying, those two were out walking all the time.

When the Hollingsworths arrived at the laundry, Narlene eagerly told Dixie about seeing the two teens on the road. But Dixie had her own story to tell. Narlene's seventeen-year-old nephew, L.G. Hollingsworth, had just stopped by the laundry in a strange car. Over the next several days, the two women would repeatedly hash over what they had seen that night, as word leaked out to neighbors and friends about events in the woods. L.G., who ran in the same circle with Damien and Domini, was washing muddy clothes that night in the laundry, one tipster would tell police.

Near the sewage pipe over Ten-Mile Bayou, Ritchey and Robbie finally met up again with Brit and Ryan. Had they heard the gunshot? the older boys asked. What about the eerie splashing? asked the younger boys. By now, several neighbors and police had joined the search. A gathering of people had congregated by the Mayfair Apartments. Officer Meek was there for a moment. She walked over the pipe and into the woods, but quickly retreated. The mosquitos were so thick, she was "breathing them in," she later remarked. The boys wouldn't have gone in here to play, she thought.

Accompanied by the two younger boys, Ritchey and Robert decided to go back into the woods. A little spooked, they told Brit and Ryan to follow closely behind, so each would know where the others were. They crossed the pipe again, and entered the woods. This time, it was uneventful. Finding nothing, they left, going back to Brit's house.

It was 10:35 P.M.

After changing clothes, John Mark Byers came back to Robin Hood wearing bib coveralls and boots. He had his long blond hair tied back into a ponytail. Byers reentered the woods at the dead end of Fourteenth Street, where Brit and the others had gone in. He was in the woods until well past midnight, he later told police. Byers started in alone, walking deep into a gully, but the darkness drove him back in search of a flashlight. Climbing back into his Isuzu, Byers was backing off the dead end when a police car pulled up. It was Patrolman John Moore.

"Did you find anything?" Moore asked Byers. It was hard to see without a flashlight, Byers said, asking the cop to help him look. Moore got out his flashlight and the two men walked down a trail, into the woods. They walked down to Ten-Mile Bayou, past the tree with the hanging rope, where Moore went down the bank while Byers searched the water with the policeman's flashlight. Together, they walked in a wide loop through the woods, circling back to the concrete slabs, where Brit and Ryan had heard the splashing. There they saw what looked like two sets of bicycle tracks.

"It looks to me that maybe they were headed in

that direction," Moore said, pointing west toward the Blue Beacon truck wash at the edge of the interstate. Moore told Byers to call the officer who first took his missing-child report. The shift changed at eleven, and patrolmen working the night beat would cite the curfew law and pull over any kids they saw. The two men left the woods, and Moore got in his squad car.

Back home, Byers made a call to the sheriff's office.

"Look, I've had one police officer out here helping me look for these boys," Byers said. "I called once and y'all told me what to do, and I did that. And I'm calling now, and I want to know why the search-and-rescue squad won't come out here and help me look for my boy."

The voice on the line told Byers not to worry.

"I'm damn worried about it," Byers replied. "My kid don't stay out. It's eleven o'clock at night—they're not at somebody's house."

Byers and Ryan went back to Robin Hood in the Isuzu, pulling off the road at the Blue Beacon onto the grass behind the truck wash that leads to the edge of the woods. Ryan began honking the horn as Byers walked to the edge of the woods and yelled into the darkness. Byers walked down a trail into the woods. Standing near the edge of Ten-Mile Bayou near a steep teakettle-shaped knoll called Turtle Hill by local kids, Byers yelled for Chris for several minutes. Finding nothing, he and Ryan went back home.

As Byers and Ryan pulled back in the driveway, Steve Branch's old grandpa, Jackie Hicks, pulled up in a truck. Hicks, a large, bald man with dark, penetrating eyes, drove fifty miles from Blytheville Arkansas, when he heard his grandson was missing. It was now about midnight, but Hicks, a burly ex-cop and wrestler, was eager to make another pass.

Several family members congregated under a streetlight as Hicks walked up to Byers, his wife, Melissa, Diane Moore, and Terry Hobbs. There was some debate about whether the boys had fallen into the bayou and drowned. The bayou, which actually was a dredged-out ditch built to improve drainage after construction of the levee had cut off the natural runoff into the Mississippi, was brimming with water.

"We couldn't see how both bikes could have run off in the bayou," Byers said. "I knew my son was a real strong swimmer. The only way he could have drowned would have been maybe trying to help one of the other kids that fell in. I said, 'Let's make another pass through.' So we all did."

About two in the morning, Byers and his wife pulled up to a stoplight. A police officer pulled alongside, offering a word of encouragement. "We'll find 'em," the cop reassured the family. The officer suggested the boys might have crawled into an abandoned house for the night. Encouraged by new possibilities, Byers began checking vacant houses in the neighborhood. They passed a van with Illinois plates but thought little of it at the time. It was warm, and the mosquitos were out in droves. After checking several doors, they drove back home about 3 A.M. and sat up, waiting for daylight.

It was a long night for Jackie Hicks. A week earlier he had given his grandson a new Renegade bicycle, and he couldn't forget Little Stevie's reaction. Grandpa got a big hug, a thank-you, and a slick proposition. "You know, Grandpa," the cute rascal had told the big guy with the soft heart, "I'm going to need some other things now, too."

Hicks, a hunter and tracker, followed two bicycle tracks through the woods at about eleven that night. Along the way, he slipped down a ravine and sprained his back. When Hicks saw the water in Ten-Mile Bayou, he got a bad feeling. More than a year later, he said he felt an "evil spirit was just bouncing off them trees down there." His later thinking likely was colored by what he eventually learned, but his family became gravely concerned that night as the hours passed and Little Stevie didn't turn up.

Searching until the wee hours, Hicks and Terry Hobbs spotted what they thought was an "oil slick" on Ten-Mile Bayou about 3 A.M. "Terry asked me, 'What's that on the water?'" The men couldn't tell. They went home, and Jackie decided he should brace his daughter.

"We better prepare for the worst," he told her.

Terry Hobbs rapped on the Byerses' front door about six that morning. Byers slipped on his boots and went out to look some more. Byers had talked again with the sheriff's department. He was finally told the search-and-rescue team was on its way, and would meet him later in the morning.

Driving back to Robin Hood, Byers looped around to Seventh Street, where the road bridges Ten-Mile Bayou west of the woods. As Byers crossed the bridge over the drainage canal, he saw Terry Hobbs and two others who had joined the search. Michael Moore's father, Todd, was there, back from his job, a night of truck driving. Little Stevie's natural father, Steve Branch, who drove down from Osceola, Arkansas, was there, too. The party told Byers they had just walked up and down both sides of the bayou, and didn't see anything.

THE BLOOD OF INNOCENTS

To keep the searchers from piling "on top of each other," Byers told the others he was headed to the place in the woods he'd been last night.

"Maybe I missed something. Maybe there's a cap or a piece of clothing or something I didn't see," he said.

At West Memphis police headquarters, the department's twelve detectives were gathering for their daily eight A.M. briefing. Filing into a tiny room in the small, aging O.I. Bollinger police building, the detectives listened as Inspector Gary W. Gitchell passed on the morning's top priority: Three small boys were missing. They hadn't been seen for twelve hours. Every available detective would be deployed for the search.

Since high school, Gitchell had wanted nothing more than to be a lawman. Now he was living a dream. His office walls were covered with photographs of Bonnie and Clyde, Pretty Boy Floyd, Al Capone, and other past public enemies. J. Edgar Hoover himself had granted Gitchell a clerk position with the FBI in 1972, the year Gitchell graduated from West Memphis High School. Hoover's letter of acceptance hung in a frame on the office wall among Gitchell's other memorabilia.

Gitchell joined the West Memphis Police Department in 1974, then rose to head the department's detective division after helping solve a sensational triple-murder case in 1985 when two elderly women and a twelve-year-old boy were brutally stabbed to death. The case put West Memphis—and Gitchell—on the map when the suspect, a black teenager in the seventh grade, was convicted and became the youngest person in the country on Death Row. Since then, Gitchell had served as police spokesman—the public face of the West Memphis Police Department.

Still, the department's reputation wasn't shining. There was a definite air of inattention, almost neglect at police headquarters, a cramped, two-story building erected in 1939, originally serving as City Hall. Smudged walls, bare electrical wires, leaky roofs, and a lack of central heat and air-conditioning blemished the upper floor, where the criminal investigation division was housed. On the back side, jail trustees washed police cruisers, or sat smoking or tying up the pay phone. But on this Thursday morning, as local news media outlets began making their first checks of the day, Gitchell wanted to make sure the police were on top of things.

He had a plan: saturate the city's northeast quadrant with detectives. Some would check the residential neighborhoods around Robin Hood Hills. Others would go immediately to the woods and join the search there. Sergeant Mike Allen, a boyish-faced detective with five years on the force, got the assignment: check vacant houses in the area to see if the boys might be hiding in one of them. The city's utility department workers would be assisting the police, Gitchell said. Together, they'd find these boys.

The morning brought a flurry of activity. The county's search-and-rescue squad trucks rolled into the boys' neighborhood. A blue-and-white police helicopter from Memphis crossed the river to join the search, hovering above treetops, floating over curious onlookers, and darting past houses around Robin Hood Hills. By midmorning, police were passing out photocopied pictures and descriptions of the three missing boys. News camera crews had joined the spectacle. Search parties congregated at Weaver Elementary and near the laundry at Ingram and Barton. Byers again badgered the authorities.

THE BLOOD OF INNOCENTS

"When are y'all going to put a boat in the bayou?" Byers said, demanding an answer from search-and-rescue leaders. "If they've drowned, let's get a boat in the bayou."

Byers got his boat. The search-and-rescue squad launched a fourteen-foot orange john boat in Ten-Mile Bayou. The water along most of the drainage canal was too shallow to drop a motor. Rescue workers poled through the water, looking for clues in the muddy flow. Meanwhile, thirteen search-and-rescue workers, decked in orange caps and shirts, began combing the trails through Robin Hood.

As the boat made its way down Ten-Mile Bayou, Byers and others sat near the pipe over the ditch, resting on the bank. Byers decided to look one more time in the woods on the other side, directly behind the Blue Beacon. Walking over the pipe, Byers climbed up steep Turtle Hill, where he'd stood the night before, then went down a steep embankment on the other side. Gazing down onto the forest floor of sprouting ferns and poison ivy, he spotted something. It was a brown coat. Byers picked it up. There was a disposable Schick razor in one pocket. Byers wasn't sure what it meant. Drifters came in and out of the woods all the time. He took the coat back to show the others.

Several residents who owned all-terrain vehicles were conscripted to pitch in. Motors buzzed and mud splattered as four-wheelers and dirt bikes whizzed along the banks of the bayou and out onto the winding trails of Robin Hood. Neighbors around the woods also chipped in, many on foot, searching under bushes, through backyards, and over playgrounds. Others joined the search in Robin Hood, walking the trails, wading along the banks of the drainage canal, and traversing large pools of rainwater.

Twenty-six-year-old Tim Cotten was looking for a job at the Blue Beacon that morning when he was asked to join the search. Cotten went home and retrieved his four-wheel all-terrain vehicle and headed for Robin Hood, throttling down the mud-caked trails and boggy undergrowth. Near the east end of Robin Hood, two women watched as Cotten, covered in mud and water, emerged from the woods. He was a strange sight, the women thought. Pale blue eyes staring out behind the mud and funk that enveloped him. Cotten told search-and-rescue workers he had fallen into the bayou and was going home to change clothes.

Like most folks who grew up around West Memphis, Cotten had often played in Robin Hood as a child. A high-school dropout, Cotten had spent many a day here skipping school, swinging on ropes from trees, and swimming in the bayou. But his swim today was unintended. The two women observers couldn't put their finger on it, but there was something about Cotten that bothered them. They made a mental note. Meanwhile, Cotten was having strange thoughts of his own. He couldn't get over how the wooded area north of the pipe seemed to smell like blood.

Across the woods, police detective Bryn Ridge was finding the going similarly unpleasant. Ridge had spent most of the morning trudging through a swampy area east of the woods, clearing vines from his path like a subtropical explorer, searching ditches, culverts and dips between the hills. Later, Ridge went home to retrieve his three-wheel dirt bike, then began exploring a large field along the bayou about a mile west of the woods, behind the local Wal-Mart. Ridge headed a couple miles to the west, farther from the woods, as the large concentration of searchers at Robin Hood scattered.

As the day advanced, part of the search-and-rescue team left Robin Hood, expanding their exploration east of town. Some rode in trucks on the gravel road atop the Mississippi River levee, the earthen embankment that provides protection against flooding. Searchers checked wooded areas and river bottoms along the levee for several miles.

A prevailing thought among the search party was that the boys could have run off and camped somewhere. If that was the case, the search party faced a massive effort. For starters, there were a number of fishing holes and patches of woods within the two miles of flat cotton land between the river and the levee, plenty of places to attract three kids with a sense of adventure. At the moment, it all seemed fruitless.

Authorities suspended most of the search by noon, sending neighbors home to rest and allowing the volunteer rescue squad members to report to their regular jobs.

Far from the woods, Sergeant Allen was checking doors and peering into vacant houses according to plan when he received a radio call a few minutes after one P.M. Report to Robin Hood Hills, he was told. Someone had spotted something.

Detective Ridge, motoring through muck on his three-wheeler, now some three miles to the west, received a call as well. Allen drove to the north end of West McAuley, the street that dead-ends at the sewage pipe running over Ten-Mile Bayou. Allen crossed the pipe, and walked up the trail past Turtle Hill.

Walking thirty yards across the rolling woods floor, he came to a gully, the one some local children knew as the Devil's Den. The rugged ditch was eight-feet deep with steep embankments leading down to a shallow creek that was dry part of the year but now well-stocked by the recent rains. Allen stood above the stream, some thirty yards north of where it poured into Ten-Mile Bayou.

There, he met county juvenile officer Steve Jones. Teeming with people and all-terrain vehicles two hours earlier, Robin Hood had emptied, but Jones had continued searching along. A small balding man with intent blue eyes, Jones took Allen to the edge of the ditch's tall bank, and pointed down into the stream.

There was a boy's tennis shoe floating in the water.

Sergeant Allen scaled down the steep bank to get a closer look. Wearing a button-down white shirt, striped blue tie, and gray dress pants, Allen wasn't prepared for slogging through the mud as he gingerly made his way down the steep bank to the edge of the dirty brown water. Now he could see two small black tennis shoes floating there. He needed to get closer. Carefully, he stepped out to try to find a footing on debris in the creek. Seeing a tree branch hanging overhead, he stretched to reach it.

"I leaned over to that tree thinking I could grab ahold of that tree and pull myself over," he recalled later. "I didn't make it."

Allen lost his balance and fell into the stagnant hip-high water. Shocked for a second, Allen tried to find his footing. But he wasn't sinking into the mud. He was standing precariously on some solid object. Allen shifted again, raising his right foot.

The water gurgled and Michael Moore's body floated to the surface.

Three

Police Case 666

Sergeant Mike Allen scrambled from the ditch, looking back in horror. The boy's hair waved silently in the murky brown water. The small body was naked. The boy's skin appeared ghostlike, blanched an alabaster white from hours submerged in water.

Panic and indecision struck the investigators at once. Steve Jones, the juvenile officer who'd spotted the tennis shoes in the water, felt his legs go numb. A call was placed to Inspector Gitchell: They'd found the boys— one of them, anyway. It didn't look good for the others. The officers suspected the other bodies would be close by.

Gitchell and other officers quickly arrived on the scene. They still weren't sure what they had. It could be a drowning. But it was beginning to look like murder.

Uniformed patrolmen were summoned to string up yellow crime scene tape south of the sewage pipe and at the other entrances to the woods. Neighbors who might still be searching parts of the woods had to be removed to preserve any evidence. At this point, however, that measure was relatively futile.

Any footprints or other evidence had long since been destroyed by the search parties.

Officers turned to the most immediate task: Someone had to go back into the water to search for the other bodies.

Bryn Ridge volunteered. The straitlaced detective, dressed in the jeans and white Arkansas T-shirt he wore on the morning search, stepped into the creek, several feet downstream from the small floating body that remained in the ditch. The water was colder than he'd expected. Sticks, leaves, cans, and splintered tree bark cluttered the slow-moving stream, concealing anything more than three or four inches below the surface. Ridge lowered himself to his knees. Kicking his legs out behind him to assume a belly-down floating position, Ridge stretched his hands down until he could feel the mushy bottom that ranged two to three feet below the surface.

Slowly, he started upstream. Raking his hands along the muck below, Ridge swept the creek bottom, bank to bank, meticulously covering the stream's six-foot width. Inching forward, he'd repeat the sweep again and again as he felt his way back toward the boy's body.

He was nearly there when he came across a stick that had been stuck in the bottom of the streambed. It was standing upright in the water. When it was dislodged, the full-length of the tree limb buoyed to the top. A muddy white shirt was wrapped around one end. It looked as if the shirt and stick had been "jabbed down into the mud," Ridge said later.

Soon, Ridge was back to the floating body. Tenderly, he scooped up young Michael Moore, cradling the boy in his arms. Clouds of brownish blood billowed in the water. The body lay stiff and rigid,

THE BLOOD OF INNOCENTS

more like a plastic doll than a child. Ridge waded to the side of the stream, raising the body up onto the bank.

Now they all could see the horror. His arms and legs were bound together behind his back. A shoelace linked Michael's left wrist to his left ankle. A second shoelace bound his right arm and leg. His face was swollen and purple. His head had been beaten in.

Ridge scooped Michael's yellow-and-blue Cub Scout cap from the stream where it had floated near his body. He also pulled two pairs of floating tennis shoes— one white, one black— from that spot. Now there could be little doubt the other boys were here, too.

Ridge set to the grim task again, paddling, raking, feeling for evidence. Piece by piece it came: Michael's blue Cub Scout shirt. His small blue jeans. More sticks with clothing jammed into the muck. A white polka-dot shirt. A striped shirt. Two more pairs of pants. A pair of child's underwear. The pants were a particular puzzle. Two pairs of trousers had been turned inside out, zippers shut, as if someone had just ripped them off the boys.

Turning downstream again, Ridge continued feeling the bottom. Some ten yards south of Michael's body, he stopped. There was something clammy there, pushed down into the muck. Carefully, Ridge grasped and pulled. Coming up, he had the body of little Stevie Branch in his hands. The boy had been lying facedown in the mud.

He, too, was nude. Ridge laid the small body on the bank. This child, too, had been hog-tied with shoelaces. Left wrist to left ankle. Right wrist to right ankle. Blunt trauma wounds— wounds of a beating— appeared about his head. But there was an even greater horror.

The left side of Steve's face was laid open from cheek to jaw. The flesh was laid ragged around the wound, as if ripped open by a wild predator.

A few feet from Steve, Ridge found Chris Byers. He, too, lay facedown on the bottom. Like the others, he was nude, hog-tied with shoelaces. Most of his penis and scrotum had been cut off. There was little left but a bloody wound.

Ridge came at last from the water, pale and shaky. The officers needed to regroup. Gitchell decided the stream would be dammed with sandbags and drained to allow his men to sift back through any evidence that might lay at the bottom of the creek bed.

Plainclothes cops rested against trees and smoked cigarettes as city utility workers arrived and began laying sandbags at the mouth of the creek. A pump whirred, spitting the stream's dark broth over the sandbag dam and down into Ten-Mile Bayou. Ridge would not rest. Still drenched from his grisly swim, the portly detective worked alongside the city workers, adjusting sandbags in the dam as Gitchell and the others watched uncomfortably from the banks.

The bodies of the three boys lay stiff and white in the dirt beside the creek bed.

On the stream's east bank, Michael lay curled on his side in a fetal position, knees drawn toward his chest. His head dipped gently, his face seemingly at peace.

Stevie was on his back, listing sideways. His arms reached up in the air before him, frozen, straining against the shoelaces that had bound his wrists and ankles behind his back. Stevie was a scrapper. His grandfather would later say he felt certain the boy gave quite a fight to whoever had killed him. Nearby lay Chris, legs spread, his arms twisted behind him.

A videotape was made of the crime scene. It

THE BLOOD OF INNOCENTS

would be replayed over and over again. The images could not be easily shaken. Their skin. It was brilliantly white, not unlike marble. Flies buzzed around their eyes.

Allen, his gray pants still soaked up past his knees, leaned uneasily against a tree and examined a blue canvas wallet found in Michael Moore's pants pocket. Inside, a mud-smeared color photo showed Michael with his father and sister, Dawn. Smiles, all smiles. Their daddy, Todd Moore, wore a suit and tie. They all seemed to be chuckling. Also in the billfold was Michael's Cub Scout card from Pack 3294. It was to expire in August. There was another photo, of Michael, decked in his baseball uniform, grinning widely, his T-ball bat slung over his shoulder.

Nearby lay a shiny toy badge that Michael's dad had bought him a week earlier. Sheriff Mike, it read in broad letters etched across a six-pointed silver star. It wasn't worth much, but the shiny little badge had empowered a boy's dreams.

Pam and Terry Hobbs had grabbed some lunch and a few moments of uneasy peace up at Catfish Island when they grew weary again. It was closing in on three P.M., but they still hadn't heard the news. They figured they'd drive by the school one more time to see if, by any chance at all, their son and his friends had shown up there.

At Weaver Elementary, where the boys went to school, the couple headed for the principal's office. School was out, and children ran yelling from under the entrance canopy. Pam was looking for Steve's classmates to ask if any had seen him. Then she overheard someone say, "They found three boys up at Robin Hood." Pam didn't wait around for explanations. She and Terry hopped in the car and raced toward the woods.

As they pulled up, things didn't feel right. A crowd had gathered on the south bank of Ten-Mile Bayou near the pipe. Yellow crime tape was up. Big Steve Branch, Pam's ex-husband, was there. His eyes were red and clouded.

"Lord, no!" Pam shrieked, collapsing to the ground. A circle of people picked her up and carried her back to her Buick. Her husband ran toward the crime scene tape, determined to hear for himself what had happened.

"You can't cross that line!" Big Steve yelled at Hobbs.

"Watch me," he shouted back. Terry Hobbs ducked under the yellow tape and made only a few more steps before Gitchell came racing up, blocking his progress.

"Who are you?" Gitchell demanded.

"The boys. Are they our boys?" Hobbs replied in a frantic tone that clearly identified him as a parent.

"Yes, they are," Gitchell said, subdued, stumbling for words. "It looks like a homicide. It looks like they've been murdered."

Terry sat down right there on the ground and cried. He fell back against a police car, and lay there, sobbing.

Gitchell had seen this sort of reaction before. It was never easy to deal with. Gitchell turned away for a few moments, then came back and handed Terry a Pepsi. At times like these, being a cop was tough. Gitchell— part social worker, grief counselor, media spokesman, and crowd control organizer— now was called upon to solve the crime.

Just outside the plastic tape, the scene was a madhouse. Television news crews, newspaper reporters and still photographers covered the bank. Everyone demanded at once to know what had happened. They stuck cameras in Gitchell's face.

"One of my men noticed a shoe," he said in a steady voice. "Being inquisitive, he jumped in the water and started feeling around," Gitchell told the throng of reporters. "People have been walking through here all day. We were lucky he saw one shoe." Gitchell's account wasn't entirely accurate, but it made as much sense as everything else going on around him.

As cameras snapped, Gitchell approached Byers, who leaned solemnly against the hood of a police car. Awkwardly, Gitchell raised a hand to Byers's waist to embrace him. Nearly a foot taller, Byers dropped his large left mitt firmly onto Gitchell's shoulder. The two men looked squarely into each other's eyes. The two men exchanged some uncomfortable words.

For Gitchell, he'd seen it all before. On a gray April day in 1985, he had stood outside a tiny crackerbox house on the city's southeast side and told a grieving father about the murders of his son and two aunts. Gitchell had blocked Bobby Simmons that day at the yellow crime tape, telling him he could not go in. As the man broke down and cried, Gitchell hugged him. "Can I see him? Can I see him?" Simmons had begged, asking to view the body of his twelve-year-old son, Chris. Gitchell had learned then how to be both tough and soft at the same time.

Had it really been eight years since the gruesome Ronald Ward murders? The case had captured local attention like no other. Two elderly women and a small boy, all white, stabbed to death during a house break-in by a juvenile black male. An all-white jury gave Ward the death penalty, and for a time he was the youngest Death Row inmate in the United States. The NAACP had protested, and the state Supreme Court eventually overturned Ward's conviction. But Ward received life imprisonment following a second trial, and Gitchell's reputation was secured.

Gitchell became something of a local celebrity. The Ward murders, though unusual for a city this size, certainly were not unique in West Memphis, the scene of several gruesome multiple murders through the years.

In 1960, a fourteen-year-old juvenile delinquent named Gurvis "Buddy" Nichols took a shotgun and blew away two boys, age eleven and nine, then calmly marched into the police station and confessed. "I want to die," he told police. "I do not belong to this world. I want to go to heaven." In 1988, forty-year-old Barbara McCoy and a female accomplice were charged with killing McCoy's two small children, then burning their bodies in what friends later characterized as an intense Christian spiritual fixation that went off the deep end. McCoy, an ardent practitioner of the Pentecostal "gifts of the spirit" doctrine, eventually was diagnosed as having a "bipolar affective disorder" and was found not guilty by reason of insanity.

Away from Gitchell's grasp, Byers no longer was downcast and solemn. He was the center of attention. When the news cameras turned on, Byers poured out his soul. Whoever did this was an "animal," Byers told reporters, expressing himself with wide eyes, a bobbing head and menacing tones.

"I hope God shows a little mercy on his soul, because I sure wouldn't," he said.

"I was out looking until four-thirty A.M. I walked

within ten or fifteen feet of where they were found and I didn't see them," Byers was quoted as saying on the front page of the local *Evening Times,* which also caught the Byers-Gitchell embrace.

Byers also told reporters he wondered why the Crittenden County Sheriff's Office did not join the search until Thursday morning despite his repeated requests. It was not their jurisdiction, authorities told him. "If they had brought them out there last night, we would have had a chance of finding those boys alive," he said, although he praised the all-night search effort by West Memphis police officers. "They could have used some help. Hell yes, they could have used some help."

By the end of the day, Sheriff Richard Busby, who said he knew Byers and considered him a friend, was on the defensive. "If anyone had called us last night, we'd have been glad to have helped them. We didn't get a call from West Memphis or anyone."

Holding back the crowd along the yellow crime tape, Patrolman G.C. Masengale was getting an earful. Some people demanded to know just what had happened. Others offered their own theories and tips. Cathy Myrick, victim Steve Branch's aunt, who had driven down from Blytheville, told Masengale a bizarre tale.

"Ms. Myrick was told (by a neighbor) that some kids were practicing Devil worship in the general area of the homicide," Masengale wrote in a report that night. "Ms. Myrick did not know the lady that made the comment . . . (but) stated she lived in the Mayfair Apartments." Myrick gave a physical description of the mystery lady and a companion, noting both had left in a blue Ford Taurus.

Independent of Myrick, Masengale received another tip regarding bizarre rituals in the woods where the boys' bodies were found. "A neighborhood resident also stated to me that her younger brother told her of Devil worship in the same area," Masengale's report read. The report did not elaborate on the supposed Devil worshiping, but it would set a tone for the investigation that lay ahead.

Something else also helped set that tone—an apparent, if chilling, coincidence. After the bodies were found, Gitchell called the records division and asked for the next chronological case number to be assigned to the investigation. A few moments later, a records clerk called back.

"You won't believe this," the clerk said. The case number would be 93-05-0666.

Six-six-six. The numbers rang out like a clarion call, warning of great evil. In the book of Revelation, the last book in the Bible, 666 was "the sign of the beast," the Antichrist, the evil one.

The number was straightforward enough. Ninety-three signified the year, 1993; 05 denoted May, the fifth month; 0666 showed this case was the police department's 666th of the year. The case came right on the heels of 93-05-0665, a 1:15 P.M. car theft that day.

It had to be a coincidence.

Back in the woods, police and city workers piled a wall of sandbags across the stream in the Devil's Den, several feet south of where the bodies had been found. Workers dropped a large suction hose into the pool. A gasoline-powered pump sucked out the water, exposing the puddled, muddy bottom below. Detectives combed through the muck, looking for clues that had eluded them when the ditch was full of water. A handheld metal detector was deployed to search for a weapon or other evidence that might have been concealed in the creek bed. The search revealed nothing.

Police created a new path for officers to travel in and out of the woods, in an effort to avoid destruction of any more evidence on the several trails that crisscrossed the woods. A decision was made to meticulously search the forest floor around the Devil's Den, north of the bayou. Lining up shoulder to shoulder with an arm's length between each officer, about ten detectives marched the length of the woods.

Starting at a point where the north end of the woods met the interstate, the officers covered some four hundred fifty feet to the point where the bodies were found, then marched on another sixty feet to the bayou. Forming another chain, they walked down another section of the woods. They found nothing. An adjacent soybean field was searched in a like manner but, again, turned up nothing.

In the Devil's Den, attention was turned to a small bank that lined the creek. The bank sat like a shelf on the ditch's earthen east wall, several feet below the crest and some three feet above the ravine's bottom, where the creek had flowed before it was pumped. With the steady roar of eighteen-wheelers behind him, Detective Ridge studied the shelf. It appeared something had happened here. Unlike the rest of the forest floor, there were no leaves or debris here. Tall reeds of grass lay bent over, their tops buried in the mud. It was as if someone had scraped off this surface with their feet, Ridge thought. But why? Were the kids murdered here? Was the killer trying to cover evidence? Yet there was no sign of blood.

The flattened area at the bottom of the ravine seemed an ideal spot for a murder. Traffic noises from the interstate disguised noisy screams and shouts for help and, from the ditch bottom, nothing could be seen except the steep earthen banks.

Even at the top of the ditch, the thick vegetation that had been growing since early spring blocked nearly everything outside the woods from view. Through a hole here and there in the leaves, cars and semitrailers could be seen whizzing down the freeway, eastbound toward Memphis. Employees at the Blue Beacon truck wash just west of the woods said they had seen nothing suspicious the night before. Other than the many inquiries by family members and friends who were out looking for the boys, the night had been uneventful, they told police.

Ridge spent most of the day dripping wet. He didn't quit after finding the bodies in the Devil's Den. Police had the bodies, but where were the bikes Mrs. Moore had seen them riding? Once again, Ridge volunteered for an aquatic investigation. Climbing down into the Ten-Mile Bayou, just yards from where the bodies were found, Ridge again felt for evidence. He walked into the bayou up to his neck. Forty feet across, the drainage ditch was much wider and deeper than the rainy-weather ditch in the Devil's Den. This time, Ridge's search was fruitless.

A boat was dropped again in Ten-Mile Bayou. Dragging a grappling hook, the boat churned westward down the ditch. Near the pipe, the hook hit a snag. There, some thirty yards southwest of the bodies, officers found Michael's green bike with the sissy-bars and Steve's new red Renegade dirt bike. Officers walked the bikes out of the woods and loaded them onto the back of a pickup truck behind the Blue Beacon as news photographers shot pictures from the perimeter. The next week, a photo of a deputy carrying one of the boys' bikes would appear in *People* magazine.

THE BLOOD OF INNOCENTS 63

A black hearse also backed up to the woods behind Blue Beacon. The boys' bodies, now covered in dark plastic bags, were loaded in the hearse to be taken to the state crime lab in Little Rock for autopsies. Reporters demanded to know more, but Gitchell, now firmly in control, declined to reveal anything.

The detectives continued searching for evidence in Robin Hood until darkness fell shortly before eight that night. They were exhausted, emotionally and physically. But there was more work to do. Bojangles manager Marty King was continuing to tell people about the man covered in mud and blood who had stumbled into the restaurant the night before. Ridge and Allen decided to check it out.

Unfortunately, there was little left to investigate. The bathroom had been mopped up the night before, and there was nothing on the floor.

But on the walls, the clean-up crew had missed a spot of what appeared to be dried blood smeared above the toilet. Ridge scraped the material into a container. Despite King's description, the detectives weren't impressed that this could be a strong lead for them. King offered them a pair of sunglasses the man had left behind. Ridge and Allen weren't interested. Back at police headquarters, Ridge, with a million thoughts on his mind and preparations for tomorrow, stored the blood scrapings in a drawer and did not follow up on them.

All day the people of West Memphis talked about the case of the three little boys. There were many rumors but little concrete information. But that night, twelve miles east across the river in the fluorescent-lit newsroom of *The Commercial Appeal*, veteran newsman James Kingsley got a tip from a source in Arkansas law enforcement that the Arkansas State Police were about to put out a broadcast about the killings over police radio frequencies. He and several others listened in.

"This department has a case of three male juveniles being abducted," a dispatcher said over the scanner. "They were found with their hands tied behind their backs and their genitals had been removed with a sharp instrument. Their bodies had been dropped in a remote area. Any department with a case similar to this, please advise this department. Attention: Inspector Gitchell. All information appreciated. Authority: West Memphis Police Department."

The police clearly were exploring the possibility that a child serial killer was at work. The information put a shocking spin on the newspaper's headline the following morning: MUTILATED BODIES OF 3 BOYS FOUND IN BAYOU.

Now it was public knowledge that the murders, grisly enough on their own, had included sexual mutilation. The police scanner broadcast had not been entirely correct— only one of the boys had been sexually mutilated. But more horrific details would emerge. For months to come the story would grip Memphis, the Mid-South, and the nation.

Four

The Promised Land

I'm Not
I'M NOT DEF
I can hear it coming. It sounds
like thunder intermingled with a
small child's cries.
I'M NOT FRANTIC
I can feel it coming. It violently
shakes every molecule of my body
as if it is rushing to reach me personally
I'M NOT CRAZY
I can see it coming. It sees me with
its one piercing eye. Its huge metal
teeth appear to be smiling. It
knows I can put an end to its madness
by just stepping aside. But no I think
I can win. It Reaches me as I
jump. And sends me out of my state
of utopia and face first into a
painful black reality.
— From the notebook of Damien Echols

Friday morning brought its usual blur of activity, as Mid-Southerners rose to face one final workday before the weekend. The truck stops and restaurants along the interstate buzzed with breakfast crowds hunched over biscuits and gravy, sausages, grits, and the morning news. There was a talent show that night at the West Memphis Civic Auditorium; a barbecue was on tap up at the Marion Shopping Center north of town. Across the river in Memphis, the annual Beale Street Music Festival would be blowing throughout the weekend in Tom Lee Park, under the bluffs along the Mississippi River.

But the big news was the unsolved triple child-murder case.

Weaver Elementary held classes as usual, but there was nothing ordinary about the morning. Television crews, reporters, and newspaper photographers stood vigil outside the single-story brick school building. Cautious parents escorted children on their morning walks to classrooms where social workers waited to provide grief counseling. Principal Sarah Kirkley asked her staff "to be as normal" as possible, for the children's sake.

"Do not go anywhere without telling me unless I'm there with you at all times," a young mother told her three children. She told a reporter, "And I'm making a special trip to get them on the school bus and pick them up—at all times."

At police headquarters, the phones had been ringing almost nonstop. Law enforcement agencies across the country offered assistance and made inquiries to see if the West Memphis case might shed any light on unsolved murders in their areas. In Little Rock, Gov. Jim Guy Tucker offered West Memphis the assistance of state police investigators to help "catch the person or persons responsible for this horrible crime." The murders were also attracting national attention, and a CBS news crew was in town to report on the case.

At a morning news briefing, Gitchell expressed guarded optimism about the direction of his day-old investigation. "We are leaving no stone unturned," he said. "We have some hopeful leads that we are checking on."

Actually, his detectives were inundated with leads. Encouraged by a reward offered by City Hall, the local Chamber of Commerce, and others, residents had phoned in nearly three hundred tips. By Friday afternoon, the reward fund stood at $7,000, and the tips kept coming.

Gitchell confirmed that the boys had received multiple head blows and had been bound hand to foot, but he declined to elaborate. The broadcast the night before by the Arkansas State Police regarding sexual mutilation was a particular sore point for Gitchell.

"Not all of that report was accurate. I've refused to comment on what part was inaccurate, for investigative purposes," he told a reporter. To guard against possible false confessions and ensure the real killer could be detected when police finally caught up with him, Gitchell did not want it publicly known that just one boy had been sexually mutilated.

"We have some major trucking in the nation going through here," Gitchell said, addressing one theory that the killings may have been the work of a psychotic truck driver by now miles down the blue highway from the crime scene. "It's frustrating. We will rely heavily on the crime lab to bring forth some information to sort of steer us in one direction or the other."

The state crime lab in Little Rock had dispatched a team of trace-evidence technicians and serologists to inspect the crime scene. Gitchell also acknowledged assistance from the Arkansas State Police, the Crittenden County Sheriff's Office, the Memphis Police, and the FBI, which had been asked to tap behavioral sciences experts in Quantico, Virginia, to develop a psychological profile of the killer or killers.

But Gitchell hedged at an offer by the State Police to play a hands-on role in the investigation. Colonel Tommy Goodwin, commander of the State Police, had called West Memphis police chief Bobby Sanders shortly after the bodies were found to commit assistance from among his twelve patrolmen and investigators in East Arkansas. "I have offered everything—anything that we've got, they can have," Goodwin was quoted as saying. Gitchell told reporters that, for now at least, he didn't need any more detectives. "We've got fifteen people on this now, and if we get too many, we'll be tripping over each other," he said.

The truth was, Gitchell had his own plan. Behind the scenes, the hottest tip his detectives were working involved reports of a mysterious white van seen in the neighborhood around Robin Hood Hills Wednesday before the boys disappeared. Over the coming weeks, white van sightings would continue pouring in. One woman, a thirty-eight-year-old maintenance employee at the dog-racing track, Southland Greyhound Park, told police her mother had seen a white van "circling around the area," a police report showed. A fourteen-year-old boy said he and a playmate had seen a white-panel van with apparent front-end damage that seemed to be roving the neighborhood, looming behind some teens as they rode bicycles. The driver, heavyset and in his thirties, wore a "red man cap" while a passenger with a long sandy brown ponytail wore sunglasses on the top of his head. "He is not sure if the van seemed to be following them or not," a police report read. In nearby Bebee, Arkansas, a woman told police that a man with "straggly blond hair" driving a white van had slowed down and was watching her thirteen-year-old son. The van then sped off.

There was nothing certain about the white van tips, but there were enough of them to merit checking. By eleven o'clock Friday morning, the Arkansas Crime Information Center had faxed West Memphis police thirteen pages of data listing some five hundred white vans registered in Crittenden County. Checking their own computer records, West Memphis detectives compiled information on several recent arrests and traffic stops involving white vans.

The volume of tips was dizzying. One sheet of messages alone Thursday night included two reported sightings of the boys (one of them occurred impossibly at 8:15 Thursday morning) and a tip from a Navy sailor on leave who said San Diego had had a similar incident in March involving two young males who were beaten to death in a rural park. A West Memphis woman passed on another tip: She said she saw two transients Wednesday night carrying red bedrolls near Earl's Hot Biscuits, a restaurant along the interstate. She saw them again Thursday heading east toward Memphis, then saw one of them later in the day heading north.

Just before midnight, the State Police broadcast a message asking law enforcement to be on the lookout for the two "dirty-looking" characters.

Gitchell wasn't concerned with all of that now. He would concentrate his efforts by launching a door-to-door canvass of the neighborhoods around Robin Hood. Nine detectives, each armed with questionnaires, were dispatched to find out anything neighbors might know or might have seen.

The tactic had worked beautifully in the Ronald Ward case. Hours after the bodies were discovered in the 1985 case, police conducted door-to-door interviews in a four-block area around the murder site. Pounding on doors, Gitchell and another detective had located a resident who said he talked to a black teenager the night of the murders. The teen, who appeared to be intoxicated, had been loitering behind the man's house, Gitchell learned. The man could not identify the youth from a photo lineup. But, knowing that most teenagers attend school, Gitchell returned to the resident's house a couple days later with some school yearbooks. In the East Junior High annual, the man spotted a photo of the youth who'd been behind his house. It was Ronald Ward. Gitchell was more than eager to try the approach again.

An eleven-question survey was drawn up. Much of it involved basic information: Name, address, place of employment, home and work telephone numbers. How long had the resident lived at this address? Who lived in the home? Did any children live there? The detectives also would seek the names and addresses of recent visitors, and ask if residents had seen any strangers or strange-acting people in the neighborhood recently.

Three of the questions seemed aimed at specific leads: "Ask: The type of vehicles they own and get complete description: color, year, make, model, tag numbers."

"Ask: If they or anyone they know in the area is a Vietnam veteran."

"Ask: If anyone in the area wears a uniform, any kind of uniform."

Gitchell wasn't leaving his detectives any room for interpretation of his orders. "Make sure that all this information is written down!!" the questionnaire read at the bottom.

Beating on doors down Goodwin Avenue, Det. Shane Griffin had some luck. He found a resident who said his daughter had seen the three boys on bikes about six P.M. Wednesday at the entrance to Robin Hood near the Fourteenth Street dead end. Griffin's notes show most of the homes on Goodwin either had no one home or no one available who could help. But there were some leads. A neighbor two doors down voiced concerns about two hitchhikers, both white men, that he'd seen Thursday morning crossing the old bridge into Memphis.

Over on North Fourteenth, detectives were getting even better details. A man said he'd seen Michael Moore in muddy clothes near Robin Hood a week earlier. Also, a white woman in a brown Chevy had been driving around looking at children, he said. Down the street, a neighbor said he saw Michael Moore on the night of the disappearance taunting two young black men, calling them names. Another neighbor reported a suspicious maroon Buick.

On an adjacent street, Ridge and Stan Burch were catching nearly everyone at home Friday afternoon. One man said his daughter, a classmate of the boys, had seen Michael playing in the area about four P.M. the night he disappeared. Michael told the girl he had "a secret hideout" in the woods directly behind the Mayfair Apartments and was going to go there. The detectives seemed to be onto something. Going next door, a neighbor said he had heard five gunshots between ten and eleven o'clock Wednesday night.

Over at the Mayfair Apartments, detectives Allen and Bill Durham had a rough day. Hardly anyone was home. There were several vacancies throughout the run-down apartment complex. One man who was home made a shocking statement. "Subject stated he would like to kill someone to see what it's like," their notes show. There was no indication whether they took the comment seriously.

Yet the Mayfair complex yielded tips that would color the investigation from this point forward. Several residents said that over the years, they'd seen strange groups of people going into the woods. "There's Satan worshipers back there," one Mayfair resident told the officers. Another said a white man "with black and red long hair hangs out in that area (in) some type of cult." A third Mayfair resident talked about "kids with black and red hair" that "hang out there." Two others mentioned they, too, had heard gunshots Wednesday night.

Mayfair provided the perfect vantage point. Located just a couple hundred yards from the spot where the boys' bodies were found, the apartment complex and the woods were separated only by a small open field and Ten-Mile Bayou. The pipe over the ditch, the point where the boys' bikes were found, runs right onto the Mayfair grounds.

As detectives compared notes, they found similar accounts throughout the neighborhood. One homeowner near Fourteenth and Goodwin advised police to check out a white man in his late teens or early twenties sporting reddish, shoulder-length hair and a pentagram, an occult symbol. A neighbor talked about three white youths, supposedly drug addicts, who lived near the woods and practiced "voodoo mutilation, everything evil—don't get much sun." A woman on Goodwin summed up her observations in less ominous terms: "Heard that a gang meets in Robin Hood."

But the most detailed tip came from a woman on Barton Avenue who lived less than two blocks from the homes of Michael and Chris. The woman said a thirteen-year-old neighborhood boy who often played with Chris Byers had been in Robin Hood recently. In the woods, the boy saw "a Star of David crudely made out of the leg of a child's swing set." A sign read something like, "Leave Now or You Won't Get Out," the woman told police.

And she also passed on names. She told about a family in Mayfair and said that the police should check out two sons in the clan. "Those boys have dropped out of sight last couple of days! A boy and girl have been in the neighborhood looking for them. This boy has a tattoo on his left forearm of a devil with a hood on" and has "scratches on his chest."

A theory was blossoming on the police station's second floor. The house surveys had produced no fewer than six tips involving strange youths holding mysterious meetings in and around Robin Hood. Two other residents had told Officer Masengale similar stories the day the bodies were found.

One woman said she heard about several black men supposedly engaged in "Devil worshiping" in Robin Hood the previous autumn. "Her husband found dead sacrificed animals in Robin Hood around this time. She stated that during the nights she could smell smoke and hear chanting and strange music," Detective Griffin wrote in a report.

A twenty-one-year-old neighbor told police she'd seen pentagrams and crosses drawn in the dirt in the woods, and said a friend had claimed five years earlier that she'd seen a dead baby hanging from a tree there. Debra O'Tinger, a nineteen-year-old neighbor who later would testify as a trial witness, told police "there has always been talk of satanic cult activities for years" but said she had never seen anything except, on one occasion, a cross carved in a tree.

It was difficult for police to know how much stock to place in the tips. But by all accounts, the three victims either were headed toward the woods or were entering it sometime after six that night. What if they had crossed paths with these ghouls, this phantom cult? The volume of tips could not be ignored. It was definitely something to check into.

Reporters and television crews pounded the West Memphis streets with a particular frenzy Friday afternoon. Weekend deadlines were fast approaching. It was the biggest story going, but the going was rough. The Moores weren't giving interviews. Over at the Byers home, John Mark and Melissa had gone into seclusion. Reporters in search of quotes at the Byers home were met at the door by a wiry little bearded man named Andy "Opie" Taylor.

Taylor, an old family friend, had designated himself the family's "official spokesman." In his thick Baton Rouge drawl, Taylor entertained media types with earthy quips. He said he'd known Christopher "since he was a curtain crawler. He was the kind of little kid who could climb in your lap and make you feel good right off the bat. He not only could do it; he would do it."

Steve Branch's parents gave media interviews that Friday. As would happen time and again over the coming months, Pam and Terry Hobbs found talking therapeutic.

"He liked older women," Terry Hobbs joked, recalling Stevie's little crush on Michael's ten-year-old sister, Dawn.

A small man with dark, brooding eyes, Hobbs looked sad even when he wasn't. As Terry spoke, his wife sat with her hands between her knees. Her round face, blond hair, and large blue eyes made her look more like a doll than a twenty-eight-year-old mother of two.

"He was going to be my little Elvis someday," she said. "I told him how Elvis bought his mama Graceland, so he'd have to buy me a Promised land."

The weekend came in a mad rush. Tips continued to pour in. Officers, working with little sleep, began interviewing the first wave of suspects. A caller to the city Crime Stoppers line told of a "very brutal, bisexual" man "who has had virgin girls but would like a virgin boy."

Police scrambled to locate the suspect, and the only one they could find who fit his description was a local schoolteacher. He was summoned to the police station for questioning. "I confronted him with the information," Detective Ridge wrote in his report. "He said that he didn't know why anybody would say anything like that about him." Ridge concluded he "could not even be sure that this is the suspect" that the tipster had mentioned.

In Little Rock, police questioned a man who'd picked up a hitchhiker and let him out about 3:30 P.M. Wednesday near the Blue Beacon off Interstate 40 in West Memphis. The hitchhiker had bushy sideburns, long "carrot-red" hair and an eight-inch tattoo on his left arm depicting a devil with claws. "Into Devil worshiping," Sergeant Allen wrote in notes from a phone conversation with Little Rock police.

The driver told Little Rock police he had offered to take the hitchhiker to a restaurant on the north side of the freeway, but the man insisted on being dropped off at a convenience store on the south side, near Robin Hood woods. "He wanted to go specifically to the south side of the freeway and he wanted off right in this, at this one place," the driver said. The hitchhiker also had told the driver he was a tree trimmer "who had gone broke in Little Rock trying to get tree-trimming work" and was headed to Knoxville, Tennessee. The tip stirred a wave of excitement. Notes show Lt. James Sudbury called twenty-nine tree-trimming and lawn-service companies in Memphis and West Memphis, but apparently learned nothing.

In the dingy West Memphis police station, Mike Allen manned the phones, chasing down more tips. One caller said a Memphis cabdriver had hauled a strange character out of town Thursday. The suspect, a white man with long hair and cutoff jeans, "paid the cab driver $390 to carry him to Centerville, Tennessee," the tipster said. The suspect had hitched a ride from West Memphis to Memphis and "needed to get out of town."

When Allen found the cabdriver, he told a strange tale. The suspect first "wanted to go to a hotel near the airport," but changed his mind and said he wanted to go to Nashville, the cabbie said. On the 210-mile drive from Memphis to Nashville, the two had a weird conversation. "I bet you did kill the three kids," the passenger blurted out. "No," the driver said, "but I'd like to kill the SOB that did it." Just as suddenly, the passenger quit talking and fell asleep. When the cabdriver stopped in Centerville, Tennessee, for gas, the passenger got out, paid the driver $390, and said he'd take another cab. Whoever this strange character was, the police never found him.

Gitchell worked other angles. A list with scores of recently paroled sex offenders was compiled. Each was to be checked out. Mounds of credit card purchase slips from local truck stops were examined. The names of drivers who recently used truck stop showers were run through FBI offices in Chicago for criminal background checks.

Down the hall, the short, intense detective Bill Durham was wiring a potential witness to a lie-detector machine. For years, if the West Memphis Police Department wanted someone polygraphed, they had to ask the Arkansas State Police. But the department bought its own polygraph machine in 1992, and hired Durham, a certified polygraph operator and former Memphis police officer. Over the next four weeks, Durham would conduct about fifty polygraph tests. His lie-detector machine would become the barometer for deciding who to dismiss and who to pursue as a suspect.

"Did you know these boys were dead before Thursday afternoon?" Durham asked the witness. A compact man with close-cropped hair and dark, stony eyes, Durham studiously monitored his charts, awaiting an answer.

"No." Tim Cotten sat stiffly, wires taped to his chest. Two days earlier the twenty-six-year-old had been riding trails in Robin Hood on an all-terrain vehicle, searching for the boys. Someone had called the police station and said Cotten was "a weird-acting guy." He became a suspect.

"Were you present when those three boys were killed?"

"No."

"Did you kill those three boys?"

"No."

"Do you know who killed those three boys?"

"No."

Durham checked his charts. There was no sign of deception. For Cotten, it seemed there was more than a little truth in the adage that no good deed goes unpunished. But the police couldn't afford to overlook anything. The officers dismissed Cotten, thanking him for his time.

The workload wouldn't ease as the officers labored into the weekend. Sitting at a computer keyboard, Mike Allen entered a code number to access the National Crime Information Center, known in law-enforcement circles as the NCIC, a nationwide data bank of criminal records and fingerprints maintained by the federal government. Following the prompts, Allen typed in his request:

"Byers, Mark. Race, white. Sex, male. Date of birth, 03-08-57." Allen plugged in Byers's social security number and other identifying details. In a moment, a response came back. There was a hit. The FBI had a file number on Byers, with his fingerprints.

"The criminal history record is maintained and available from the following: FBI," the response read. "The record(s) can be obtained through the interstate identification index by using the appropriate NCIC transaction." There were no further details.

Allen tried again. Twice more, he got no details. In a moment, the information came:

"Byers, John Mark . . . Arrested or received 7-29-92, Agency: USM (United States Marshal) Memphis . . . Charge 1: Conspiracy to commit Felony— Cocaine, Charge 2: Carrying dangerous weapon."

Things were beginning to get deep.

By Sunday morning, police had questioned more than fifty people.

"Naturally, some leads haven't panned out," Gitchell told reporters at his daily media briefing. "We have ruled out more things, or more appropriately, many different people."

Gitchell asked anyone with information about vehicles or individuals seen in the area to come forward. "I definitely feel we are closer," he said, expressing optimism. But he had to admit that police didn't really have a clue who committed the murders. "It's like a great puzzle," he said. "It would take the whole front courtyard to put together all the pieces."

The murders were the topic of sermons throughout the city that morning.

At Holy Cross Episcopal Church, Rector Fred H. Tinsley, Jr., called the murders the "incarnation and manifestation of evil." His heart was especially heavy. Out among the congregation, Todd and Diane Moore sat with their daughter, Dawn. The family leaned on each other, huddled at times in a lump. Around them, congregants dabbed their eyes with handkerchiefs. There had been a tremendous outpouring of compassion and support. In addition to the reward fund, West Memphis residents had started a second fund to help pay for all three families' funeral expenses. It stood at $15,000.

"While I do believe to the very core of my being in God the Father, Son, and Holy Spirit, I freely admit to you this morning that my heart is sorely troubled," Tinsley told his congregation. "We're not dealing with the garden-variety sin here. Anyone who would do something like this is not like you or me. They've reached the point that they refuse to recognize that anything wrong was done."

Despite their immense pain and loss, the Moores could not afford to be weak. They faced serious business. They had to plan Michael's funeral. And the police had begun questioning the victims' family members in an effort to learn more about the boys' disappearance and deaths.

Todd Moore had brought Dawn to the police station Saturday, where father and daughter met with Ridge. Most of it was painful. Todd talked about his son. The way he was dressed the day he died. The blue Cub Scout shirt. The little wallet he insisted on carrying. The toy sheriff's badge his dad had bought him just a few days before the murders.

Dawn told how she went out looking for her brother that night. She was riding her bike near the pipe when three teenagers came out of the woods, one white and two blacks. "You want a shot?" one of the boys had asked her. "She felt they were talking about drugs," Ridge noted. He kept the interview brief. After all, they were victims.

But as a result of that interview, police contacted a teenage girl, who had been with Dawn and saw the same three boys come out of the woods. She, too, heard the comment about "the shot." Whoever they were, the girl didn't feel good about them. Like so many others, she passed on disturbing rumors about what went on in Robin Hood. There's "cult activity" there, she said, adding that some members blackened their faces.

There were too many stories of satanic activity for police to dismiss the tales out of hand. But like the shadowy demons that possessed both people and swine in the Bible, the cult members seemed intangible and without face or form.

Devil worshipers. Blackened faces. Chanting. Bonfires. A hitchhiker with a devil tattoo who wanted to be left off near the woods. What did it all mean? Was there really some evil cult operating in West Memphis? Or was this simply hysteria mixed with weird coincidence? Having three boys murdered in their midst can do strange things to people in a small town in the Bible Belt.

The questions would be tested that afternoon, Sunday, May 9, 1993. Police would look their demon in the face.

It was five minutes after two when Det. Shane Griffin finally caught up with Dennis Ingle, a man police had been trying to reach for two days. Ingle was a preacher at Lakeshore Baptist Church. On Sundays the one-room church burned with fire and brimstone, and on election days it doubled as a polling place for those who lived in the Lakeshore Estates mobile-home park, a sprawling assortment of junked trailers and better-kept homes that surrounded a shallow lake just north of the West Memphis city limit.

A tipster on Friday had told police a group of people at Lakeshore were into Devil worship. "The pastor at the church is real concerned," the tipster had advised. Confronted by Griffin, Ingle eagerly confirmed the tip. A strange young man named Damien Echols, who hung around Lakeshore, was "supposed to be involved in cults," Ingle told Griffin. "The cult is supposed to meet somewhere by the Mississippi River," he said.

Ingle told Griffin that Damien wore boots with the numbers 666 written on the side of them. Pastor Ingle didn't have a lot of biographical detail but he knew that this Damien had a girlfriend in the park, a teenager named Domini. Griffin jotted down the information and hurried back to headquarters.

Damien Echols. The name kept popping up.

Five

Damien

Self-Portrait
*Hello, can anyone hear me. Can anyone see me.
Maybe I'm just a character in someone else's dream.*

For proof you set on a tree stump and tie tin cans to a string and hope the wind will blow them and make some kind of noise.

The only problem is that it only lasts a minute and once it stops you're not even sure you heard it in the first place. Face it it's my destiny to be flipped, ripped, copied and at times completely overlooked. I'm flat and without life. The thought sickens you so much you can't take it anymore until you snarl so hard and turn away so fast you don't even realize you're looking into a mirror.

— From the notebook of Damien Echols

He was born Michael Wayne Hutchison, but in an adolescent whim of reinvention, changed his name to Damien Echols. It sounded dark and mysterious, and it suited him well. Like so many of his generation, with little parental supervision or interest,

Damien grew into a surly, moody teenager. He kept his distance from most kids his age, but, as several adults would later remark, he seemed to maintain an astonishing control over a small circle of teenage misfits who looked up to him. He was their leader, their role model. They mimicked him thoroughly, from his odd fascination with the occult to his fondness for black clothes. Some even dyed their hair the same shade of jet-black.

Still, Damien didn't look the part of a leader. He was slender yet flabby, a layer of baby fat coating his sturdy frame. His face was handsome, yet strangely pale, and he had dark, penetrating eyes. He learned to stare with a menacing air that could raise hairs on the necks of rivals. Yet at other times people would look into Damien's eyes and marvel at his vacant, distant look, as if nobody was there. In May 1993, he was an eighteen-year-old high-school dropout with no car, no driver's license, and no steady place that he called home. Recently he had moved back with his mother and father, a career gas station attendant, living in a cluttered mobile home in the Broadway Trailer Park in West Memphis's dismal east end.

Despite all they thought they knew about him, Damien remained an enigma to police, just as he'd always been to those around him.

His station in life wasn't much different from many in the trailer-park crowd. His parents, Pam and Eddie Joe Hutchison, were married in 1974 when they eloped to New Mexico as teenagers. On December 11, 1974, Damien was born in Memphis. The movie *The Exorcist* was playing in a Beale Street theater. His younger sister, Michelle, was born several years later.

They lived a working-class life. It was a rather typical West Memphis family, with parents who were reasonably intelligent but without a lot of formal education. From the beginning he was a bright, precocious child. But he also could be sullen and cold.

Pam Hutchison divorced Joe Hutchison in September 1986. A few days later, she married a roofer named Andy Jack Echols. Jack and Pam had met through another couple; eventually they became attracted and had an affair.

Joe Hutchison moved to the West Coast and had almost no contact with the children during Pam's second marriage. Michelle became embarrassed that her last name was different from her mother's new married name, and so, on Halloween 1990, Jack legally adopted both Michael Wayne Hutchison and Michelle Hutchison: they became Echolses. For the occasion Michael changed his first name, too, and from then on was legally known as Damien Wayne Echols. Though classmates said they thought the name was taken from the Antichrist character in the Omen movies, Damien would always say that he took the name of his hero, Father Damien, the nineteenth-century Belgian missionary priest who worked with Hawaiian lepers. His family would continue to call him Michael.

Both children harbored some resentment toward their biological father. They were upset at the fact that he didn't stay in touch, and they blamed him in part for the family's breakup. Discipline was not very harsh in the household.

Later Jack would describe Michael as a "backward child," fairly happy, but a loner when it came to the rest of the family. He rarely participated in family activities. He preferred to keep to himself, by reading or watching television. And, Jack said, throughout their childhood, Pam openly favored Michael over Michelle.

Jack Echols came from an itinerant background; many in his family were migrant workers and he never felt he belonged anywhere. He grew up easily able to meet girls, but had few male friends and even years later he would have trouble trusting anyone. He received little formal education and became a roofer, nailing shingles for more than a quarter of a century.

Jack considered himself a religious man. He had at one time attended the local Nazarene Church, but he and his former wife quit the denomination for the Church of God. Their reason, he explained: Nazarenes do not believe in speaking in tongues. He also attended the Assembly of God Church following his separation from Pam.

When one day Michael announced he was joining the Catholic Church and felt called to become a priest, Jack supported him. He told Michael to follow the call. Michael went to Roman Catholic classes in the Rite of Christian Initiation for Adults at St. Michael's Catholic Church in West Memphis, and appeared intrigued.

In September 1990, the family would move in with Frances Gosa Haynes, the maternal grandmother of the children. She had had a stroke and lost her legs, and was now in a wheelchair. The family was thus made up of Jack, Pam, Michelle, Damien, and Mrs. Haynes.

In 1991, Damien started a sexual relationship with a fifteen-year-old girl who drew him deeply into the occult. But over the months, pressures from the girl's family made it very difficult for them to stay together. Swearing to stay together against all odds, they even made a suicide pact.

THE BLOOD OF INNOCENTS

But on March 3, 1992, she told Damien it was over— partly because of her mother's insistence she leave him, and partly because of his increasingly obsessive, moody attitude toward her. Shortly thereafter Damien's behavior became bizarre. Echols jumped on her new boyfriend at school and reportedly tried to tear the youth's eyes out with his long fingernails.

On the morning of Friday, March 6, 1992, Damien told his ex-girlfriend he would kill her new boyfriend, dump him in her front yard and come back to burn down her house. The girl's mother called the police. A report was filed describing Damien's behavior as "terroristic threatening."

Over the next few months, Damien and this girl resumed their relationship in defiance of her mother's wishes.

Then, on May 19, 1992, her mother called the police to report that her daughter had run away and that she believed Damien was with her. The subsequent Marion Police Department report noted the two were found in a closet of an empty trailer at Lakeshore Estates, partially nude from the waist down. Echols was charged with burglary and sexual misconduct.

The youth authorities ordered Damien to stay in the Juvenile Detention Center at Jonesboro on May 26, 1992 as a result of the incident.

Damien had also begun to see another girl, Domini Teer, a skinny, freckle-faced sixteen-year-old redhead with a very peculiar laugh. Another denizen of Lakeshore, she lived with her mother, Dian. Damien would ultimately make the Teer trailer his home. On a bedroom floor of the trash-strewn trailer, he and Domini would share a soiled mattress. A homemade Ouija board lay amid the clutter, under a bare red lightbulb hanging from the ceiling.

Domini was a temperamental girl, often jealous, sometimes hurtful. Like so many other lower-class juveniles in Crittenden County, she was already known by local police. Once, she and her mother got into a fight when she would not go to school. The cops were called. The mother later said that Domini had accidently struck her aunt in the arm. On the other occasion, she violated curfew in Kewanee, Illinois, where she had gone to stay for a while with her father.

Marital problems served to break up the Echols family finally. Jack Echols moved out and on May 27, 1992, their divorce was finalized.

It was also around this time that Michelle, out of a bit of desperation, made contact with her biological father, Eddie Joe Hutchison. She had not seen him in five years, but wanted his help. Eddie Joe came to Arkansas to investigate the family's situation, and just like that, he was back in their lives.

As Michelle became a young woman, Damien apparently began to recognize the attractiveness of his younger sister. In fact, at his insistence, Michelle dated Damien's friend Jason Baldwin for a week. Jason was nice to her, she said, and would go out of his way. She never had sex with Baldwin, although she liked him. On the other hand, Jessie Misskelley, Jr., another friend of Damien's, had made rude sexual advances toward her on the school bus. He was always, rather clumsily, hitting on her, but she never had anything to do with him.

The family's troubles, and Damien's encounters

with the law, led Damien Echols inward. In one prescient account, he wrote:

> The introduction to this heartache began as a child
> So it's no wonder he grew up to be so wild.
> So he protected his feelings in walls he imagined
> But castles crumble, exposing the frightened child
> Fire in the sky, can't you see that all my castles are burning?
> Won't you help me down? My castles are burning.
> In solitude he couldn't deal with his own existence,
> The burning questions in the castles have still remained.
> God only knows he searched in vain
> Now the castles crumble
> Exposing his naked flames.
>
> They're gonna put me away, God damn them.

Damien was a nobody, just another loser out at Lakeshore. Yet, by the spring of 1993, Damien's reputation was growing. He was a spectacle. He kept his fingernails long—"talons," one person called them. Though he had bouts with acne, he didn't have a bad complexion, and he always kept himself well groomed. His hair was longish, and he always kept it clean and combed. He changed hairstyles by the week. At times he slicked it straight back. Sometimes, borrowing a style popularized by California surfers, he'd shave part of one side of his head and let the rest hang long. His attractiveness to girls was important to him, and he knew he had to take care of himself to make them notice him.

Throughout West Memphis and Marion, it became common, day or night, to see Damien Echols out walking. Sometimes he was by himself, sometimes with a friend. Nearly always he wore a black trench coat, even in the moist, sticky summers of the Mississippi River Delta.

"He wore that coat down to his knees if it was ninety degrees," a resident of Lakeshore Estates trailer park, Anita Brewer, remembered.

Damien was a cigarette smoker but he wasn't a big drinker or drug user. He had tried pot, speed, LSD, and he had even sniffed gasoline— a practice the trailer-park urchins called "huffing." But it wasn't an ongoing thing with him. For Damien, nothing held his interest for long.

Nobody who saw Damien described him as a normal teen. And in a sense, he encouraged people to misunderstand him. He was bright, sarcastic, cynical. But by and large he didn't like people; didn't trust them. He could match anyone's contempt with a streak of obnoxiousness and hatred that could be quite intimidating. Before he was tossed out of Marion High School, he had been in constant turmoil there. During one particularly troubled streak, he was suspended seven times. He fought. He spat on a teacher. He started a fire in his science classroom. Throughout this time, he was tortured by growing thoughts of suicide and destruction.

Increasingly, he turned his mind to dark considerations.

Though he said he did not consider himself a worshiper of the Devil, he didn't particularly mind it if others thought he was. For him, that just displayed others' ignorance, and if someone thought he was potentially violent, he wouldn't argue. In his world, the appearance of a menacing specter could be a good self-defense.

Damien's interests were the fairly typical, antisocial or antiestablishment preoccupations of a teenager in the early 1990s. He often enjoyed mainstream rock music, listening to Tom Petty or Dr. Hook or Led Zeppelin. He even liked some country performers like Garth Brooks and Billy Ray Cyrus. But, increasingly, he drifted toward dark, hard-rock artists like Metallica and Ozzy Osbourne. Death and horror became a morbid curiosity, then an obsession. With a razor blade and India ink, he tattooed the letters *E-V-I-L* across the knuckles of his fist. He liked to read, and two of his favorite authors were the horror writers Anne Rice and Stephen King. Schoolwork didn't interest him, but he did have a studious nature that led him first into reviews of the world's religions, then into Wicca, the New Age nature religion which claims roots in the paganism of prehistory.

While many Wiccans will dispute it, theirs is a neo-pagan religion that mixes the traditions of what's known of Celtic shamanism with the beliefs, or research, of an Englishman named Gerald Gardner, who died in 1964. Gardner, who claimed to be related to witches and later joined Aleister Crowley's "tantric sex-magic group," the Ordo Templi Orientis, wrote several books asserting that modern witchcraft is the remaining remnant of the pre-Christian European pagan religion.

Witches and covens exist, but the popularity of Wicca is best explained by an interest in crystals and pyramids and a fascination with astrology and the unknown cosmology of ancient peoples. Often intense proselytizers, these earthy nature-lovers glory in their surroundings, and insist that a basic tenet of their belief is to not harm others. Searching for something that the Judeo-Christian tradition and organized religions don't offer, they explore a spirit world strictly off-limits to those of most mainstream faiths.

For Wiccans, or white witches, nature is supreme. Good and evil exist, but not as God or the Devil. Damien believed in a series of gods and goddesses who influenced impulses or events and resided in the woods or the crossroads. To some he acknowledged he worshiped the Devil; to others he insisted he was only a Wiccan. He studied turn-of-the-century occultist Aleister Crowley, but at the same time would play down Crowley's influence on him.

Yet despite Damien's claims, he was clearly fascinated with the Devil. In a notebook where he logged his thoughts and impressions, Damien kept a list of names for the ancient fallen angel and some Biblical terms. Alongside the terms, he listed the seven deadly sins:

    lucifer - pride
    mammon - avarice
    Asmodeus - lechery
    Satan - anger
    Beelzebub - gluttony
    leviathan - envy
    Belphegor - sloth

Police suspicions about Damien actually had started the moment the boys' bodies were discovered in the ditch. It began with the numbness that had overcome juvenile officer Steve Jones as he watched Det. Bryn Ridge pull the bodies from the ditch. Jones's horror was more than just a reaction to the grisly scene. His fears had come true, he would tell others. Damien Echols, that dark, moody teenager from Lakeshore, had finally killed somebody.

Jones and his boss, Crittenden County chief juvenile officer Jerry B. Driver, had spent the better part of the past year investigating Damien. Their fascination with the teen had started on May 19, 1992, when Damien and a girlfriend were arrested after they had run away together and were caught living in Lakeshore in an abandoned trailer whose only furniture was an old piano. In interviews with Driver and sheriff's deputies, Damien began talking about his dabblings in the occult, asserting there was a dark underworld at work in Crittenden County. Conducting a consent search of Damien's home, authorities confiscated some macabre artwork from his bedroom walls, including an artist's rendering of winged demons and unsightly creatures circling a robed figure with a goat's head who held aloft two lighted torches.

Driver also came into possession of Damien's notebook, which included some dark, disturbing writings, including this passage:

> Jackyl speeking [sic] with my tongue. Roach egg laying in my brain. I once stalked beneath your shadow. Sleepwalking to the gallow. I'm the sun that beats your brow in till you finally threw the towel in. Never knowing if I'd wake up. . . .

The discovery intrigued Driver, a tall, bulky ex-football coach and former airline pilot who switched careers in 1989 when he took this job with Crittenden County Juvenile Court Services. Driver and Jones took their work seriously, aggressively maintaining a network of "informants" who kept them alerted to the doings of the Crittenden teen scene. They were an odd couple—the large-framed Driver, fifty-three years old in 1992, with his white hair squared in a crew cut; and the small, wiry Jones, then thirty-five, who was most comfortable in blue jeans and a T-shirt. At the time of Damien's May 1992 arrest, Driver and Jones were taking careful inventory of what they determined was a marked increase in occult dabbling among local teens.

Across the county, in abandoned cotton gins, inside vacant country homes, and under viaducts, the juvenile officers found their evidence. Scattered animal carcasses. Remnants of bonfires. Spray-painted graffiti. Tips poured in about wild parties with drugs and group sex. Teenage fascination with the occult was nothing new, and the officers recognized that most of it amounted to troubling but harmless experimentation. "What it's mainly an excuse for is to take drugs and have sex," Driver would say, explaining the phenomenon as a periodic waning and waxing of interest. Still, there were more ominous signs. During the summer of 1992, Driver asked a Little Rock consultant to inspect the graffiti sites to help interpret what was going on.

Increasingly, Driver said, his informants passed on disturbing information about Damien. He planned to sacrifice a baby, teens said. Damien denied it. But then, among the teen's effects, Driver found a pencil drawing that the juvenile officer believed hinted at a possible sacrifice. Word had it that Damien had tried to impregnate the girl he ran away with in order to sacrifice the baby.

Days after the triple murders—and again in follow-up interviews—Driver explained to police investigators that during the summer of 1992 he felt a portentous evil was lurking around the corner.

"That child was to be sacrificed," Driver told the West Memphis detectives. "We got that information from some informants and from some drawings that we had confiscated from Damien at the time." The drawings included "four tombstones and a baby's foot from behind it and a rattle and power emanating up into the moon or something," Driver said.

Driver told the detectives he feared that sixteen-year-old Domini Teer—pregnant with Damien's child in May 1993—now carried the potential sacrifice. The young couple had had a rocky relationship the year earlier, Driver explained to the detectives. Damien and Domini had dated in 1992, broken up, but then got back together. "Several people very close to them, confidential informant people, said that's what was going on, and when Domini and Damien get back together, what happens? They have a baby. I'm very concerned about that."

On the day after the boys' bodies were found—Friday, May 7, 1993—juvenile officer Jones escorted Lt. James Sudbury to Damien's home in the Broadway Trailer Park. Allowed into the home, Jones said he noticed something unusual right off the bat. By the door sat Damien's black combat boots beside a pair of tennis shoes. Both were caked in mud, the juvenile officer later would recall.

Jones had brought Sudbury here to feel out the teen. The two officers came prepared. They had reviewed a consultant's literature obtained by the juvenile officers during their occult investigation. The materials, dealing with occult killings, discussed overkill, the need to defile a victim. This could include urinating in the victim's mouth, the materials said. Jones and Sudbury floated the details by Damien. They apparently made no record of this visit, but

Jones would later say that Damien's reactions were suspicious enough to warrant further inquiry.

The visit also served to kindle more interest in the juvenile officers' theories.

At the least, Driver said, he feared Damien was bound to hurt someone someday. On at least two occasions, Driver had driven Damien to a mental hospital and a reform school following arrests. One arrest involved a fight between Damien and a rival for a girl's affections when Damien was still attending Marion High School.

Some sensed bad blood existed between the teen and Driver and Jones. Damien told his friends the pair were obsessed with him. Once, Jones had warned him to leave the county, Damien claimed. On another occasion, Damien claimed he received a telephone call from a television network doing a special on witchcraft after Jones had given them his name. Jones denied the teen's claims. But the juvenile officers' interest in Damien was clear.

Driver explained to the detectives that during the summer of 1992, Damien had hinted at a pending sacrifice.

"He said he was involved in the occult, not as a Devil worshiper as such, he said he was a gray witch," Driver recalled. A "gray witch" was one both black and white, good and bad. Driver said Damien told of "three or four groups" in Crittenden County involved in "cult activities." The groups comprised mostly teenagers, but in some cases, a few adults participated, Driver said. Damien had talked of one cult group that was involved in animal sacrifice, Driver said. The cult, he said, had reached the end of their animal-sacrifice phase, and "the next logical step" would be the sacrifice of a human being.

"We asked him if he knew who it was going to

be, and he denied that he knew who it was," Driver told the detectives. "He said that one of the cults in particular was waiting for the return to Crittenden County of, I believe, the number was seven individuals (from the Chicago area) who had been involved before here and they were out of town and they were coming back in the summer of ninety-two to participate in a sacrifice. Shortly after that, we did have, I think, about seven kids showed up down at West Memphis P.D. who had all the earmarks of it, with the tattoos, and the devil rings and this, that, and the other. But it turns out they probably weren't the same ones."

Driver had studied voodoo and had plenty of interesting theories. The interstates seemed to attract plenty of weirdos, networks of people dealing in child pornography, the occult, drugs, and other sadistic practices, he said. Reviewing reports that passed across his desk, he believed there were an unusual number of underage runaways passing through Marion and West Memphis. He was not sure what it all meant. "Every kind of weirdo at one time or another has passed through these truck stops here," he said. He did not take it lightly.

In his office in Marion, Driver kept a calendar where he took note of lunar cycles and dates said to be of importance in occult circles. Throughout the summer of 1992, Driver and Jones kept watch for those dates; then, when the sun went down, they'd hit the roads into the countryside, to local woods, spots under viaducts and other locations where they believed groups of youths gathered for rituals.

"We went everywhere in the world that summer, every time there was a witches' Sabbath, we were out in force," he told the detectives. "And whether that did any good or not, I don't know, but to my knowledge, nothing happened that summer."

At first, it may have all sounded like the paranoid quackery of a novice lawman. But after the murders, the juvenile officers, with badges on their belts and guns in holsters, became a resource. After all, there were three dead boys, senselessly mutilated and drowned, murdered on the night of a full moon. At the moment, no one had any better explanations.

Driver told the detectives more.

On a grayish day the previous November, he saw Damien Echols and two companions walking down a street in the Lakeshore Estates, each dressed in black and carrying a long stick that he referred to as a "staff." It was the first time Driver had seen the three youths together, and it made him even more determined to keep a closer eye on this strange, pasty-faced, black-haired kid.

Driver, compelled by the sight of the three youths, pulled over. Damien, he would recall later, was wearing a long black coat and a "black slouch hat."

"What are you guys doing?" Driver called to them.

"We're going to watch TV," they said, and laughed.

Driver left them alone, but he said the incident served to whet his interest once again.

Driver told the detectives that Damien's group involved seven to ten members. There were indications that some adults were involved as well, he said.

"I've probably talked to Damien twenty times in the last two years, and he's always maintained that there was an older woman that brought him into it, but he would never tell me who it was," Driver said. Echols gave the indication the woman was in her "late twenties or early thirties," Driver said. But over time, Driver would make it clear that, in his immediate circle of peers at least, Damien was in charge.

"He wanted to have the ultimate control over these people," he said.

On the morning of May 9, 1993, as the West Memphis detectives prepared to interview Echols in depth, Driver and Jones passed more information on to Sudbury. They gave the detective a list with some ten names of teenagers who they believed were involved in occult practices. Among them was Damien's best friend, sixteen-year-old Jason Baldwin. A thin, quiet kid with long blond hair and a brooding face, Baldwin lived in one of the ratty trailers of Lakeshore, down the street from Echols's girlfriend, Domini Teer. Jason Baldwin was a puzzle. Shy and artistic, Jason had always denied any involvement in the occult, Driver said. But his associations with Damien and Domini made him suspect.

Also on the list was Domini Teer. Domini had been on probation for shoplifting, and Driver said he'd once transported her for commitment to Charter Hospital in Little Rock. On the ride, Driver said, Domini told him she and her friends were witches and that they worshiped nature. They also worshiped Hecate, a Greek goddess of the moon, earth, and underground realm of the dead who was later associated with witchcraft and sorcery; and Diana, the Roman moon goddess. Driver said the girl also claimed to drink blood. "She discussed with me the blood-drinking and said, 'Why should I not drink blood, because my mother drinks blood?' And I thought, now that's a strange thing to say."

Lieutenant Sudbury, who typically worked narcotics cases but, like every other available man, now was in the thick of the triple-homicide investigation, drafted a thirty-two-point questionnaire to confront Damien and his companions.

Detectives Griffin and Durham hopped in a car

and drove to Lakeshore. Located some two miles north of the police station, Lakeshore trailer park sat between West Memphis and Marion, Arkansas, a small, tidy bedroom community that serves as the county seat. To get to Lakeshore, a motorist must drive down a two-lane service road running north along Interstate 55, then take a hairpin turn and pass under the interstate through an overpass.

Spray-painted graffiti covered the concrete pillars there. Fuck The World, read one greeting. Stray dogs— scrawny, sad-eyed, some diseased with mange— lay in the road or loitered throughout the trailer park. Long-haired teens— nearly all poor and white and most sporting sleeveless T-shirts— walked in groups, peering suspiciously at strangers. Narrow lanes of curbless asphalt ran past rows of trailers packed tightly together. Trailers ringed a large, shallow man-made lake at the center of the trailer court, giving the park its name.

It was around five P.M. when Griffin and Durham drove toward the back of the trailer park and stopped at Jason Baldwin's home, a rusted yellow-and-white trailer with a sagging porch of unfinished, rain-warped wood. Jason, Damien Echols, and Domini Teer were all there, and they stepped out into the yard to speak with the detectives.

Damien, dressed in a black Portland Trail Blazers T-shirt, looked ill. His face was bone-white, as if he never got out in the sun. His hair, jet-black, was slicked back. His cheeks were pudgy, his forehead high. He gazed about him with black, dead eyes that seemed to focus on nothing. The detectives wasted no time, and began asking him questions.

"Did you know the boys?"

"No," Damien answered, registering no emotion.

"What should happen to someone who did something like this?"

"They should get the death penalty."

"Why would someone do this?"

"Thrill kill," Damien said.

As Griffin went down the line of questions, he jotted down Echols's clipped answers. Who do you think did this? Don't know. Did you do this? No. Would you take a polygraph? No, he didn't think they were accurate. How do you think it would feel to kill or watch someone die? Scary. No, he didn't believe in God or the Devil. Where was he May 5? With his parents.

Red flags went up on the next couple questions.

"How do you think the person who did this feels?"

"They liked it— happy," Griffin jotted down.

"Have you ever wondered what it would be like to kill someone, even if you didn't go through with it?"

"Yes."

Damien went on to tell the cops he'd never been sexually abused, but he knew a relative who had. He was a manic-depressive, he told them. He said he took an antidepressant medication. He saw a therapist and a psychiatrist.

"Have you ever experimented with controlled substances?" he was asked. He'd breathed gasoline fumes, he said. Gasoline was poured into cupped hands and held under the nose. It seemed clear that this kid was weird but, for the most part, he gave candid answers.

The detectives turned their attention to Jason. He seemed more alert, more on edge. No, he didn't know the boys, he said. The killer should get the death penalty. How does being questioned make him feel?

"Like a suspect," he answered.

But when the detectives asked the probing questions—the trick ones designed to elicit a response that could make him a suspect—Jason didn't hand them anything like Damien had.

"Why would someone do this?"

"I don't know," he answered.

"How do you think they died?"

"I don't know."

Yes, he believed in God. No, he hadn't tried drugs. No, he'd never thought of killing anyone. Griffin was getting ready to ask Jason if he believed in white or black magic when the teen's mother drove up and came into the yard. A small, bony woman, Angela Gail Grinnell flew into the officers like a whirlwind.

"You're picking on my son," she yelled at the officers. She didn't want them talking to him, she shouted.

"I attempted to reason with her, but to no avail. We then left," Durham wrote in his report.

Later, driving down the street to a trash-strewn trailer, the officers got a brief interview with Domini Teer. A freckle-faced girl with orange-red hair flowing onto her shoulders, Domini was an intriguing sight. Pale and thin, she stood nearly five feet eight inches tall but weighed just a hundred pounds. She sure didn't look four months pregnant.

Griffin took down basic details: She was in the tenth grade at Marion High School, but her mother took her out of school because of her pregnancy. Griffin asked where she had been May 5. She provided the same basic alibi Damien and Jason gave: She, Damien, and Jason Baldwin had walked to Jason's uncle's house in West Memphis to mow his lawn early that afternoon. She went home at six P.M., and stayed there the rest of the night. Her mother, Dian, a short, round, partially disabled woman of forty-four, verified the story. Griffin didn't push it. He noted the girl had her initials tattooed on the inside of her left leg above the ankle, and had a teardrop-shaped tattoo above the web of her left hand between thumb and forefinger.

He snapped a Polaroid of her and left. But police weren't through with Domini or Damien. Within hours, they would make the couple the focus of a deepening inquiry into witchcraft and the occult.

Six

"I'll Eat You Alive!"

On June 1, 1992, Echols was placed on a year's probation and was ordered sent to Charter Hospital in Little Rock, one of the state's leading mental health facilities.

It was during his stays at Charter Hospital that Damien grew more introspective, writing dark poetry and short essays. He kept a journal as part of his therapy. He also drew upon other sources, including occult writings and rock music lyrics, that he sometimes copied and sometimes paraphrased to fit his own ideas. Soon after he was admitted, he began meditating in his room in a bizarre and unusual fashion. He also drew pictures of occult symbols. His writings revealed his dark moods and perhaps his innermost thoughts.

> I am writing in my journal today. I don't really have anything to say. I'm just writing to take up space. I just really hate people. They all think the earth rotates around them. They all just have over inflated egos. They need to just shut the hell up and die a slow horrible painful death.

Damien admitted to suicidal ideation for two weeks prior to admission. He told the staff he ran away with his fifteen-year-old girlfriend because her parents forbade them to see one another. They had been having sex, he said. Damien denied involvement with Satanism, but said he was a witch. Damien recounted chasing a younger child with an ax and attempting to set a house on fire.

Damien spoke about his history of violence, and about his poor attendance at school. He was suspended on seven different occasions during the school year. He was disruptive. His habit of staring was described as odd.

"Neither Side Wins"
Some idiots only believe one sided. That will be their death. They think there is none greater than theirs. They couldn't be any more wrong. I know both sides. I believe neither. Without them I can breathe up the universe. I fly above them and laugh in their retarded faces.

For nearly thirty days Damien was kept at Charter Hospital. He grew to like it. He told friends he felt safe there. Damien was discharged from the adolescent psychiatric unit on June 25. Upon his discharge he was prescribed imipramine, and his discharge summary said he had improved in eye contact, expression of positive feelings, and communications with staff. Yet next to the communications item was the caveat "some."

On the last day of June 1992, as part of his probation, he was given permission to live with his biological father, Joe Hutchison, in Aloha, Oregon, in the suburbs west of Portland. It was there that Pam,

Michelle, and grandmother Frances had decided to go to escape their problems in Arkansas.

There, the family made an uneasy life. Fairly readily, Damien accepted Joe Hutchison as part of the family fold. With his dark eyes, large nose, and bent but sturdy frame, Joe closely resembled his son. But Michelle was still resenting her father for what she considered his earlier abandonment.

Even after the move to Oregon, Pam recognized that her family wasn't entirely whole. She kept in contact with social workers and she tried to arrange for follow-up counseling.

Damien and his family lived in a small, two-bedroom apartment in central Aloha. In addition to Damien, his parents, Michelle and their grandmother, there was also his half-brother on his father's side, Timothy Hutchison, aged six. Eddie Joe Hutchison worked at several gas stations in the Portland area, and Damien got full-time employment in the Raleigh Hills BP. There, he was known as Michael. He worked forty hours a week and got $5 an hour. It at least gave him some spending money. He didn't like it, but he didn't have anything better to do. It appears he made no close friends in Oregon.

It was while he was in Oregon, he said later, that he sold a collection of knives he had gathered. A former girlfriend would later testify that, before he went to Oregon, he was in the habit of carrying a huge survivalist's knife in the pocket of his long black raincoat when he wandered the streets of West Memphis.

On September 2, Damien and Joe Hutchison got into a terrible fight. Damien was demanding more freedom, but Joe wasn't willing to grant it. The whole family was traumatized. Damien, believed to be both violent and suicidal, was taken to St. Vincent's Hospital in Portland. It was there that he became delusional and paranoid. He screamed at Joe, "I'll eat you alive!"

Joe Hutchison would later recall that night, downplaying it, claiming his son had not threatened to kill him. The argument had started simply. Damien's grandmother told Joe she saw Damien with a knife. When his father confronted him, Damien denied it. Then he grew angry. His dad was siding with his grandma. He didn't believe him.

Joe called the police. He went back to his son's bedroom. Damien had three knives. Each was strapped to his body in a holster.

"They're not going to take me," Damien told him.

"Who is gonna take you?" Joe asked blindly.

"The police. You called the police."

"Son, I ain't trying to have you locked up." For a minute he pleaded with his boy. "Give me the knives," he said. Then, without resistance, his father recalled, Damien gave up the knives. They took him to the hospital.

His parents, believing him dangerous, readily agreed to his wishes to go back to Arkansas. Within days, he left Oregon for good, by bus, via St. Louis.

But unknown to Damien, Officer Driver was aware, through Oregon authorities, that the youth was on his way home. Returning unsupervised was a violation of his probation, as was his violent confrontation with his father. On September 9, Driver filed a violation of parole report on Damien Echols. Shortly after he returned to Arkansas, he was taken into custody.

* * *

When Damien returned to Arkansas, he took up with his old pals. He'd soon turn eighteen. Some folks never knew he'd gone, he would testify later. Many residents had reported seeing him around town anyway, even though he'd been in Oregon— "Damien sightings," he called them. And it was as if he had never left in another sense— within days, he was back in police custody and on his way to the Juvenile Detention Center in Jonesboro.

About three hours after Damien arrived at the detention center, he was sitting in the recreation area with several other boys. One boy had scraped his arm. It was bleeding.

Without any warning, Damien grabbed the bloody arm and began to suck the blood. The boys all said he told them he had not taken his medication the night before, and he was "about to go off on them."

Damien was asked why he sucked the boy's blood, and he replied, "I don't know."

He was sent to his room and stayed there until he was picked up for court. "It is our opinion that Damien needs mental health treatment," wrote Joyce Cureton, juvenile director.

On September 4, Damien was sent back to Charter Hospital in Little Rock for his second stay that year. He'd be there two weeks.

This time, the admissions form listed a slightly different chief complaint from him: "They say I suck blood."

Damien came to Charter with a host of physical and emotional problems. Medically, he suffered from severe allergies, migraines and heart palpitations. He smoked two packs of cigarettes a day but denied he used drugs currently. He admitted to having sniffed paint, glue and gasoline in the past and to using speed and marijuana. His problems in school and at home were fairly routine in the lives of troubled teens.

Several aspects of his case did seem unusual to the staff at Charter. Damien showed no remorse for the blood-sucking incident, laughed at the thought of being called a "blood-sucking vampire" and denied rubbing the blood all over his face. He stated that he did it to get into a gang, not as part of an occult ritual.

When he was released from Charter, he was placed in the custody of Patricia Ann Liggett, his paternal aunt. But he rarely spent much time with her. Instead, he spent nearly all his time with Domini in her mother's trailer, sleeping on that mattress under the bare red lightbulb.

Seven

"Chris . . . turned his head, knowing he was next."

He was a large kid, with jet-black hair and a pentagram medallion dangling from his neck. He came into the West Memphis police station for questioning Sunday night, about fifteen minutes before nine, some three hours after officers had questioned Domini Teer out at Lakeshore.

The cult theory now was in full bloom, and Murray Jay Farris was a witness who could possibly shed more light on it. Farris told police he was "in a group of so-called white witches" who studied the first ten books of the Bible and "prepared the readers for purity," Detective Ridge wrote in his notes. "He explained that the group believes in harming no one and gave a list of four members."

The young man made clear his reason for showing up at the station. "Farris came to the police department because his friend Damien had told him that the police had been talking to him," Ridge wrote. Farris's name was on the list of ten youths that Driver and Jones had shared with Lieutenant

Sudbury earlier that day to provide homicide investigators with information on local teens believed to be dabbling in the occult. Bryn Ridge noted the seriousness of this meeting: "Farris came to the West Memphis Police Department to answer question(s) about his whereabouts" the night of the murders.

Farris passed a polygraph test and was quickly dismissed as a possible suspect. He told police he and a friend had attended the First Baptist Church revival the night of the killings, and his alibi checked out. But he passed on some curious information. He told detectives Ridge and Allen about "a black witch," a teenage girl who lived in Marion. She was Damien Echols's former girlfriend, the one he'd dated before Domini Teer. Farris offered other peculiar details, including a description of a possible suspect: a white male, with blond hair, thirty-seven years of age. He wore reading glasses, Farris said. He stood about five feet nine inches tall and weighed 240-260 pounds. The man was heavyset, with a beer belly, and was going bald. He lived outside West Memphis near Earle, Arkansas. Farris went on to say the man "leads an evil cult" and drives an "off-white van or cream van."

If nothing else, Murray Farris was imaginative. A member of the drama club at West Memphis High School, where he was a senior, Farris also worked part-time as a carnival barker. He'd dyed his blond hair black. He was large, six feet one and 247 pounds, but gentle and warm in demeanor. Farris seemed polished beyond his eighteen years. He could converse easily about world religions, aviation, and his desire to someday become a criminal psychologist. Intelligent and articulate, he was a notch above the trailer-park crowd. His father ran a print shop and his mother was a registered nurse.

And intellectually, at least as far as this case was concerned, he was also several steps ahead of the West Memphis police. He tried to explain the medallion around his neck, which Ridge's notes described as a "star in a circle." Although it was a pentagram, a five-pointed occult symbol, Farris described it more accurately as a "hex mark." He elaborated on its meaning by spelling it in Hebrew for the police, then translating to English. The medallion depicted a pentagram positioned upright, the fifth point facing up. That was the mark of good magic. A black magic pentagram contains a fifth point facing down and can be taken to look like a goat's head, with horns atop its head.

Police didn't really know what to make of Farris. They fingerprinted him and sent him on his way.

It was pushing midnight when First Baptist youth pastor Jim Agee stirred from his bed to answer the phone. The voice over the line was shaky and uneasy. Agee recognized it as that of Bob Loomis, a sixteen-year-old boy he'd known for several years and who had come to church off and on. Just Wednesday, the night the boys had disappeared, Bob and his close friend Murray Farris had come to the revival at First Baptist, and Agee noted their visit as the first time he'd seen either in church in a year. Agee once had spent a great deal of time with Bob and Murray, sharing the gospel of Jesus Christ. But for their part, the youths had engaged in intellectual jousting, sharing their growing interest in white witchcraft, or Wicca.

This was an unusual call, Agee thought. Bob never called. It was almost midnight. Eventually, the talk turned to the murders. Agee asked Loomis if he

THE BLOOD OF INNOCENTS

knew who did it. "Maybe I do, and maybe I don't," Agee recalled Bob saying. Sensing trouble, Agee called the police.

"Bob is scared about something," Agee said as Det. Tony Anderson scribbled down notes. "This is his gut feeling after dealing with young people for fifteen years. Both of these two boys (Bob and Murray) go to WMHS and are noted for being involved in cult— white witchcraft!"

Working into the wee hours of Monday morning, the detectives on the second floor at police headquarters laid plans for the coming daylight. The talk of Wicca, witchcraft, sacrifices— stuff normally to be dismissed as nonsense— had solidified their suspicions. They would go straight for Damien. They'd summon him downtown for questioning. They'd get a second statement from his girlfriend Domini, too. And, after Agee called, they decided to throw Chris Littrell into the mix as well. They were casting a dragnet. Hopefully, they'd pull in something.

As the detectives filled out their day's reports, they routinely jotted down the case number assigned to the investigation on each slip of paper. Repeatedly, the numbers stared them in the face: 666— the mark of the Beast. It was like a clue straight out of the Book of Revelation. *Here is wisdom. Let him that hath understanding count the number of the beast. For it is the number of a man. And his number is Six hundred threescore and six.* Some would later question the assigning of the case numbers, suggesting they came by design rather than chance. But Gitchell stuck by his story: That's just the way the case number came back from the records department.

At this point, anything seemed possible. Three

dead boys. A full moon. The chief juvenile officer passing on tips about human sacrifices.

By now, the speculation of a cult motive was no secret in town. Throughout the city's churches, restaurants, and community grapevines, prevailing rumor had it that the boys had been the victims of a satanic sacrifice. Exactly how much of that rumor was based on knowledge about the direction of the police investigation is uncertain. But by now it was reaching some news reporters. Most discounted it as hysteria. And Gitchell would help others to the same conclusion. Gitchell told *The Commercial Appeal* in Memphis that, despite wide speculation, police had no evidence the boys were killed during a cultlike ritual.

For the record, Gitchell said in the West Memphis *Evening Times* that preliminary autopsies showed the boys had died from blows to the head. The reward fund, thanks to roadblocks that solicited numerous contributions from motorists over the weekend, stood at $16,000. There was no mention in the West Memphis newspaper of a possible cult link.

Damien Wayne Echols arrived at the police station a little before noon that Monday, looking peaked, as usual. He walked in a hunch, as if falling forward, his large feet plodding in an awkward swagger. His eyes, when they registered anything at all, flashed a hint of arrogance. "Damien was very cold and unemotional at the time of the interview," Det. Bryn Ridge later wrote in his notes. His demeanor at this interview would help propel the entire investigation.

The interview started at 11:54 A.M., with Ridge and Lt. James Sudbury jotting down biographical details and observations. Damien was five feet eight inches tall, 175 pounds. He had several tattoos: *Domini* on his right arm. A pentagram on his chest. The letters *E-V-I-L* were across his left knuckles. An Egyptian ankh, a T-shaped cross with a loop on top, also adorned his chest. None of his tattoos looked particularly professional. Damien had made them himself, cutting himself with a razor blade and injecting India ink under the skin. Ridge noted the pentagram was "faded." Damien also wore a necklace with a pentagram pendant. He explained that was a symbol of "Wicca magic."

He had dropped out of the ninth grade, but obtained a general equivalency high-school diploma. He listed his occupation as "roofer." His vehicle was a bicycle. Damien had no driver's license. Officers examined Damien's Arkansas identification card. In the photo, his eyes peered intently, almost transfixed, into the camera. He had some sort of early-Beatles-style haircut at the time, bangs dangling below his eyebrows.

Damien rehashed his alibi for May 5. He and Domini Teer accompanied Jason Baldwin that afternoon to mow grass for Jason's uncle in West Memphis, he said. His mother then picked Echols and his girlfriend up outside Alexander's Laundromat, then took Domini home to Lakeshore, north of town. Damien said he and his parents and sister then visited a friend's home from three to five P.M. Damien said he then went home, and got on the phone with a girl he'd met at the local skating rink. Damien said he stayed on the phone with the girl until about 11:30 that night.

He told the detectives he didn't hear about the boys' disappearance until Thursday afternoon, when Jason's mother told him about it at her trailer in

Lakeshore. Over the course of the interview, Damien agreed to give hair and blood samples to the officers. At times he appeared uninterested in the questioning, offering what seemed to be comical quips. Police asked at one point if he hunted, fished, or enjoyed camping.

"I tried fishing once but didn't like it," he said. "I don't have any outside sports."

The better part of the interview focused on Damien's beliefs. "He stated he is a member of a white magic group in which he named members including Murray Jay Farris and Bob Loomis," Ridge wrote in his notes. "He stated that his belief was there was a goddess and not a god. He stated that everyone in the group works toward a divine light and upon reaching that stage they become like gods themselves. He has been a member of this group for about five years, he stated."

Ridge's notes continued: "Damien stated that he had met one person that he considered to be a priestess. This was an ex-girlfriend." He stated that she worshiped cats in what she did with her form of witchcraft." Officers, who had found an empty package of Doral cigarettes at the crime scene, asked Damien what type of cigarettes he smoked.

"The cheapest brand I can find," he answered in his soft, controlled voice.

Damien also liked to read books, the officers noted. One of favorite authors was Anton LaVey, the so-called "Black Pope" who founded the Church of Satan in California in the 1960s and authored the controversial *The Satanic Bible* in 1969. "Damien wants to be a writer of scary books and poems at some time," Ridge noted.

Over the next few hours, police grilled him for answers, again running him through the thirty-two-

THE BLOOD OF INNOCENTS 117

point questionnaire, then giving him a polygraph test. Police made no tape recording of the interview, leaving only handwritten notes and a typed report as their record. According to those records, Damien made several alarming statements that led police to believe he knew more about the murders than he was letting on.

"Damien stated that he figured that the killer knew the kids went into the woods and even asked them to come out to the woods," Ridge typed in his report. "He stated that the boys were not big, not smart, and they would have been easy to control. He also felt the killer would not have been worried about the boys screaming due to it being in the woods and close to the expressway. He further stated that the killer probably wanted to hear the screaming."

When the detectives asked why someone would do this, Damien said the killer was someone "sick" who was seeking a "thrill kill." When asked who he thought did it, he responded, "Satanists." In discussing the mutilation, Damien "stated that the penis was a symbol of power in his religion known as Wicca. He also stated that the number three was a sacred number in the belief."

He also told the detectives that juvenile officer Steve Jones had visited him one or two days earlier and told him the boys' testicles had been cut off and that "someone had urinated in their mouths," then tossed the bodies into the water to wash out the evidence.

Because there was no tape recording, the precise give-and-take between Damien and the detectives cannot be known. According to the report, here's how some of his comments came out:

"When asked about what he had heard about how

the murders had occurred, he stated that they probably had died of mutilation. He stated that he heard that some guy had cut them up. He heard that they were placed in the water, and that they may have drowned. He stated that because of what he had heard, he believed that at least one of the boys had been cut up. He stated that one of the boys may have been cut more than the others. Damien felt that the homicide may have been for the purpose of trying to scare someone.

"Damien stated that he felt it was probably only one person because if it were more than one person somebody would probably tell about it sooner or later. He said that there would be a fear of squealing by one of the person (sic) in the act if it were more than one person.

"When asked if the water had any type of meaning in the Wicca or black magic, Damien stated that water was a demon type symbolism and that all people have a demonic force. He further stated that people have control over the demonic force in them.

"When asked how be thought the person felt that had done the homicides, he stated that the person probably felt good about what he had done and that he felt good that he had the power to do what he had done.

"When asked why he thought the victims were so young, he stated that the younger the victim, then the more innocent the victim would be. That in turn meant that the more innocent the victim would be, the more power that the person would have gotten from the sacrifice. . . .

"When asked what kinds of items we should be searching for, he stated that we should be looking for stones in the area, candles, a knife, and some type of crystals.

"Damien went further to explain that in his Wicca religion he knew that evil done comes back three times. He stated that meant that any evil done by a person would be rewarded by the person doing the deed having three times the evil done to him in revenge.

"Damien stated that his favorite book of the Bible was that of Revelation because of the stories in it about what was being done by the Devil and the suffering done by people at the hands of the Devil."

Since Sunday, Damien apparently had given more thought to the question, "Have you ever wondered what it would be like to kill someone?"

"Only out of anger, to beat someone up," he was quoted.

Then the detectives asked a couple of key questions.

"How do you think the person who did this feels?"

"Probably thinks it is funny and that he won't get caught and won't care one way or the other if he did," Damien said.

"Do you know who did this?"

Damien offered the names of two people who "could have" done it. One was Jason Baldwin. Not his friend, the skinny kid from Lakeshore, he explained. But another Jason Baldwin from West Memphis who weighed about three hundred pounds. "He claimed that the other was mean and that he has been known to kill snakes, which he claimed was just for the 'hell' of killing," Ridge typed in the report. Police later checked out the "big" Jason Baldwin, but never linked him to the murders.

Damien's other suggested killer was L.G. Hollingsworth, his girlfriend's cousin. There had been bad blood between Damien and L.G., though the two teens frequently hung out together. In addition to being Domini Teer's cousin, L.G. also dated her best friend. Somewhere in the mix, L.G. had ticked off Damien. "He stated that L.G. was kind of weird in that on one occasion he wanted to trade girlfriends with Damien for a night," Ridge wrote in his report.

As police prepared to polygraph Damien, they found they wouldn't have to go far to check out part of his story. Detectives had L.G. down the hall in another room, where they had begun working on him.

L.G. Hollingsworth, Jr., sat awkwardly in the interview room. Initially, he had become angry when he learned the police wanted to talk with him. Now the brown-haired skinny kid with *Little Gangster* tattooed on his bicep was just scared. At seventeen, he was a high-school dropout who didn't make it past the ninth grade. Just last week, he'd landed a job as a grocery store sacker. Now he was in the middle of the area's biggest murder case in years. As he sat before two detectives, the allegations were mounting all around him.

In another room, Sgt. Mike Allen was jotting down an anonymous phone tip from "what sounded like an older white female." Allen wrote: "She had overheard that a Domineck (sic) and a Damion (sic) killed the three little boys and that LG (sic), last name unknown, took and laundered their clothing. Caller stated that Damien had body parts in a box from the children."

Down in Horn Lake, Mississippi, a young relative of L.G. told a schoolteacher that an aunt said L.G.

had come home Wednesday night with blood on him. The talk among the family was that L.G. had come home over the weekend carrying something "stinky" in a box. Startled, the Mississippi teacher promptly called West Memphis police.

But as L.G. sat nervously in the interview room, denying any involvement in the murders, police were getting a different account from his aunt out at Lakeshore.

Narlene Hollingsworth sat amid the clutter of her double-wide mobile home as West Memphis police detectives Charlie Dabbs and Diane Hester tape-recorded her account of seeing Damien near the crime scene the night of the murders. Narlene had alerted detectives a day earlier, calling the police station on Sunday to inform them she had seen Damien and Domini walking away from the Robin Hood Hills area about 9:40 Wednesday night as she drove down the interstate service road. "They looked dirty," Narlene had said. But her story was as much about her nephew L.G. "Her nephew L.G. made the statement on Thursday that he knew about what happened before anyone else." One cop jotted down in notes as Narlene talked.

Now, with two detectives and the tape recorder in front of her, Narlene excitedly told her story in her high-pitched twang. In a sixteen-minute interview, Narlene would talk herself into becoming a cornerstone of the investigation, sending authorities on a months-long search for a widespread conspiracy behind the murders.

According to her account, she left her trailer about 9:30 Wednesday night to pick up Dixie Hubbard, a friend who was getting off work at ten. Narlene, her husband Ricky, her son Anthony, and daughters Mary and Tabitha all piled into Narlene's

1982 red Ford Escort station wagon. As they drove east along the service road lining Interstate 40, Narlene spotted Damien and Domini walking west, toward her car and away from Robin Hood Hills. Narlene placed the couple in front of Love's convenience store, some five hundred to one thousand feet east of the Blue Beacon truck wash and Robin Hood. As Narlene drove by, the couple walked past a yellow road marker. Narlene said she turned on her bright lights, and Domini grabbed the road marker, which Narlene described as "some stick standing up." Then, "she pointed the stick out to us," Narlene said.

With her bright lights on, Narlene said she could clearly see Damien and Domini, whom she referred to as "Dominique."

"I've known her all of her life," she said. "I used to hold her on my hip when she was a six-month-old baby." Narlene and Domini were distantly related through marriage. In recent years, Narlene and Domini lived within a few hundred feet of each other at Lakeshore. Domini lived with her mother in a trailer they rented from Narlene's sister. The detectives asked Narlene what she did "right after you saw" the pair.

"Well, I was upset about it, for them being out that late and around that area, but you know I was wondering what they were doing out at that time of the night. My husband told me to quit worrying about it, 'cause they are out all the time. He said that he sees them all the time."

According to her account, Narlene then arrived at the Flash Market laundry, about a mile southeast of the point where she'd seen Damien and Domini. At the laundry, Dixie told Narlene that her nephew L.G. "had just left from there in some car." Narlene said she and Dixie grew more concerned about the night's events after the three boys turned up dead.

"I said, 'Dixie, that's kinda odd for them to be out that time of night and those little kids were dead, don't you think?' She said, 'Yes, I do. Yes, I do.' I said, 'Let me ask you something,' I said, 'You know Damien better than me, do you think he's capable of anything like that,' and she said, 'Yes, I do.' She said: 'Because he's in with the Devil.'"

As the tape recorder whirred, Narlene turned her attention to Thursday, the day after the bodies were found. L.G. drove out to Lakeshore that day in "a yellow car," she said. Some of Narlene's young nephews there noticed L.G. had "some boxes" in the back, she said.

"Now, what was in the boxes, I don't know. The kids said that the box was about this big (indicating a box a little wider than a shoe box) and they didn't know what was in the box. But he said, 'Don't look at it, don't touch it, don't step on it or I'll hurt you.'" Narlene went on to tell the officers the box "smelled horrible."

Narlene next told the officers she had just seen L.G. earlier this Monday morning, up at the police station where he was about to be questioned. She claimed her nephew had begged her to change her story.

"He said that, 'I wasn't at no laundromat Wednesday night.' I said, 'Yes, you was.' He said, 'No, I wasn't. Go in there and tell them that I wasn't.' I said, 'You better stop lying or they are going to get you for murdering these children and they are going to know why you lied.' He said, 'All right, I was there.' I said, 'I know you was.'"

Any policeman knows that a witness placing a suspect near a crime scene can make a case. But how solid was Narlene's claim?

Her husband, Ricky L. Hollingsworth, told police he saw two people walking along the service road, but couldn't be certain it was Damien and Domini. "Narlene thought it was strange and asked if she ought to turn around to give them a ride," Ricky Hollingsworth, then thirty-seven, said. "I told her no, that I had seen them walking all over the place and that they are always walking."

Narlene, her daughter Tabitha, and her son Anthony all identified the pair on the road as Damien and Domini. Also riding in Narlene's red Ford Escort were daughter Mary and son Rick. Police and prosecutors later would accept a portion of Narlene's account, and dismiss the remainder. They contended the Hollingsworths correctly spotted Damien, but had confused Domini with Jason Baldwin. Both thin, Jason and Domini each had long, light-colored hair at the time. They said Domini was wearing black pants with holes in the knees. But Tabitha and Anthony said the person they saw walking on the road had "white flowers" covering the black pants.

According to the full context of her statement to police, Narlene had seen a lot of things that night and in the days after the murders, all of which could have been related to the killings. She told police she had even seen the three boys on their bikes a couple hours before they disappeared.

However, something didn't add up. Echols contended he was at home at the time that Narlene and her family claimed they saw him on the service road, a couple miles from his home at Broadway Trailer Park. A witness confirmed his claim. A Bartlett, Tennessee, girl, who was twelve years old when Echols met her at the West Memphis skating rink, told police she was talking on the phone with Echols around 9:20 or 9:30 P.M., the approximate time the Hollingsworths spotted Echols on the road.

Several members of the Hollingsworth clan also said they doubted Narlene's statements. They said her possible motives for lying included jealousy and revenge. Although Narlene was L.G.'s aunt, she once was married to L.G.'s dad, L.G. Hollingsworth, Sr. Explaining her twisted family tree to a reporter one day, Narlene said she split with L.G., Sr., after he became romantically involved with her best friend. Seeking revenge, Narlene said she married Big L.G.'s brother, Ricky. "I wanted to hurt him the way he hurt me," she said. "I married L.G.'s brother to hurt L.G."

Narlene also was indirectly related to Domini Teer. Dixie Hubbard, the woman who worked at the Flash Market laundromat, was Domini's aunt. And Dixie once was married to Big L.G.'s father. In a May 20 statement to police, Dixie warned that Little L.G.'s mother would cover for her son, but she also said Narlene "will exaggerate."

Down in Horn Lake, John Hollingsworth had similar sentiments. John Hollingsworth claimed Narlene was only interested in the reward money. "The only thing she knows is what she made up," he said. "I can understand them checking all these leads but if they're listening to Narlene Hollingsworth, he's wasting his time."

But Narlene Hollingsworth had handed police the first evidence outside pure speculation that could link Damien Echols to the murders. For that, they were grateful, and unlike some Hollingsworth family members, they didn't take her information lightly.

For her nephew L.G., that spelled a lot of trouble. After several hours, he was released that Monday afternoon. But other details concerned investigators. A consent search of L.G.'s house that day revealed a knife in a sheath, among other things. Hollingsworth steadfastly denied any involvement in the murders. But if there was anything to a cult connection, it seemed to some officers that L.G. Hollingsworth knew more about it.

As the day wound down, police explored another link to witchcraft provided by Bob Loomis. Like his close friend, Murray Farris, the sixteen-year-old junior at West Memphis High School was large for his age. He stood six feet two inches and weighed 270 pounds. And like Farris, Bob explained he had been at the First Baptist revival the night of the murders.

Bob told detectives he had picked up Damien to go to the mall the day after the boys' bodies were found. Bob said he knew nothing of the murders, and passed a polygraph test. But over the coming weeks, as police pressed witnesses for leads on a possible cult connection, Bob would tell them about a secret club of teens called the Order of the Divine Light. They met in Farris's bedroom and backyard, practicing "the religion of nature" and vowing to "do whatever you want as long as it harms no one," he said. That pledge is the cardinal rule of Wicca. Loomis provided a list of members— Damien Echols among them.

New members of Loomis's club were blindfolded and bound with their hands behind their back during initiation rituals the group adopted from a 1990 book, *Buckland's Complete Book of Witchcraft* by Raymond Buckland. A compendium of the history and philosophy of witchcraft, the book describes a coven initiation rite in which the subject, preferably nude, is bound at the wrists with a nine-foot red cord. The cord then is looped and fastened around the neck.

It was interesting to read. But police knew they had nothing solid.

As reporters checked with police on the case's progress, Gitchell expressed optimism that his detectives were on the right track. He said detectives had interviewed six or seven people, including four on Monday, who were shedding light on circumstances surrounding the murders.

"The pieces are beginning to fit together a little better," Gitchell said. "I'm confident we will solve this. We're talking with some individuals. We don't know what direction it's going to lead us in. We're making steady headway and progress."

Domini Teer was interviewed at ten minutes after eight that night on May 10. Although Domini made several statements that appeared to conflict with Damien's account, police records don't indicate that officers were alarmed by anything she said.

According to Ridge's notes, Domini said she and Damien went to a nearby laundry where Damien's mother picked them up. But differing sharply from Damien, who indicates this happened before three P.M., Domini said they were picked up "just before it got dark." The sun set at 7:49 P.M. that day.

Domini went on to tell Ridge and Mary Margaret Kesterson of the Arkansas State Police that she called Damien later that night and he said he was tired and was going to sleep. "Domini's mother stated that Domini came in when *Time Trax* was on TV on Wednesday night," Ridge wrote in his notes. *Time Trax* aired at seven that night. The officers apparently didn't confront Domini with Narlene's contention that she saw her with Damien along the service road the night of the murders.

As for Damien, he failed his lie-detector test earlier, according to polygrapher Bill Durham. The two engaged in a forty-five minute conversation which, according to Durham's notes, produced more curious statements:

"What are you afraid of?" Durham asked at one point.

"The electric chair," Durham recalled Damien's answer. Damien said he liked the hospital in Little Rock where he had been treated for manic depression, Durham noted. After a short period, Damien "ceased to deny his involvement," making "admission through absence of denial," Durham wrote in his notes.

"I will tell you all about it if you will let me talk to my mother," Damien told him. Detective Ridge quickly drove out to the Broadway Trailer Park and brought Pam Hutchison back to the police station. A large woman with dark hair and eyes like Damien, she spoke with her son for several minutes. The cops got the tape recorders ready.

But when Damien spoke to them again, he denied involvement in the murders.

"You're never going to tell anyone about this but your doctor, are you?" Durham impatiently asked.

"No," Damien answered.

It almost seemed Damien Echols had slipped through their fingers. The disappointment would only intensify the next day, Tuesday, May 11, when detectives learned more people had at least a gut feeling Damien had killed the kids. Within hours, two witnesses would fail polygraph tests, then tell police they believed Damien committed the murders.

The first was none other than L.G. Hollingsworth.

He showed no signs of deception when answering questions about whether he'd played a role in the murders. But when L.G. said 'no' in answer to question No. 10— "Do you know who killed the boys?"— it threw Bill Durham's polygraph machine into fits. "In the posttest interview, the subject said he suspects Damien Echols," Durham reported. However, if L.G. explained the reason for his suspicions, they didn't appear in Durham's report.

Police also interviewed Damien's former "priestess" girlfriend, a cute brunette from Marion who had been arrested with him a year earlier. In a polygraph test, Durham felt the girl lied when he asked, "Do you know, for sure, who killed these boys?" Durham detected deception in her negative answer.

"In the posttest interview, the subject stated that she is convinced that Damien Echols is involved," Durham wrote in his report. He didn't go into details.

"Did you say that the death of these boys was ordered by a friend of yours at school?" Ridge asked her.

"I said that Damien would not have been there. He is a coward and would be afraid of going to jail, but he could have ordered it done and so probably Jason Baldwin would have been the one. He is a follower."

The girl, just sixteen years old, described a bizarre subculture of teenagers in Marion and West Memphis involved in what she called "the cult." Confirming Murray Farris's tip, she told police she had been a "black witch" when she'd dated Damien a year earlier. "It was a game people get into for the power and stuff," she said.

But not all of it was a game, she said. And in lucid detail, she confirmed juvenile officer Jerry

Driver's seemingly wild account of a planned human sacrifice.

"I found out that he planned to kill our firstborn if it was a girl. Damien would not do it. He is a coward, and would have tried to get me to do it. That's when I knew he was nuts and I had nothing else to do with him."

She said cult members carried weapons, preferably knives and staffs. If the cult committed the murders, it would have been between eleven P.M. and one A.M., most likely at midnight, she said. The group did drugs in wooded areas and planned activities around full-moon phases. New members "would have been stripped," she said, and "might have been made to drink blood."

"Damien is crazy, mixed up with drugs and the cult . . . Damien says he is into white magic, but that is a lie. He is into black magic and sometimes says he is into gray magic. I hate I was stupid enough to get involved in this stuff."

And still, all the interviews—the around-the-clock work, the investigation of the endless stream of bizarre tips—had turned up nothing solid. For the time being, the Damien trail, which had seemed so hot a day earlier, was cold. Over the next several days, it would be back to chasing phantoms.

Then came one of the strangest incidents of the entire case. Out in Phoenix, Arizona, a resident walking down a street found a mysterious notebook containing news articles about the West Memphis triple murders, along with maps and handwritten notes that appeared to detail the boys' deaths. The resident turned the papers over to police.

In the notebook, officers also found a bank deposit slip that led them to a Glendale, Arizona man. On Wednesday, May 12, Glendale Police Department detectives interviewed a local upholsterer who told them the notebook was a chronicle of a dream.

The man, who said he had read about the case in the newspaper, dreamed of an unpainted barn with wooden slats. Then he saw a van and a white male, but they weren't very clear to him.

The notes the upholsterer had made of his dream were chilling:

"Got them at nite time. Moon is shining on river. . . . Steve was killed first. 5 min Michael.

"Chris did not want to look, turned his head, knowing he was next, man."

He then went to the library and photocopied a map of the West Memphis area. Over the next couple days, Glendale police checked into the upholsterer's story. Acquaintances said he had not been out of the state on May 5 and 6, though he was studying to get an airplane pilot's license. His girlfriend said he once had dreamed about "somebody winning big on a slot machine" at a nearby Indian reservation, and "sure enough, somebody won real big." The upholsterer fell from the list of suspects.

Almost as soon as it had appeared, police's optimism turned sour. "I think we're looking at a long investigation," Gitchell told reporters at one of his daily news briefings. The police were grasping for leads, and they knew it.

Eight

My Little Angel

The funerals for the boys would give police another opportunity for insight into their murders, maybe even clues. They knew that some killers, trying to draw some strange satisfaction from their crime, will sometimes come to their victims' funerals. So detectives posted a video camera outside Holy Cross Episcopal Church in West Memphis, watching as two hundred mourners filed into the tiny church for James Michael Moore's funeral on May 11. Police officers, family members, two dozen children, several Weaver Elementary teachers, and Mayor Keith M. Ingram came to say goodbye to the little Cub Scout with the big imagination. The media, too, were out in force.

"It's just hard to imagine that something like this has happened in our small community, where almost everybody knows each other," said Lou Cook, a substitute teacher at Weaver. "It just doesn't seem real yet." Along with grief, fear consumed the city. Cook said her children "won't hardly leave the house." Two days earlier, at a Mother's Day picnic, the Cook family ate fried chicken in their backyard, but as soon as they finished, the children "wanted to go back in the house," she said. Charles Norris, a twenty-three-year-old ice cream truck driver, said that, despite the heat, his Popsicle business was at a standstill. "On the east side of West Memphis, kids weren't even coming out, and if they did, parents were watching 'em from the window. I think everyone's suspicious of everyone."

The impact of the murders ran deep. *People* magazine and nationally syndicated television shows, including *America's Most Wanted* and *Inside Edition*, were preparing features on the case. Flags at Weaver Elementary flew at half-staff. The reward fund climbed to $25,000. The marquee at Second Baptist Church made public the feelings of thousands: "To the Families of Christopher, Michael, and Steve. We Are Praying for You."

True to his calling, the Reverend Fred Tinsley attempted to find something positive, something comforting in this great tragedy. "It was scarcely a year ago that this young lad was standing at the baptismal font," he told the mourners sitting out before Michael's small, cloth-draped casket. "We know that today, right now, Michael is the resurrection and the life."

Todd Moore, dressed in a dark suit, listened stoically. His wife, Diane, her brilliant red hair drawn up in a bun, held her arm around their daughter, Dawn, drawing her close, as if shielding her remaining child from a vicious world.

Tinsley also urged the parents of the three boys not to blame themselves, not to delude themselves into thinking they had failed to properly supervise their boys. "Such self-deprecation and blame at this particular time only serves to draw our attention away from why we are here," he said, "celebrating the gifts of Michael's life."

But self-forgiveness would come hard for Pam Hobbs. She would blame herself for months, and no one could reason with her. She had let Stevie go for an hour. Just an hour. For now, she found comfort with relatives in her hometown of Blytheville, Arkansas, in the northeast corner of the state. The family had decided to bury Stevie in Steele, Missouri, a town of 2,400, fifteen miles north of Blytheville. Jackie Hicks, Stevie's grandpa, grew up there and owned eleven burial plots in a cemetery just off Interstate 55.

Hicks, too, had been beside himself since Stevie's death. He could not rest. When the boy's body came back from the crime lab in Little Rock, Hicks insisted on inspecting his grandson's wounds.

Hicks watched helplessly as funeral director Charles Adams pulled Stevie's broken body from a plastic bag. This wasn't his grandson. It couldn't be. Just a week earlier Stevie's little face had smiled into his, blue eyes flashing, when his grandpa gave him the new Renegade bicycle. Now the face was unrecognizable. It looked to Hicks as if Stevie's jaw was nearly torn from his face. The shiny blue eyes were busted. "Some son of a bitch has done a number on this baby with a pair of combat boots or engineer's boots," Hicks told himself, then others.

He looked over the body carefully. He could see no marks on his grandson's wrists where he'd been bound, but he saw that one ankle had a bruise "about as deep as cigarette burns pulling into his skin." Hicks could not stifle his curiosity. He inspected his grandson's privates. There was a scratch beside the boy's penis, Hicks noted. But he assured himself his grandson had not been raped. "I'm not a professional. I'm not a doctor," he said later. "But I don't believe it. I don't believe Steve was raped."

Jackie Hicks ached. His body was still sore from his slide down the ditch in Robin Hood, but it was more than that. He was at a loss. This mountain of a man, this ex-cop, a former wrestler—he now felt utterly helpless. "It was inhuman the way Stevie looked," he said.

Tuesday brought more pain and another funeral. Scores of people attended services for Christopher Byers at Ingram Boulevard Baptist Church, where the singing and tears contrasted sharply with the reserved Episcopal service of the day before. A dark oak casket, flowers, a baby quilt, and a photo of Chris sat at the front of the auditorium.

"This is one of life's most painful experiences, the homegoing of a child or a little one," the Reverend Sonny Simpson told the gathering. "We are reminded that our life, even at its longest, is still very short."

By the night of May 12, it had been a week since the killings, seven days of fear and uncertainty. Shortly before the sun set this night, seven men slipped under the yellow crime tape around Robin Hood Hills and went back to the ditch where the bodies were found. They were looking for blood.

Leading the group was Donald E. Smith, a criminalist with the state crime lab in Little Rock, and Kermit Channell, a lab serologist. They were accompanied by five West Memphis police detectives.

The team sprayed a chemical reagent called Luminol in the area where the bodies were found, then waited for darkness. Luminol is a solution that glows in the dark when it comes in contact with blood, even trace amounts not visible to the eye. Investigators requested the test because they found no blood on the ground at the crime scene. They needed to know what that meant. If Luminol testing turned up negative, it might mean that the boys were killed somewhere else and dumped in Robin Hood. Under Arkansas law, Luminol test results are not admissible in court because they are considered unreliable, suggestive, and highly prejudicial. But police often use Luminol as a tool to guide them in investigations.

When the sun went down, an eerie glow shimmered from the ditch. Starlight and brightness from the surrounding city dimmed the glow, and the team would return the next day with a funeral tent awning and black plastic to block out the light so they could photograph the reaction.

In all, Luminol reacted positively in eight spots in and around the ditch where the bodies were found. Three of those spots involved points where the boys' bodies were discovered in the stream or where they were laid after being pulled from the water. Three of the spots—at the bluff on top of the ditch, a point on the ditch slope, and a point on a trail leading to the ditch—appeared to contain blood transferred by the shoes of rescue-and-recovery teams, Smith later said in a June 10, 1993, report. Two spots, both on the "scuffed-off" bank immediately east of where Michael Moore's body was found, were believed to be points of attack.

"The areas . . . indicate activity prior to recovery of the victims and relate to activity to the victims when perhaps they were being attacked," Smith's report said. "It is our opinion the crime had taken place where the bodies of the victims were recovered."

* * *

THE BLOOD OF INNOCENTS 137

Partly because of the town's hysteria, the swirl of leads wouldn't stop. Police were asked to check out a fifty-four-year-old paroled sex offender from Oregon who may have been in the area. On Thursday, May 13, Gitchell asked detectives to call the Veterans Administration hospital in Memphis to see if any Vietnam veterans were living in the Mayfair Apartments. VA officials were asked particularly to be on the alert for any patient with an injury to his penis.

The last to be buried was Stevie Branch. At the funeral in Steele, Missouri, Stevie's mother, Pam, and his uncle, Jackie Hicks, Jr., sang one of Stevie's favorite songs, "When the Children Cry," by the band White Lion. Jackie accompanied on electric guitar. "Every time I picked up my guitar, he wanted me to play that song," Stevie's uncle said. "Bless his heart, he knew every word." A spray of white carnations and purple ribbon covered Stevie's coffin. Two poems by his mother were read, including one called "For My Little Angel" that ended with the line, "Baby, we will always love you."

By the morning of Friday, May 14, Gitchell had discontinued his daily press briefings. A sign newly posted on the door to the criminal investigation division read: Do Not Enter.

Gitchell had issued a terse press release that anticipated reporters' routine questions: No, there are no suspects. No, police do not believe the case is related to a similar double homicide in San Diego. FBI officials were still assembling a profile of the killer or killers. Police would not discuss a possible murder weapon. Commenting briefly on weapons, Gitchell told a reporter he didn't want to hand details to several "crackpots" who were calling in to confess.

Part of Gitchell's frustrations involved delays in the return of evidence from the state crime lab, where materials had been sent for analysis. Police still had no idea if they had any substantial physical evidence from the crime scene.

That same day, a story on the triple murders aired nationally on *America's Most Wanted*, triggering more than one hundred calls and seventy-five faxes to West Memphis, none of which proved useful.

Then on Saturday, May 15, the case took another turn. Damien Echols's mother, Pam Hutchison, drove to the police station to give a statement and wage some complaints.

Over the next forty-five minutes, the short, dark-haired woman gave a detailed accounting of her son's whereabouts, maintaining the police were unfairly focusing on her son as a suspect. It would be the first of many charges in the months to come about the police focus on Damien. It would come to be called "Damien tunnel vision."

"I feel we are under watch because my son has mental problems," Hutchison told detectives Ridge and Sudbury. Like her son, Pamela Joyce Hutchison had dark, intense eyes. She was cool under fire. She had dropped out of school after the eighth grade, yet, at thirty-four, she came across with a certain sense of intelligence and self-confidence.

She explained that her son was different, and had been hospitalized three times for mental and emotional disturbances. "And I think that every which way he turns, somebody is going to blame him for anything that happens."

"Are you talking about this particular incident or anything?" Sudbury asked.

"Anything in general that happens in West Memphis," she told them. "And I know that Jerry Driver does not like him."

Pam Hutchison told the officers that juvenile officer Driver had it in for her son. When Damien had been arrested a year earlier with the girl in the abandoned trailer, Driver listened only to the girl's family, blaming Damien, she said.

The speed at which the investigation came to focus on Damien was startling, she said. Mrs. Hutchison claimed that Steve Jones and a police detective came to question her son on Thursday, May 6, the afternoon that the bodies had been found. Jones recalled the visit happening a day later, on Friday. The officers interviewed Damien in his room, then took pictures of him out in the yard, Mrs. Hutchison said.

"Do you personally feel that your son has nothing to do with the death of these boys?" Sudbury asked.

"I know for a fact that he doesn't."

"Okay. You feel very strong about that?"

"Yes, I do. And not just because he's my son. But because I know his whereabouts, and everybody else knows his whereabouts."

She provided this account that became Damien's alibi: On Tuesday, May 4, Pam and Joe had another falling-out and Joe walked out, moving in with his mother. Damien took it hard, and began crying.

"He usually tries to suppress (his emotions) but their natural father had deserted them when they were both real small and I guess he felt like he was doing it again," she said.

The next day, May 5, Damien had a doctor's appointment at the East Arkansas Mental Health Center. She stressed that her son had been suicidal in the past, and was receiving medication. He was not suffering any particular duress this day, she said.

About 12:30 P.M. that day, Pam, Damien, and daughter Michelle left the clinic and went to a drugstore in Marion to fill a prescription of imipramine for her son. The drug makes her son sleepy, she said. But the line was long, so they decided to pick up the prescription the next day, she said.

About one P.M., the family swung through Lakeshore trailer park, where Pam dropped Damien off at Jason Baldwin's trailer. Pam went back home. About 3:45 P.M., Pam received a call from Damien. He was at the Alexander laundromat on Missouri Street with Domini and needed a ride. They had just been with Jason, who was mowing his uncle's yard in West Memphis. Pam said she picked Damien and Domini up, dropped the girl off at Lakeshore, then returned home about four P.M. at the Broadway Trailer Park.

About 5:30 or six, the family— Damien included— dropped by the home of some friends on West Memphis's northwest corner. They stayed about an hour, then went home. Damien spent the better part of the night on the phone, she said, talking part of that time with a girlfriend from Bartlett, Tennessee. Police later interviewed the girl, who said she was on the phone with Damien at about 9:30 P.M.

Detective Ridge saw a problem with Pam's account. Ridge knew that Domini had said it was dark or getting dark when Mrs. Hutchison had picked her and Damien up at the laundry. The sun set at 7:49 P.M. on May 5.

Ridge tested her.

"Were I to inform you that the time period of when you picked him up at Alexander's has been explained by other methods and other witnesses to say that time . . . was between seven-thirty and eight, are you steadfast it happened at three-thirty?"

Mrs. Hutchison said it was about quarter to four.

"So these other people are in error?" Ridge pressed.

"Most definitely. They don't know what they are talking about."

Over the course of the interview, she explained that her son was introverted and had a high IQ. He had been suicidal because of his breakup with the girl last year. Contradicting Driver's claim that Damien and the girl had planned to have a baby to sacrifice it, Mrs. Hutchison said their plans were driven by love.

"They were in hopes she would get pregnant because the girl's mother had forbidden Damien to see her and they thought if she got pregnant, that she couldn't keep him away."

Mrs. Hutchison conceded that Damien could have a violent temper if he's "continually pushed." He does practice white magic, she said. When asked for names of his associates, she could think of only three: Jason, Murray, and Chris.

But, she insisted, the police were way off track.

"I think that you should be checking on something other than these young teenage boys," she said. "I think these boys are maybe a little mischievous or something like that, but as far as doing anything like murdering these boys, I don't think that is right."

Somehow, the police needed to get on track. But how? They seemed to be making the right moves. They checked the truck stops, even checked truckers' shower records. They inventoried local sex offenders, and questioned many of them. They consulted the FBI. They chased leads about wacky hitchhikers and bizarre cults. They even had national TV programs going to bat for them. They went door-to-door, surveying scores of residents all around the woods. The house surveys had worked so well in the Ronald Ward triple-murder case, but now, it seemed, there was nothing.

John Mark Byers sat uneasily before the two detectives. His big face seemed strained, as one might expect of a parent under such circumstances. But there was something else. His green eyes were pale and dull. His head seemed oddly misshapen. The left side of his forehead seemed to bulge on one side like a cheap softball that had been smacked lopsided by a bat.

Over the next hour and eighteen minutes, detectives Bryn Ridge and James Sudbury would try to get inside this man. It was a delicate task. On the one hand, here was a grieving father, still mourning the loss of his stepson. It could be considered rude and indecent to pump him for information. On the other hand, there was something about him that stirred questions. The detectives knew about his past.

"Um, first, one of the first questions we need to know is, where were you when you first found out the kids were missing?" Ridge asked, initiating a tape-recorded interview May 19, 1993, fourteen days after the murders.

Byers proceeded to give his account of May 5: how he had disciplined Christopher that day, how the boy later disappeared from under the carport, and how Byers, his wife, Melissa, and son, Ryan, spent the next several hours looking for him. Byers told how he went into Robin Hood woods a little after eight that night and stayed out looking until three or four in the morning. At one point, Ridge asked if Chris frequently went to Robin Hood, and Byers said he had told the boy the woods was "off-limits" because last summer Ryan and a friend had seen "a bum or a junkie" there.

Sudbury asked if Byers was taking medication. Byers said yes, that he had a brain tumor, which explained the lopsided head. Byers said he frequently broke out in sweats, got migraine headaches, suffered tunnel vision, and experienced "blackouts." To combat all that, Byers said he was taking Valium and Tegratal, an antiseizure medicine. He'd taken a ten-milligram Valium tablet three hours ago, before Gitchell called and asked him to come to the station. Sudbury then asked if Byers had any life insurance on either of his kids or wife. Byers said he had a life insurance policy at one time, but lost it because of mounting medical bills. He'd filed for bankruptcy in 1991, he said.

Byers talked about frequent parties in his backyard, explaining that they had stirred ill will with Todd and Diane Moore.

"I wouldn't say we were close friends and we weren't enemies," he said. "We had had some backyard barbecues where we would get together and have friends over. I quit inviting them. And the reason I quit inviting them was because they would get a little too much to drink, and they would get belligerent and loud."

But it seemed there was more to their differences.

"And then this past summer, they called the police on me four times." Sometimes, the complaints involved Byers's guests parking on the Moores' lawn. "Once they said the music was too loud. And then the time they complained about that, and the police came out, there wasn't even any music playing."

That was interesting, but the detectives knew the real reason Byers was here. Byers likely knew it, too. It involved drugs. Sudbury cut to the chase. He floated the name of a sixty-one-year-old Memphis man who was busted in 1991 by West Memphis police after Byers cooperated with an undercover officer in the arrest.

Byers repeated the man's name four times, as if he couldn't place it. Finally, he recalled the man and the incident.

West Memphis police busted the man on November 18, 1991, after he bought three "bricks" of marijuana for $6,500 at Byers's house, where an undercover officer was posing as a drug dealer from Heber Springs, Arkansas. The man was later convicted and received a five-year suspended sentence. Sudbury asked Byers if he thought the man might hold a grudge against him for the bust.

He "definitely had suspicion," Byers said. "Hell, he left my house and got on Broadway and, boom, you know, it's just one of them things." The man, a Marine veteran, also kindled police interest because he had pleaded guilty in 1991 to a misdemeanor violation of Tennessee's "Homosexual Acts" provisions for engaging in sex near a public boat ramp in Memphis. However, there is no indication in police files that they ever talked to him about the triple murders.

Byers also acknowledged helping narcotics officers arrest a Crittenden County man in 1992, and to targeting a methamphetamine laboratory near Marion in that same period. The 1991 narcotics case file listed Byers's address, noting it as the home of "confidential informant No. 175."

For good reasons, Byers's life as an informant had

been kept secret. For months to come, he would remain known in public only as the tragic father of a murder victim and a former jeweler who once ran a shop in the Holiday Mall in West Memphis.

But Byers had other enemies. One was a former business partner who, among other things, claimed to be in a federal witness protection program. Byers told Ridge and Sudbury that he had operated a West Memphis pawnshop with the man until he learned his partner was "just bogus." Byers said his partner had claimed to be a lawyer and drove around with "Tennessee House of Representatives tags on his car." Byers said he got wise to the man when Crittenden County sheriff Richard Busby told him his associate was "not a good business partner to be in business with."

"He conned the crap out of me," Byers told the detectives.

Police had been loosely building a circle around Byers but, apparently, it was nothing he didn't know about. A week earlier police had interviewed Opie Taylor, the "official spokesman" of the Byers family who showed up at their house after the murders and began giving media interviews. Originally from Louisiana, Taylor, a thirty-four-year-old Memphis machinist, told police he'd been arrested about seven times for drunken driving and twice for possession of marijuana. He had fourteen tattoos, apparently too many for any to be specifically described on a police report.

Taylor also offered police an intriguing theory: The killer likely was a white male who was sexually abused and possibly has military training, he said. The killer gained the boys' trust but probably was smart enough to get out of town. In his own interview Byers acknowledged talking with Taylor about the detectives' earlier inquiries.

As the officers wound down the interview. Ridge got the biggest reaction from Byers when he asked if he had anything to do with the murders. It was a calculated question, not based on evidence, but designed to elicit a response.

Q: I may have information; this information suggests strongly that you have something to do with the disappearance of the boys. And ultimately, of the murder. What is your response to that?

A: My first response is I can't fathom where you would get that . . . And it makes me so mad inside that I kind of got to hold myself here in this chair.

Q: Okay. Who, of all the people you know, might make that kind of suggestion?

A: I wouldn't have the slightest idea. If I did it would make me want to hit 'em. You know, it would make me mad to think that someone maybe has said something like that about me. It makes me mad.

Ridge went on to tell Byers the question was aimed "to get a response" and not "to hurt" him.

Byers said he understood. But he wanted the detectives to know there was no way he could have killed little Chris.

"Just tell me one thing," he said. "Man to man, you tell me man to man, I don't care on the record or off the record . . . You know I didn't have anything to do with the murder of my son and those other two boys."

"Man to man, I know that," Ridge said.

Byers shot back: "And I could literally squeeze the life out of the animal that did it."

The investigation foundered again. It yielded nothing solid on any legitimate suspects, yet a host of weirdos, wackos, perverts, lunatics, and eccentrics poured forth from the Arkansas Delta, ready to take credit for the murders.

Police thought they were onto something May 18, when a man dashed into a local woods after a state trooper stopped him along a road and mentioned the triple-murder case. Michael Headlee got his picture on the front page of local newspapers after authorities turned loose tracking dogs and a Memphis police helicopter to flush him from the woods. After a two-hour search, Headlee, a twenty-one-year-old stock boy with Harley-Davidson wings tattooed on his chest, was found hiding in a treetop. But he knew nothing about the murders. "He apparently has the habit of doing that whenever the police talk to him," Gitchell told the *Evening Times*.

In Memphis, police took note of a mental patient who lay in bed muttering over and over, "I know I didn't do that. I couldn't do something like that."

In Oceanside, California, police grilled a former West Memphis ice cream truck driver who, curiously, had known Stevie, Chris, and Michael, and, after lengthy questioning over two days, broke down and shouted, "Well maybe I freaked out . . . then blacked out and killed the three little boys and then fucked them up the ass or something." Police never established anything linking him to the crime.

Police questioned a thirty-year-old schizophrenic living in the Mayfair Apartments, next to Robin Hood, who had a cross tattooed on his left wrist. He passed a polygraph and had an alibi, although a hair at the crime scene later was found to be microscopically similar to his.

Police interviewed a thirty-three-year-old Marion man convicted of child molestation in Colorado who was familiar with the Robin Hood area and who told them the killer could have played a molesting game with the boys—"cops and robbers, cowboys and Indians, whatever"—when one of the boys decided not to play.

"All perpetrators have to keep in control," he said, saying the molester may have "had to kill them to keep them quiet." He also said the boys would have been killed elsewhere and dumped in Robin Hood. Asked why he thought that, he said, "If you have to think like this man, you have to be a sick individual, and I've been around some sick individuals, and I was myself sick, so I can think like this guy." The ex-con told Ridge and Sudbury he had stepchildren and still fantasized about molesting children. They may have been disgusted, but they could not link him to the murders.

All the while, new tips came in on Damien Echols. A former girlfriend told police on May 18 that Damien had talked of sucking blood out of raw steaks. The fifteen-year-old West Memphis girl, who broke up with Damien a year before, said she heard Damien now was claiming he'd been a knight in a past life when he had killed several people. Recently, she heard he'd written some books on witchcraft.

"He used to always talk about how much he hated little kids and he used to always say this, saying about cutting all of your fingers and toes off one by one," the girl wrote in a statement to police. The girl also heard that Damien and Jason Baldwin "always have their Devil-worshiping meetings in that park and those little kids were riding over there and they saw something they were(n't) supposed to of (sic) seen so Damien killed them."

But as the days passed, they had nothing solid. Each tip, no matter how promising, fizzled. By May 26, Gitchell was getting worried. "We need information from the crime lab desperately," Gitchell wrote serologist Kermit Channell in Little Rock. The letter was loaded with more than twenty questions:

Were the kids sodomized? Which clothing belonged to which boy? Any blood on the clothing? Were the boys forced to perform oral sex? Could police get a description of fibers found? Was there any residue under the boys' fingernails? Does anything indicate involvement by a black man? Gitchell noted that Dr. Frank Peretti, associate state medical examiner, "mentioned finding urine in the stomach of two boys." What has been determined regarding the urine? he asked. Which boy was killed first? What was the time of death? The cause of death?

"This case has received national recognition and without the crime lab's help our hands are tied," Gitchell wrote. "We feel as though we are walking blindfolded through this case at this moment."

It was clear the case needed a compass. Three days after the bodies were found, Gitchell had likened the investigation to so many puzzle pieces, enough to fill a courtyard. Three weeks later, the puzzle had grown considerably, and few pieces fit together. But there was no quit in Gitchell. His confident outlook with the press was just an outward sign of an intense desire to succeed.

Nine

An Orgy or an Esbat?

"You're lying!" Gitchell yelled, thrusting a hand toward the frightened teenager. "You're lying!"

Bob Loomis sat in a daze, his heart pounding. On May 10, police had asked if he was involved in the occult. He was back again seventeen days later because police had received another tip. That, and because he carried the unfortunate label of being an acquaintance of Damien Echols.

Police asked Loomis to retrace his steps of May 5 once again. Despite Gitchell's objections, Bob eventually satisfied police he'd had no involvement in the murders. But, Bob also told police more tantalizing Damien stories.

Bob gave police a list of five teenagers who met at Murray Farris's house as part of a "witches' coven," known as The Order of the Divine Light. The "coven," which he said practiced white magic, was started three or four months earlier, Bob told Det. Bill Durham. Damien attended one meeting a month or two ago, and since that time, Bob had heard plenty of stories about Damien. He drank blood out of a gang leader's wrist while in reform school in Jonesboro, Arkansas, Bob said.

"Also, Damien likes to put sharpened sticks through frogs to see how long it takes them to die. Once, he burned down his father's garage and, after the roof collapsed, stood in the flames and chanted," Bob told Durham.

A day earlier, on May 26, police nearly got their smoking gun on Damien when they interviewed William Winford Jones, a skinny teenager who claimed Damien had confessed to him a week earlier out at Lakeshore.

"He said that he had sex with them, that he molested them, and had sex in the rear with them," said Jones, eighteen, sporting a three-letter tattoo that, at the moment, he probably wished he could hide: *FTP*— Fuck The Police.

"Okay, you said that he said that he cut them," Det. Bryn Ridge asked.

"Yeah, that's all he said, that he cut them. He didn't go into no details."

"Do you know what he cut them with?"

"No, he said just with a knife, you know, a little knife."

Ridge seemed a bit skeptical. Jones illustrated the "little knife" with hand gestures that made it look ten to twelve inches long.

"He was drunk," Jones said, explaining that Damien had called it little but had gestured big. But Jones assured Ridge he knew what he was talking about. "Well, first he wasn't weird or nothing, but now he's got into the satanic cult stuff," Jones told Ridge.

A phone call on May 27 sent Gitchell, Allen, and Ridge to Marion, where that city's assistant chief of police, Don Bray, had a surprise for them. In Bray's office sat a pale, redheaded woman, slender and nervous, clinging to a fidgety, round-faced little boy. What the mother and child told the officers over the next two days would propel the case toward a sensational crescendo.

They offered more tales about Damien drinking blood—bizarre, yet nothing to hang murder charges on. But as the detectives listened, this woman and her eight-year-old son raised hairs, claiming they had witnessed satanic meetings where cult members painted themselves black, mutilated animals, chanted incantations, and engaged in wild group sex.

The door to Crittenden County's satanic underworld opened to her about two weeks after the murders, Vicki Hutcheson told the detectives. Hutcheson said she had heard so many rumors about Damien, she decided to "play detective" and try to solve the case herself. She said she invited Damien into her home to feel him out on the subject.

"I had gotten some satanic books and witchcraft books and all this and we were sitting on my couch and I had laid them out where he could see them," Hutcheson said. She told officers she checked the books out of the local library to bait Damien.

There were a couple reasons behind her bold move, Hutcheson said. For one, she had a hunch the murders were part of a "Devil-worshiping thing," and she wanted to find out for herself. Secondly, she had a friend, a teenager named "Little Jessie" Misskelley, who told her some strange tales about someone he knew.

"Jessie told me about a friend of his named Damien and this friend drank blood and stuff," Hutcheson matter-of-factly told the cops. "He just

THE BLOOD OF INNOCENTS 153

kept going on and on about how weird he was and stuff."

According to Hutcheson's account, she befriended Damien, gained his trust, and engaged in long conversations with him.

"He kept telling me about the boys' murders and how he had been— he never said questioned— he always said, 'I was accused for eight hours. I was accused of killing those three little boys,'" Hutcheson said. "And I said, 'Well, you know, why would they pick you in West Memphis, you know, there are beaucoup people, why would they just pick you out?' And he just looked at me, I mean just really weird. And he said, 'Because I'm evil.'"

Damien never admitted to the murders, but he never denied it either, she said.

Victoria Malodean Hutcheson had a certain air of mystery about her. She was thirty years old and a mother of two, yet lacked any apparent anchor in her life. She had moved to West Memphis nine months earlier in the fall of 1992, coming across the state after quitting her job as a legal secretary in Fayetteville, Arkansas. She and Tony, her second husband, moved into a comfortable, three-bedroom house with her two sons, a block down the street from the Byers family.

Her youngest son, Aaron, now at her side, became close friends with Christopher Byers and Michael Moore. With Stevie Branch, they all attended Weaver Elementary and joined the same Cub Scout troop. But as Vicki's second marriage broke up, she had to move again. On April 19, sixteen days before the murders, she moved two miles up the road into a rented trailer in Highland Trailer Park, south of Marion. She quickly got to know the boys in her neighborhood, including a friendly but tough teenager called Little Jessie, who lived a few doors down.

After the murders, Little Jessie passed on several strange stories, Vicki said. The teen claimed he saw Christopher Byers alive behind the Blue Beacon the day the bodies were discovered, she said. He also talked frequently about Damien. Vicki claimed Damien was a member of a gang called the Dragons who held cult meetings where they were "sacrificing genitals" from animals.

Vicki first came to the Marion Police Department at City Hall, a two-story brick building that once served as a bank, because she was in trouble with the law herself. On May 6, 1993, assistant chief Bray interviewed Vicki about a $200 discrepancy in a customer's credit card that occurred on her watch as a clerk at a local Delta Express convenience store. Bray eventually found there was insufficient evidence to charge her, although her employer fired her. But as Bray talked with Vicki and her son, he became interested in her stories about Damien and decided the West Memphis police should hear them.

The homicide investigators listened to Vicki's account over two days, tape-recording a forty-six-minute interview on May 28 in the West Memphis Police Department's drug task force offices. There, Vicki told detectives Ridge and Sudbury that Damien took her to an orgy in an open field two weeks after the murders.

Her venture into the shadowy world of sex mixed with Satanism started with the witchcraft books she had spread on her coffee table for Damien, she said. Among the books, Vicki had a magazine with an advertisement in the back about a "witch school."

"I told him not to worry, this is what I'm wanting to be," she said. "And he just looked at me really weird and he said, 'You don't have to go like that. You don't have to go there to do that. . . .'

"The next day, after he finds out that I'm wanting to do this, he told me and asked me did I want to go to esbat. I didn't know what esbat was. I looked it up in the book and found out that it was a (witches') meeting and I thought immediately, 'Yeah, this is where I want to go. I want to see what's going on.'"

Vicki said Damien, driving a red Ford Escort, picked her up the night of Wednesday, May 19, and drove her to a field near Turrell, Arkansas, about fifteen miles to the north of West Memphis up Interstate 55. Little Jessie came along, too, she said. They turned off onto a dirt road, then into a woods and an open field. It was dark, Vicki said. She could hear running water.

"It was just really dark, especially out, you know, in the woods, it was just dark," she said. "And I was scared a little bit, in fact. But we held hands, just like you would hold my hand and keep trying to comfort me. He knew I was scared."

If it seemed peculiar to the detectives that a thirty-year-old mother of two would be out in a field at night holding hands with an eighteen-year-old kid with a reputation as a blood-drinking Satanist, the point was not explored in detail in this interview.

Vicki explained that she convinced Little Jessie to introduce her to Damien by saying she thought he was "hot."

"I really want to go out with him," she recalled telling Jessie. Vicki said she and Damien became close, and that "word has gotten out that I was seeing him because I'm a, you know, older woman." Damien once smashed a board on her front porch in a jealous rage, Vicki said, after he apparently saw her with a boyfriend. But she denied having sexual relations with Echols, maintaining she was just investigating the truth.

In the field, Vicki said she saw about ten youths, all with their faces and arms painted black.

"Then these kids took their clothes off and began touching each other and I knew what was going to happen," she said. "I looked at Damien and I said I wanted to leave." Damien took her home, but Jessie stayed, she said.

Aaron told an even darker tale, a sordid story linking Damien's cult to Robin Hood and the three murdered boys.

Aaron told detectives that he, Michael, and Chris often went into Robin Hood before May 5 and spied on five men who painted themselves black, chanted in "Spanish" around a fire, killed animals, smoked strange cigarettes, and did "nasty stuff," like "what men and women do." The men each carried knives about ten inches long, he said.

Yet Aaron's story perplexed police. He and his friends spied on the men at least five times, he said, often at a range as close as five feet. It was hard to know how to gauge his account. He was a child, unsophisticated and unwise to the world of police and murder probes. Head bowed, his voice soft, he described in short, often undescriptive sentences the observations of an eight-year-old. To a child, five feet might actually be fifty feet. The "men" in the cult could have easily been teenagers, or illusions.

But to the detectives his story appeared consistent with accounts from neighbors around Robin Hood who told about youths painting themselves black and meeting in the woods. Plus, there was his mother's account to consider. And Aaron had another point of corroboration. He said one of the men in the woods wore a skull-shaped pendant as an earring. His mother gave police an inch-long pewter earring, which she said had fallen off Damien when he was at her trailer. It was just like the one Aaron said he had seen in the woods: A snake slithered out of one eye socket of the ornament and wrapped around the skull.

Vicki told police she found the pendant lying on her bathroom floor. When Aaron saw it, he became transfixed, she said. She assured detectives she had protected her son during the eight days she played detective, sending him away to relatives in Fort Smith, Arkansas, on the other side of the state. Her other son, ten-year-old Scott, also was visiting his natural father. She said she took down all photographs of her sons to keep Damien from knowing about them.

Vicki also said she recognized at least one of the kids at the orgy near Turrell. He was a neighbor in the Highland Trailer Park, she said, but when pressed for names of cult members, she could mostly provide only nicknames, including "Spider" and "Snake." She told the detectives there was an older cult member called "Lucifer," some guy with "a big nose," apparently in his thirties, who was driving through the Lakeshore Trailer Park one night when Jessie pointed him out. "Damien always says 'Lucy,' he don't ever call him Lucifer," she said.

Ridge was interested. He asked where Lucifer lived. Vicki didn't know.

"Okay," Ridge said at one point, "Lucifer. Spider. Snake. You know Snake? You ever seen him?"

Vickie had no clear answers.

Police may have been leery of Vicki's and Aaron's stories, but they weren't about to miss out on the chance they were telling the truth. With Vicki's permission, police planted an eavesdropping device under her bed at home. According to plan, Vicki was to invite Damien and some of his friends over to her house for a party, with hopes they might make incriminating statements. The only thing police ever heard that night was loud music and indecipherable voices in the background.

On June 2, the investigators decided it was time to give Vicki a polygraph test. Before hooking her up, Bill Durham quizzed her about her story. "In the pretest interview, the subject stated that she had seen Damien Echols at the skating rink about a month and a half ago, but had not met him prior to three weeks ago," Durham noted. But despite this discrepancy, she passed the test.

Ten

Inside or Outside

The Masses
   Their twisted green fingers grasp at my legs as I run across their rotted decayed bodies. Their long black fingernails dig into my flesh as I scream. Is it real? No. Another illusion shoved down my throat and ingraved (sic) into what little brain they have saw fit to give me. Does this make sense? Sometimes completely. Sometimes none at all.
   — From the notebook of Damien Echols

The sky was bright and blue the morning of June 3, 1993, just as it had been a month earlier, the day West Memphis searched for three missing boys. Another full moon was about to rise. Some believed the police were running out of time.
Sergeant Mike Allen, who had discovered the first body four weeks earlier, rumbled down the service road along Interstate 55 in his unmarked white Ford LTD. Allen was headed to Highland Trailer Park to pick up Jessie Lloyd Misskelley, Jr., and bring him back to the police station for questioning.
Allen found the teen's father at Jim's repair shop,

a tall metal building surrounded by rusting cars and wildflowers sprouting from a drainage ditch out front. "Big Jessie" Misskelley, a mechanic, told Allen he'd go down the street and get his boy. Big Jessie hopped in his beat-up Chevy pickup truck and returned minutes later with Little Jessie.

Father and son were a sight. Big Jessie, barrel-chested and tanned, wore matching dark blue work pants and shirt, his sleeves rolled up to the elbows. He was no more than five feet six. His seventeen-year-old son was about five inches shorter, but solid as a brick house. A spike of hair rose two inches off the crown of his head. An aqua blue T-shirt revealed powerful biceps, the right arm boasting his outlook on life in a three-letter, homemade tattoo: *FTW*. Fuck the World.

"Would you mind coming up to the police department to talk to me about some friends of yours out at Lakeshore?" Allen asked.

"Sure," Little Jessie answered. The police had always spelled trouble for the Misskelleys. Little Jessie had dealt with them several times for minor offenses in recent years. His father knew them even better. Big Jessie had gone to prison six years earlier for selling marijuana. The Misskelleys were uncomfortable with the law, yet compliant, respectful of its power.

Big Jessie and his son joked with Ridge about possibly winning the reward money, which now stood at almost $40,000. "Maybe I can get a new truck," Big Jessie laughed.

Mildly retarded, Misskelley often played with children half his age. Standing five-feet one-inch and weighing 125 pounds, he had fantasies of becoming a professional wrestler. When he spoke, he rarely used complete sentences. And from early childhood he'd displayed fits of violence (he once stabbed a fourth-grade classmate in the mouth with a pencil) and rage. Misskelley seemed unable to cope with a troubled home life and the various women with whom his father was connected.

Little Jessie had spent most of his life in the Highland Trailer Park. The rural subdivision sat south of Marion High School, separated by a wide, open field. On the west stretched the quiet, two-lane service road that runs parallel to Interstate 55 after the freeway makes its sharp bend north from West Memphis, heading toward St. Louis. A half-mile to the south, on the opposite side of the interstate, is Lakeshore Estates.

Highland is called a trailer park, but it's really a mixture of single-family homes and mobile homes, many sitting on larger lots than are found in traditional trailer parks. Big Jessie would later scoff at a television reporter's characterization of Highland as a "run-down trailer park" and, in truth, the upkeep of property there varied widely. Plastic ducks, decorative rock, flowering bushes, and a cement birdbath fountain decorate one close-clipped yard down the street from the Misskelley home. But just across the street, clutter abounds. A broken basketball goal, a rusty junked Ford, a discarded plastic bucket, two industrial barrels, and a pickup camper truck lay haphazardly in a single yard. Some of the narrow, curbless asphalt streets are lined with deep ditches sprouting wildflowers, cattails, and other weeds.

The Misskelley yard is decorated with roses, marigolds, and other bright perennials bedded in three car tires, each painted white. Loose landscaping timbers line a short gravel driveway. Two wooden flower troughs hang from the porch. The entire length of the three-bedroom trailer is covered with freshly painted tan wood siding. Big Jessie rents both the trailer and the lot.

Little Jessie's natural mother and Big Jessie never married. Big Jessie split with his third wife, Annie, a year before Little Jessie was born on July 10, 1975, but the divorce took several years to settle. The uncertain moorings would breed a deep-seated insecurity in the boy.

"Jessie was always a happy kid," Shelbia Misskelley said. Little Jessie was four years old when his father and Shelbia married in 1980. She was at least the third maternal figure he had known. At the time of the murders, Lee Rush was the woman of the house. But in time, Shelbia returned to Big Jessie's side. "We didn't have anything in common," Big Jessie said of Rush with a shrug, explaining the change.

Shelbia once told a clinical social worker that Little Jessie threw "hysterical fits" whenever she left his sight. "She indicated that it took her about three years to assure Jessie that she would be there, that he was afraid to let her out of his sight for fear she wouldn't return," the social worker wrote in a report, referring to Jessie's behavior at age four or five.

At the same time, Little Jessie provided his parents with an endless source of amusement, and they would chuckle when they recalled the antics. Once, as a young boy, Little Jessie wrapped a rubber band around his penis, then couldn't get it off. "It almost fell off," Shelbia said, laughing. Big Jessie recalls his son suffering from ear infections, and following a medical procedure, having tubes placed in his ears to drain them. Big Jessie, a stock car racing fan, remembered taking his son to a track in West Memphis, where the roar of loud engines hurt the boy's sensitive ears.

"We went to the pit. Whenever they cranked up, he took off running. I had to run almost to the highway to catch him. That little shit was running, I guarantee you," Big Jessie said, with a laugh.

Growing up, Little Jessie often had free rein to roam with friends among the trailer parks south of Marion, where children ride bicycles, play with the countless stray dogs that roam the streets, and venture off into surrounding patches of woods. Jessie often accompanied older relatives to fish for crappie, catfish, and brim at area fishing holes like Lake Dacus, an oxbow lake immediately west of the Mississippi River.

When Jessie was about twelve, the Misskelleys lived in Lakeshore, where Little Jessie became friendly with Jason Baldwin. They often spent the night at each other's houses.

Trouble trailed Little Jessie from a young age. When he was eleven, he was accused of assaulting a young girl in Lakeshore. His parents claim Jessie had initially come to the girl's aid after her boyfriend became abusive, but she jumped on his back when Jessie hit the young man. Jessie chased the girl, then hit her on the head with a rock or a brick. The girl "fell down and couldn't get up," according to the May 4, 1987, complaint by the girl's mother. Later that spring, Jessie was suspended from the fourth grade for splattering ketchup over a table and walls in the lunchroom.

"Jessie denied he did this, but instead implied another child splattered the ketchup," a clinical social worker wrote in a June 10, 1987, report following a court-ordered psychological evaluation.

The incident frightened his stepmother, who voiced fears about Little Jessie's explosive temper.

"He gets so mad, he's capable of hurting someone," Shelbia told the social worker. According to the report prepared at the East Arkansas Regional Mental Health Center in West Memphis, Shelbia told the social worker about Jessie's assault on the young girl and the pencil-stabbing incident. She also said Jessie had a habit of breaking windows, and once required several stitches to his left hand after he punched a window in a fit of anger. "Mrs. Misskelley reported Jessie does not own up to his wrongs," the report said, "that he always blames someone else. She denies Jessie becomes physical with she (sic) or her husband but will clench his fist and take his anger out on someone else or something like breaking the windows. Mrs. Misskelley replied, 'I don't think he can control it,' referring to his temper. 'He needs some help.'"

But Shelbia, fifty-three years old at the time of the murders, said Jessie's acts of aggression had eased up recently. Four years earlier, another evaluation had revealed Jessie had an IQ in the 70s and suffered mild mental retardation and an undersocialized, aggressive personality. Shelbia and Little Jessie jointly entered counseling in 1983, but didn't complete the sessions. A clinical report at the time indicated Jessie suffered from ear infections and had a hole in his eardrum that his stepmother couldn't afford to fix.

Big Jessie couldn't participate in the 1987 evaluation because he was in prison. He pleaded guilty that March to sale or delivery of marijuana and was sentenced to ten years in prison, with five years suspended. But Big Jessie wasn't the only one in the family to get busted. Shelbia also pleaded guilty on drug charges, was fined $2,500, and received five years' probation. Two other family members also were convicted after sheriff's deputies charged they were selling marijuana packed in fifty-five-gallon drums. Or, at least authorities believed it was marijuana. Big Jessie maintains the substance he was selling was mostly jimsonweed, a poisonous, hallucinogenic plant that Big Jessie innocently explained as a harmless filler. When authorities busted the ring, in early 1986, they confiscated four barrels of the weed, some of it stashed in a West Memphis mini-storage rental vault.

The drug bust placed great stress on the Misskelley clan. The State of Arkansas sought forfeiture of Shelbia's 1976 Monte Carlo. At the time, she still owed $875 for the ten-year-old car, records show. With her husband in prison, her sole source of income for a time was a monthly Social Security check, and she was paying $50 a month toward her fine on the drug conviction. A handsome woman, she also had a son and daughter from another marriage at home. Ellen, her daughter, had two small children of her own.

By August 1988, Little Jessie was in trouble again. Now thirteen, he was placed on a year's probation after stealing seven band flags from the high school. Big Jessie said his son wanted the flags to set up his own stock car track. The cops found the flags under the Misskelleys' porch.

After Big Jessie came home from prison, he found that his son considered him a role model. Tinkering with mechanics, Little Jessie worked on bikes and helped his father in the shop where they worked on cars together. Like his father, Little Jessie also developed a taste for pro wrestling. Many a Saturday afternoon, Big Jessie would sit before the TV set, watching his favorite wrestlers, like Lex Luger and Tetancah the Indian Chief. Before long, Little Jessie was riding with friends to the Mid-South Coliseum in Memphis on Monday nights to watch his idols, including Jerry "The King" Lawler, a Memphis institution who gained national attention once for pile-driving the late comedian Andy Kaufman onto the hard canvas of a wrestling ring.

At police headquarters, Sergeant Allen logged in Misskelley's vitals, then began questioning the teen about ten A.M. as Det. Bryn Ridge looked on. Misskelley said he worked a roofing job until about five P.M. on May 5, then spent the night at home. He said he knew nothing of the homicides. But, like others, he had heard that Damien did it. "Damien is sick," Misskelley said, telling how, after a fist fight, the strange teen once dipped his finger in Jason Baldwin's blood and licked it.

The detectives knew Misskelley from an interview three weeks earlier. On May 15, Misskelley and two friends excitedly called police after they encountered a strange, bearded man camping out in a patch of woods behind Bojangles and the Goodyear service station on Missouri Street. The man turned out to be house painter Tracey Laxton, son of Crittenden County sheriff's chief detective Ed Laxton. Police briefly considered the younger Laxton a suspect, until he produced an alibi showing he was in eastern Mississippi, more than a hundred miles away, at the time of the murders. Strangely, especially considering his links to law enforcement, the younger Laxton would tell police, and later a reporter, that he had been unaware of the murders until that day—fully ten days after the case had inflamed his community.

But today, Misskelley was not so cooperative. He denied any cult involvement. He knew nothing about the outdoor orgies. Ridge, primed by Vicki Hutcheson's

THE BLOOD OF INNOCENTS

spine-tingling tale of the evening esbat at Turrell, smelled a rat. Jessie at one point said he hadn't seen Damien in over two months. Then, he acknowledged introducing Damien to Vicki after the murders. Jessie's dark eyes fell to the floor with each tough question. "He was nervous and failed to look at me in the eye," Ridge put in his report.

At eleven A.M. Ridge decided to give Misskelley a lie-detector test, and Allen read the teen his Miranda rights. Allen drove Misskelley out toward Highland Trailer Park to get his father's approval for a polygraph. On the way, Allen spotted Big Jessie driving a tow truck up Missouri Avenue and flagged him down. Big Jessie signed a permission slip for the polygraph, and Allen returned to the police station with Little Jessie.

Now it was Bill Durham's turn. At 11:30 A.M. he hooked Misskelley up to the lie-detector machine and went to work.

"Have you ever taken a polygraph test before?" he asked the youth. Despite his tough looks, Misskelley now seemed fragile.

"No," he answered.

"In regard to the deaths of those three boys, are you going to tell the truth during this test?"

"Yes."

"Have you ever been in Robin Hood Hills?"

"No."

"Do you smoke dope?"

"No."

"Have you ever took part in Devil worship?"

"No."

"Have you ever sold any dope?"

"No."

"Have you ever attended a Devil worship ceremony in the Turner-Twist area?"

"No."

"Have you taken any drugs or medication today?"

"No."

"Are you involved in the murder of those three boys?"

"No."

"Do you know who killed those three boys?"

"No."

The stone-faced detective studied his charts. Working furiously over the next forty-five minutes, he burst from the polygraph room at 12:30 P.M. and announced his findings to Gitchell and the others. "He's lying his ass off!" Durham told them.

The detectives huddled. This was it. They'd go for the kill. They couldn't afford to miss another opportunity, not on the afternoon of a night that promised a full moon.

It was decided Gitchell and Ridge would take over the questioning. At 12:40 P.M., the pair took Misskelley into Det. Diane Hester's office and closed the door.

The room was small but tidy. Pictures of smiling children— Hester's kids— lined the desk. Crayon drawings were on the walls. I Love You, one read. Misskelley sat anxiously on one side of the table. Gitchell, his antagonist, sat across from him.

Over the next hour and forty minutes, Gitchell and Ridge pressed Misskelley for details about cult activities, the murders, and Damien. They made no tape recording of the interview. Only Ridge took notes. It appears the detectives started the interview by telling Misskelley he'd failed his lie-detector test. From the first line in Ridge's notes it seems as though Misskelley took on a different face, as if he were ready to come clean. Then it happened.

Jessie said he had received a call from Jason Bald-

THE BLOOD OF INNOCENTS 169

win the night before the murders. "They were going to go out and get some boys and hurt them," Ridge wrote.

Misskelley told the detectives about "satanic cult" meetings before the murders, including one in which pictures of the murder victims were passed around. A mysterious boy named "Ken" brought a briefcase with guns to the meetings. In open fields and local woods, the cult "will skin a dog and eat part of it," Misskelley said. He gave the officers a list of ten people who attended the meetings, including Damien, Jason, Domini, Ken, someone named Adam, two other teenage girls, a "new dude" and a "blond-haired, tall, heavyset" individual.

"Will be 8 or 9 people and they will have orgy afterwards. 3 on one," Ridge wrote. "Jason and Damien are having sex with each other."

The details were sketchy, disjointed. Police knew they weren't dealing with a genius. Misskelley, a high-school dropout, had an IQ in the low seventies. But for the most part, Gitchell and Ridge liked what they were hearing. They were getting confirmation. There were meetings in Robin Hood, Misskelley said. The day after the murders, he added, Jason called him. In the background, Damien was yelling, "We did it! We did it! What are we going to do now? What if somebody saw us!"

But Jessie steered clear of placing himself at the crime scene.

Gitchell grew impatient. With an ink pen, he drew a circle on a piece of paper and showed it to Misskelley. Gitchell pointed to several dots inside the circle. These were the bad guys, the killers. Then he pointed to several dots outside the circle. These were the good guys. Law-enforcement officers and law abiders.

"Which side are you on, Jessie?" he asked.

"The outside," Misskelley answered. He wanted to be with them.

Gitchell left the room. He came back a few minutes later and tossed a Polaroid at Jessie. There, in color, lay the mutilated face and upper torso of Christopher Byers.

Misskelley snatched the picture in his hand. He fell back in his chair and stared at the photograph in horror. The white, nude body. The lifeless face. The red wounds. Misskelley sat, transfixed, unable to take his eyes from the photo. After some moments, Gitchell took it from him and laid it on the table.

Taking notes, Ridge listened. "That's the Moore boy," Misskelley said. He gave the wrong name, but he identified the dead child as one of the boys in the photo that had been passed around in one of the cult meetings. "Jessie stated that he didn't want to be a part of this, that Damien and Jason killed, he did not," Ridge wrote.

What happened next is not entirely clear. Ridge wrote two accounts of the interview, one in handwritten notes, the other a typed report. Ridge's notes indicate the officers asked Misskelley again about taking another polygraph. Misskelley said he'd think about it. Ridge then left the room, his notes said. According to a separate typed account, Ridge said something else happened before he left:

"Jessie told of one occasion he had gone to the scene of the murders and sat down on the ground and cried about what had happened to the boys. He had tears in his eyes at this time telling about the incident. I felt that this was a remorseful response about the occurrence and that he had more information than what he had revealed up to this point."

Both Ridge and Gitchell would later testify that,

before Ridge left the room, Gitchell played part of a tape recording for Misskelley. Holding a microcassette player in his hand, Gitchell snapped on the Play button. Out came the soft voice of a young boy.

"Nobody knows what happened but me."

Gitchell snapped the recorder off. Misskelley went into near panic, the detectives said.

"I want out of this! I want to tell you everything!" Misskelley cried, again off tape.

Ridge, eager to tell Sergeant Allen the news and in need of a break, left the room.

Gitchell and Misskelley were alone. The seasoned detective and the cocky punk with the spike on top of his head. Whatever happened between the two in these moments remains a mystery.

The week before, it had been sixteen-year-old Bob Loomis. The yelling, the finger to the face. Now it was just Jessie and Gary. And whatever Gitchell said, it worked.

At 2:20 P.M., when Ridge came back in the room, Gitchell informed him Misskelley had just said he was in Robin Hood when the murders occurred. He had seen what happened.

Misskelley was crying. Ridge started crying, too. "Jessie seemed to be very sorry for what had happened and told that he had been there when the boys were first coming into the woods and were called by Damien to come over to where they were," Ridge typed in his report.

At 2:44 P.M., after Misskelley and Ridge had finished, Gitchell turned on the tape recorder to take down Misskelley's confession.

"When I was there I saw Damien hit this one boy real bad, and then, uh, and he started screwing them and stuff," Misskelley told Gitchell and Ridge as the tape recorder whirred.

On the table before him lay three photos cut from a newspaper. On the left was Michael Moore, in his Cub Scout shirt, staring grimly. In the center, Stevie Branch smiled brightly. On the right, Christopher Byers managed a grin, despite the dark circles under his eyes.

"Which one of those three boys is it you say Damien hit?"

"Michael Moore," Jessie answered. But he was pointing to the picture of Chris Byers, the detectives noted.

"That's, uh, the Byers boy, that's who you are pointing at?" Gitchell asked, and Misskelley agreed. Ridge asked him what Damien hit Chris Byers with.

"He hit him with his fist and bruised him all up real bad, and then Jason turned around and hit Steve Branch . . . and started doing the same thing, then the other one took off, Michael Moore took off running, so I chased him and grabbed him and hold him, until they got there and then I left."

The detectives listened. The recorder took it down. Until that moment, Misskelley had been a witness to something horrific. Now, probably unbeknownst to him, he was a suspect. "I chased him and grabbed him." By his own words, he was a party to murder.

Misskelley told the detectives he returned to the scene and the three boys were nude and tied up. All three were beaten "real bad" and had their clothes removed, he said.

"Then they tied them up, tied their hands up; they started screwing them and stuff, cutting them and stuff, and I saw it and turned around and looked, and then I took off running," Misskelley said, his voice a high-pitched pleading. "I went home, then they called me and asked me how come I didn't stay. I told them, I just couldn't."

Ridge, concerned about accuracy that could make or break the confession, pressed Misskelley for details.

"Okay, now when this is going on, when this is taking place, you saw somebody with a knife. Who had the knife?" Ridge asked.

"Jason," Jessie answered.

"Jason had a knife, what did he cut with the knife? What did you see him cut, or who did you see him cut?"

"I saw him cut one of the little boys."

"All right, where did he cut him at?"

"He was cutting him in the face."

Finally, some answers. In Misskelley's scenario, Damien took care of Chris Byers, Misskelley handled Michael Moore, and Jason assaulted Steve Branch. The detectives could not forget the horrid maiming of little Stevie. A ragged cut ran down the left side of his face. It was laid wide open. Who could know this but someone who was there?

"Cutting him in the face," Ridge said, summarizing Jessie's statements. "All right, another boy was cut, I understand. Where was he cut at?"

"At the bottom," Jessie answered.

"On his bottom?" Ridge asked. "Was he faced down and he was cutting on him or . . . ?" Gitchell interrupted.

"Now, you're talking about bottom, do you mean right here?" Gitchell asked, apparently pointing to his own groin.

"Yes," Misskelley answered.

"In his groin area?"

"Yes."

"Do you know what his penis is?" Ridge asked.

"Yeah," Jessie said, "that's where he was cut at."

"Which boy was that?" Gitchell demanded.

"That one right here," Jessie said, pointing to Chris Byers's picture.

Another hit. The questions seemed leading, but Ridge and Gitchell felt no one could know these details except someone who was there. Chris Byers was sexually mutilated. His penis had been removed. Stevie Branch had been cut in the face.

Misskelley also said the beatings occurred in the ravine, on the east bank of the creek. That's where the Luminol had reacted, suggesting the presence of blood. Misskelley went on to say he didn't know where the little boys laid their bikes down. But he said Damien and Jason hollered at the boys to come over, and they did.

Under close questioning, Misskelley went into detail describing the assault. The three boys were beaten over the head with sticks until they were unconscious, he said. Two of them— Michael Moore and Steve Branch— were sexually assaulted.

"Jason stuck his in one of them's mouth and Damien was screwing one of them up the ass and stuff," Misskelley said at one point. But, often, he would contradict himself.

"Okay," Ridge said, "and the one that they were cutting the penis off of . . . did they have sex with (him) at all?"

"No," Jessie said.

"Did either one of them?" Ridge pressed.

"Jason did."

"Jason did?"

"Jason was screwing him while Damien stuck his in his mouth."

"Okay, how did he have sex with that one?"

THE BLOOD OF INNOCENTS

"He was holding him down like, and Jason had his legs up in the air and that little boy was kicking, saying, 'Don't! No!' like that."

"Okay, he had his legs up in the air, all right, what was to keep the little boys from running off, but just their hands are tied, what's to keep them from running off?"

"They beat them up so bad, they couldn't hardly move, they had their hands tied down and he sit (sic) on them."

Painfully, the detectives took Misskelley over details leading up to the crime. He said Damien had been stalking the boys, apparently in connection with this strange circle of people they called a cult.

"Had Damien seen these boys before?" Ridge asked.

"Yes," Jessie answered.

"Had he done things with them before? Or had he just been watching them?"

"He had been watching them."

"Has he ever had sex with them before?"

"No, he's been watching them."

"He's been watching them. You mentioned earlier that, one of the meetings you went to with this cult thing, they had some pictures. Describe those pictures for me."

"They had some houses, trees and stuff," said Misskelley in an answer that has never been fully clarified. But the detectives forged ahead.

"Okay, had somebody taken pictures of these boys?"

"Yes." Jessie said all three boys appeared in a photo that Damien took. The photo was in a briefcase, he said.

"Have you seen them with a briefcase before?" Gitchell asked.

"I've seen them once that night, I seen them with it that night."

"Okay, what was inside the briefcase?"

"They had some cocaine and a little gun."

"Is that when you first saw the pictures of the boys?"

"Yes, out there in Lakeshore."

"And you saw pictures in the briefcase?"

"Yes, I think when we had that cult."

"Okay, now you have participated in this cult, right?"

"Yes."

"How long have you been involved in it?"

"I've been in it for about three months."

"Okay, what is, tell me some of the things that you all do typically in the woods, as being in this cult."

"We go out, kill dogs and stuff, and then carry girls out there."

"What do you all do with the girls when you're out there?

"We screw them and stuff."

"Just everybody takes a turn?"

"Everybody, and we have an orgy and stuff like that."

"Okay," Gitchell said. Ridge took over.

"When you kill a dog, what do you do with that?"

"We usually skin it, then make a bonfire and eat it and stuff."

"Okay, when you're initiating somebody new, come into a cult, what actually is done to initiate that person into a cult?"

"We usually, you know, kill an animal, you know; you have to know how to handle the meat and stuff, after we kill it to see if he knows. If he can't handle it, then he don't get in."

Ridge and Gitchell concluded the interview at 3:18 P.M., thirty-four minutes after it had started.

Eleven

Of Rope and Shoelaces

Pandemonium swept through the police station. Breathless, Allen went to the courthouse in Marion to find deputy prosecutor John N. Fogleman.

"You've got to get down here!" the detective said, telling him of the confession. Fogleman, waiting for the jury to come back in another murder case, rushed down to the West Memphis police station.

The atmosphere at the station was nothing less than jubilant. Gitchell phoned the crime lab in Little Rock to request trace evidence technicians to accompany officers on house searches later that evening. Secretaries began typing affidavits for Gitchell and Ridge to sign, attesting to the facts they had passed on. But as the officers laid plans to arrest Echols and Baldwin, they hit another snag.

Fogleman, now down from Marion, and deputy prosecutor James "Jimbo" Hale listened as police summarized Misskelley's statement. Municipal Court judge William "Pal" Rainey also came up to Gitchell's office. As the three lawyers listened to Gitchell and Ridge give Misskelley's confused account, red flags went up.

THE BLOOD OF INNOCENTS

For one thing, Misskelley's times were all wrong. He said he and his accomplices went out to the woods at nine in the morning, and were in the woods at noon. He said the little boys were in the woods then, too, because they'd skipped school. But the police knew that Michael, Chris, and Steve went to school that day. The little boys were last seen around 6:30 at night. Also, the prosecutors needed more concrete evidence. Misskelley said the boys were tied up, but with what? They knew the boys had been tied up with their shoelaces.

Rainey, sensing it would take some time before he was needed, decided to go home for dinner. But as he left, he warned the officers to have all the necessary evidence if they expected him to issue warrants. "You be sure you have got everything you have down on this affidavit," he said. "Are you sure that everything is applicable to this case?"

Gitchell, tape recorder in hand, went back in to talk to Misskelley. Again, the two were alone, the sleuth and the reluctant witness.

"Jessie, uh, when . . . when you got with the boys and with Jason Baldwin, when you three were in the woods and them little boys come up, about what time was it?" Gitchell asked.

"I would say it was about five or so. Five or six," Misskelley answered.

Nine in the morning. Noon. Now, five or six. That pretty much covered the daytime clock. But police suspected Misskelley had been confused before. By asking the time that Steve, Michael, and Chris came into the woods, rather than the time Misskelley left home to get to the woods, Gitchell felt more certain about Jessie's statement. And five or six certainly fit more closely with the known facts in the case.

"Now," Gitchell continued, "did you have your watch on at the time?"

"Huh-uh."

"Uh, all right." Gitchell decided to press again for clarity. "You told me earlier around seven or eight. Now which time is it?"

"It was seven or eight."

He did it again. Misskelley seemed either an idiot or pretty darn cagey. At any rate, Gitchell seemed confounded.

"Are you—" he started to ask, but Misskelley interrupted.

"It was starting to get dark."

"Okay," Gitchell said, sensing progress. "It . . ."

"I remember it was starting to get dark."

"Okay, well that clears it up," Gitchell said, relieved. "I didn't know—that's what I was wondering, was it getting dark or what?"

"We got up there at six o'clock and the boys come up and it was starting to get dark."

One hurdle cleared. Winding down the questioning about times, Gitchell told Misskelley, "Wait just a minute." He stopped the recorder, and went out to consult with the attorneys. Once back in the room, Gitchell asked Misskelley to detail the clothing he wore that day and the particular actions of each defendant.

"All right, who tied the boys up?" he queried.

"Damien."

"Did Damien just tie them all up or did anyone help Damien, or . . ."

"Jason helped him."

"Okay, and what did they use to tie them up?"

"A rope."

"Okay, what color was the rope?"

"Brown."

THE BLOOD OF INNOCENTS

If Gitchell stopped to consider the discrepancy—the boys were tied up with their shoelaces—it isn't reflected in the tape recording. He went on to ask how the boys were placed in the water, whether Jason or Damien wore a belt and who raped whom.

"Do you know which one raped which boy, or how did that happen?"

"Damien raped the Myers by hisself," Misskelley said, apparently referring to Chris Byers. "And Jason and Damien raped the Branch."

"All right, give that to me again, now."

"Damien raped, uh, the Myers by hisself and Jason and Damien raped, uh, the Branch."

Gitchell asked about oral sex, but after a couple of exchanges, excused himself again and stopped the tape. Contrary to common police procedure, which includes recording the time that taped interviews begin and end, Gitchell recorded no times. It also is impossible to know what, if anything, was said when the recorder was off. But it had been a crazy day of distractions, and Gitchell had a few things on his mind.

"Let me ask you something else, Jessie," he said, reentering the room. "I'm sorry I keep coming back and forth, but I got people that want me to ask you some other questions. Uh, talking about oral sex, did you see—you know we had talked earlier about how Jason and, uh, Damien do each other, have sex with each other—did they, did they have oral sex on the boys?"

"Yeah," Jessie said. "They . . . one of them stuck their thing (sic) in one of the boys' mouth (sic) while the other one got the other one up the butt and stuff."

That was not what Gitchell was getting at. The

lawyers were trying to account for some scratches and other injuries to two of the boys' penises.

"Okay," Gitchell said, "but did anyone go down on the boys and maybe sucked theirs or something?"

"Not that, I didn't see nothing, neither one of them do that," Jessie answered.

"You didn't see that?"

"Uh-uh."

"Okay, did they pinch their penis in any way, or were rough with it or anything like that?"

"I didn't see nothing like that, not rough with them, I just seen, . . ."

"You didn't see anyone go down on the boys?" Gitchell asked for the fourth time.

"Uh-uh."

"Are you sure?"

"Yeah."

Gitchell paused the recorder again. He gave Misskelley a Coke. He wasn't getting anywhere with the penis injuries. But there was one more thing he needed to cover. At least two of the boys had bruises on the tops of their ears, as if they'd been squeezed with a lot of force. If Misskelley could confirm the injuries, it would help their case.

"Jessie, the boys hands were tied up right?"

"Right."

"How did they force these boys to have oral sex on them? How did they have ahold of them?"

"One of them had holding them by the arms, while the other one got behind them and stuff."

"Did he ever hold him up here, or . . ."

"Oh, the one that was holding him up there at the front, grabbing him by his headlock."

"Had him in a headlock? Did he have him any other way?"

"He was holding him like this, by his head like

THE BLOOD OF INNOCENTS

this and stuff," Misskelley said. When the tape was transcribed onto paper, a parenthetical line was added here: "(Note: Was indicating the victims being held by their ears)."

"Could he have been holding him up here like that?" Gitchell asked again.

"I was too far away. He was holding him up here by his head like this," Misskelley said. Again, a parenthetical line was added: "(Note: Showed the same as above)."

Gitchell asked if all three of the boys were held by the ears, but Misskelley said just two. Gitchell pressed on:

"Tell me again about their hands on."

"It was just up here by their heads and stuff and was just pulling and stuff."

"All right. So they are up here, had their hands . . ."

"By their ears, and pulling them and stuff."

"Okay, all right," Gitchell said, hearing the magic word. "Say that again for me now."

"Hold them by their head, by ears and pulling."

"Okay," Gitchell said, clicking off the recorder.

The interview was over. Gitchell hustled out to pass on the news.

The moon stood high in the sky, bright and round, bathing its baleful glow on carloads of police who sat waiting for the word. Four teams of cops were dispatched to three trailer parks where they planned to conduct simultaneous raids on the homes of Damien Echols, Jason Baldwin, Jessie Misskelley, and Damien's girlfriend, Domini Teer. Out at the Broadway Trailer Park, on West Memphis's east side, close to the river, Bryn Ridge headed the team that would hit Damien's trailer.

Things had moved swiftly since Gitchell's last interview with Misskelley. A probable cause hearing was held at 9:06 P.M., where Gitchell and Ridge gave testimony about their investigation, and Rainey signed the arrest warrants and search warrants. Attached as supporting documentation for the warrants was a transcript of Misskelley's statement, along with the transcribed statement of William Winford Jones, the teen who told police a week earlier Damien had confessed to him. The warrants instructed the officers to search for boots, a briefcase, photographs of the murder victims, "cult materials (Satanic materials)," and other items.

At 10:28 P.M., the signal was given, and the house searches began.

Ridge walked through a gate in the chain-link fence and went for the front door. The lights in the trailer cut off. Ridge could hear the sound of running feet inside. He knocked on the door. There was no answer. He beat on the door several more times. Finally, it opened.

It was Damien Echols. He stared numbly through the doorway. He wore a black Harley-Davidson motorcycle T-shirt. Officers seized him, slapped cuffs on him, and placed him in the back of a squad car.

It was a lucky strike. Jason Baldwin was in the trailer, too. So were Domini Teer and Echols's sixteen-year-old sister, Michelle. Baldwin, looking frail despite his black Metallica T-shirt, also was placed under arrest. Jason's complexion, police reports would say in the description of the suspect at the arrest, was "ruddy." His hair was blond and long. He was five foot eight and 112 pounds. The arrests were made without incident. When Damien was taken to jail, he was searched and had $1 in currency on him, one earring, one pair of black shoelaces, and two sheets of typing paper.

Officers began digging through the clutter in Damien's bedroom, snapping photographs of items of interest. They found a paperback edition of *The Exorcist*, by William Peter Blatty; a skateboarding magazine; a red bandana; another book with what appeared to be red candle wax drippings; and a little cot that served as a bed. Then came what seemed to be a big find: a briefcase, or possibly a typewriter case. Was it the briefcase Misskelley talked about, the one with the photos of the boys in it? Records show officers sent its contents to the state crime lab, but there was no mention of photographs.

Over in Lakeshore Estates Trailer Park, three detectives entered Domini Teer's trailer. A stench greeted them at the door. Several cats milled about inside, their feces and urine scattered throughout the house. Clutter was everywhere. A pale, disheveled woman let the officers in. Dian Teer, Domini's mother, offered no resistance. Officers made their way to a back bedroom, where there was a mattress on the floor.

Two teddy bears sat on a nightstand. A guitar case and suitcases lined the walls. A flannel shirt served as a curtain in one window. Above the other window, a compact disc by the heavy-metal band Grim Reaper was pinned to the wall. See You In Hell, it read. Officers took note of a stain in the tan carpeting. They found a knife in a sheath and what appeared to be a jump rope.

Down the street, Mike Allen and other officers secured Jason Baldwin's trailer. Jason's stepfather,

Terry Rae Grinnell, initially balked at letting the officers in, but when they produced the search warrant, he had no choice. Officers dug through Jason's prized possessions. They took fifteen black T-shirts, most advertising his favorite bands, Megadeth, Metallica, Iron Maiden, and Mötley Crüe. Officers also found a red bathrobe, a pair of green Army-style boots, and a poem written on a piece of paper.

Jason's mother came home around 11:40, after work. A small, pale woman with sunken cheeks and a rail-thin body, Angela Gail Grinnell flew into hysterics when she learned her son had been arrested. "You turned him in!" she screamed at her husband, accusing him of seeking the reward money. Officers ordered Ms. Grinnell to sit on the living-room couch, and for a time she calmed down. She pleaded with officers, saying her son couldn't have committed the murders because he was mowing a lawn that day and later played video games at Wal-Mart.

Over at Highland Trailer Park, Jessie Misskelley, Sr., calmly let officers in. They headed for Little Jessie's bedroom. For a kid involved in a dog-eating satanic cult, Misskelley didn't seem to flaunt it. His walls were covered with posters of half-naked women in cheesecake poses. A large crimson banner hung from the wall: Alabama, it read. Roll Tide. A handmade poster by Little Jessie's girlfriend, Suzie Brewer, hung near the closet door. I Luv You, it said.

All typical teen stuff. But police zeroed in on several items, including a curious black leather mask, a pocket knife, a purple bandana, and several T-shirts, including a black one featuring country singer Reba McEntire.

THE BLOOD OF INNOCENTS

As officers searched, a tall, gray-haired woman sitting on the living-room sofa couldn't contain her thoughts. Lee Rush, Jessie, Sr.'s, current love interest, thought this was all odd. She said she'd stirred in the middle of the night several days ago, awakened by loud sobbing coming from Little Jessie's bedroom. She went in to ask Jessie what the problem was, and he said his girlfriend was moving away, Rush said. An officer jotted down her comments.

Fifty miles up the road in Blytheville, the telephone rang at the home of Stevie Branch's grandpa's. The dead boy's grandpa, Jackie Hicks, picked up the phone. It was Gary Gitchell.

"We have got three suspects in jail charged with capital murder," Gitchell said. There would be a press conference in the morning. Hicks's head spun. His prayers had been answered. He went back into his bedroom to be alone.

"I kneeled beside my bed and rededicated myself to Jesus Christ," he later recalled.

The City Council chamber brimmed with reporters, microphones, television cameras, and electrical wires. Memphis television stations went live, broadcasting news of the arrests throughout the three-state area of East Arkansas, North Mississippi, and West Tennessee. Officials held the press conference in City Hall because the police station simply couldn't accommodate the crowd.

Gary Gitchell sat alone at the council dais, the many microphones pointing to his face. His detectives stood in a long line behind him.

"The officers behind me are officers that worked

very hard on this case," Gitchell said. "I can't have enough praise for them. They're the number one group I want to thank at this time. Secondly, I want to thank the citizens of West Memphis for the information they gave, for the personal support that they gave us—cards, letters, personal phone calls, even bringing food to us when they knew we were there working all night."

Hugs and smiles were exchanged among the officers and supporters. But Gitchell provided little information to the curious public. He fielded questions from reporters, but fended off most with no comment. What was the motive? Did the defendants know the boys? Did police recover any weapons? Paul Morrison, a television reporter with the NBC affiliate in Memphis, shouted out a question that drew groans.

"Was there any evidence of cult involvement?"

"I cannot comment on that," Gitchell said. Some reporters rolled their eyes. But Gitchell didn't. He knew Morrison, a thirty-three-year-old contrast of boyish face and silver hair, was on top of something police wanted to keep under wraps.

Gitchell did answer at least one question. On a scale of one to ten, he was asked, how good was the case against the defendants? "Eleven," Gitchell answered, with a nod of confidence.

"This, I can honestly say, was the most difficult case that the police department in West Memphis has ever had," he said.

Twelve

So Close to Perfect

Charles Jason Baldwin was born April 11, 1977, in Memphis. Baldwin was the first child of Angela and Larry Baldwin. His father would say later that he and Gail should never have gotten married. They had had a platonic relationship that suddenly blossomed into romance. They were second cousins.

For the most part, Jason Baldwin had a childhood bouncing from neighborhood to neighborhood on both sides of the river. Larry Baldwin left his wife and children when the kids were very young, and Jason grew up under the care of his mother and stepfather, Terry Grinnell. As he got older, Jason developed a taste for rock music, particularly heavy metal. His black concert T-shirts advertised an obsession with the music of Metallica, Iron Maiden, and Megadeth.

Not much of a student, he distinguished himself with drawing. Using pencils, he drew complex, detailed images of eagles, owls, and other animals. He also drew snakes, skeletons, and other images that news accounts would later describe as lurid and macabre. By sixteen, he had his own stylized artist's signature, elaborating on his initials, J. B.

His family profile reads like so many other kids' in late twentieth century America. His parents were divorced. He lived in a variety of homes in lower-middle-class neighborhoods, often unsupervised. He found friendship with boys of a similar stripe. They shared an interest in heavy metal, girls, and video games. Jason, like his brother Matt, became an expert Super Nintendo player. They spent hours before the video games at the local Wal-Mart.

Five years before the murders, Baldwin had lived in a seedy section of unincorporated Shelby County, north of Memphis. The Shelby County Fire Department was called to his house June 5, 1987, when someone inside set fire to a bedroom with a cigarette lighter. A room burned but no one was injured.

A teacher from that period recalled he was a pretty good student. But something happened in the intervening years. His mother said he was improving at school, but papers seized by police from his school locker show a kid full of opinions but unwilling to work. One teacher wrote a month and a half before the murders that if Baldwin had been willing to write more than ten lines on ruled paper, he would have gotten better than the D grade he'd earned. But Baldwin didn't feel like measuring up where academic ability was measured as much by quantity as quality.

When they first moved to Marion, just a short bike ride from West Memphis, Jason's family lived in a double-wide manufactured home. They then moved to the smallish trailer where they lived when the trouble started.

Jason occupied the trailer's south bedroom, next to Matt's. It was at the end of the hall at the end of the trailer, on the opposite side of the wooden porch. He had a television set and his own bathroom.

The family settled into a fairly quiet life at Lakeshore Estates. The trailer had faded yellow trim and a piece of plyboard over a broken door window. In back, a porch overlooked the shallow lake. When they were younger, Jason and Matt used to swim in the lake, but Matt said it eventually became too "nasty" for swimming.

On January 13, 1990, Jason and some other kids broke into a shop full of vintage cars and equipment. They broke the front, rear, and right-door glass on a front-end loader, two left-side door windows, and the side vent of a 1969 Cadillac, and all the glass on a 1959 Ford. Three other kids were supposedly with him. Jason, almost thirteen years old, later admitted breaking some headlights, but also pointed the finger at another kid. He was charged with breaking and entering and criminal mischief. In juvenile court, he was placed on probation and ordered to pay nearly $450 in restitution. Court records show that, over time, $30 was actually paid. Acting on behalf of the juvenile court was the prosecuting attorney, John Fogleman.

Nearly three years later, Jason went into the West Memphis Walgreens on a Sunday afternoon. He removed from store shelves a bag of potato chips and a thirty-two-ounce bag of M&M's. He was stopped after walking past the cash register by a clerk who asked to see a receipt for the items. Jason had a receipt, but it was for a bottle of vodka. He was detained by store employees until police arrived. He promptly admitted shoplifting and later, in court, was placed on twelve months' diversion of judgement ending in January 1994.

The break-in and the shoplifting were Jason's only

recorded brushes with the law before the West Memphis killings. When the shoplifting charge came up in court, he was instructed to stay in school and out of trouble. The order was still in effect on the day of the murders.

A report card from Marion High School, for the period beginning three days before that court date and ending the day Jason Baldwin was arrested for murder, showed him to be a rather indifferent student in most subjects. He had a D-plus in Algebra I and C's in most other classes. However, in English, he was a borderline B student. And in art, he earned an A.

The Grinnell-Baldwin family were working people, holding low-paying jobs. Terry and Gail tried their best with three boys— Matt and Jason, along with the smallest, Terry's son, Terry, Jr. Until Jason's arrest, the family's most serious problems were Gail's bouts with depression.

But his mother's travails affected Jason. In a school assignment, students were asked to write their thoughts about a girl who had attempted suicide.

"I didn't know the girl very well," Jason wrote. "I seen her around every now and then, but I know how the people that knew her feel, because once my Mother tried to commit suicide, and I know how I felt when that happened. It was pretty devastating since I was the one who found her and called 911 and kept her alive. But I am lucky, my mother is well and happy now and so am I."

According to probate records, in 1992 Gail was admitted to the East Arkansas Regional Mental Health Center for a period not to exceed forty-five days. The February 5 order cited "paranoid delusions," noting Grinnell had been seen four times that January in the emergency room at Crittenden Memorial Hospital, where she was treated for self-inflicted injuries that included razor slashes to her neck and arms. She would tell authorities that she had "hallucinations of a male voice," and was afraid she was dying of AIDS.

Through all this, her sons tried to maintain the illusion of normalcy. But there wasn't a lot to do. The boys would spend their time at the VFW pool, riding their bikes, or just hanging out with Barry, their black mutt. Matt would recall later that Jason's mobility was limited after he got a flat tire on his bike. He never got it fixed.

Although Terry Grinnell tried to keep a close eye on the boys, they'd largely ignore him when it suited them. He wasn't the strictest of disciplinarians, either. According to Matt, he did not strike the boys. Sometimes he yelled; often he talked too loud, "and he got on my nerves," Matt would say. The six-foot-one, forty-four-year-old construction worker had striking looks: Under a mop of black hair, he had one blue eye and one almost-black eye.

Jason didn't much care for Terry. He rarely listened to him and found him annoying. But the brothers got along very well.

Before the arrests, as the investigation began focusing on Damien and his circle of friends, Gail became convinced that police, in their questioning, were planting ideas into people's heads. It was common knowledge that Damien—and anyone associated with him—was a suspect.

Since he was a suspect, virtually anything Jason did could be considered damning. A boy who rode the same bus with Jason Baldwin to school remembered that sometime in 1992, Damien told him that he and Jason Baldwin wanted to "catch a bum under the overpass and torture him just to see what it was like." He told Echols that he must be crazy, and Damien said he was kidding.

Jason's science and math teacher, Steve Bacca, remarked to an investigator that Jason had nodded agreement when Bacca told his students to be careful about spreading rumors of Satanism. Later, a classmate would recall that Jason said little or nothing when the murders of the boys was discussed.

Over and over, Jason was described by neighbors as a rather shy, artistic young man— polite, courteous, and responsible. Despite the run-ins with the law, no one considered Jason a troublemaker.

After his arrest, Matt and Jason's girlfriend came forward to defend him. Matt told police that Jason was never involved in the occult. He said Jason was fond of animals and would never do anything to hurt one. He scoffed at a suggestion raised in news accounts since the arrests that Jason might have eaten the leg of a dog. One of Jason's interests, he said, was veterinary science.

The arrest shocked Jason's family and friends. None thought the mild-mannered kid was capable of what many now considered one of the more gruesome murders in recent regional memory. Furthermore, they argued, he wasn't like those other boys. Of the three defendants, Baldwin was the only one still in school at the time of the murders. He'd even been in class that day.

"In my heart of hearts, I don't believe he did it. He was always respectful. He was always, 'Yes, ma'am, no ma'am,' " said Lakeshore resident Kela Marshall, who once baby-sat Baldwin. "The only thing I ever found weird about him was he drew a little skull with a knife in it." She also told a reporter he drew a picture of two cats with knives in them once. "He could draw pretty good, though."

Jason's family tried desperately to clear him of involvement. It was a big mistake, they said. Gail and Terry gave a statement to Detective Ridge on June 4 at 9:54 A.M., the morning after Jason's arrest.

Gail tried to explain, again, that Jason was in school the day of the murders. And after he left school, she said, he went to the house of his uncle, Herbert Bartoush, to mow his lawn in West Memphis.

After he was paid, Jason told his uncle he was going to go to Wal-Mart to spend some of the money on video games. Gail told Ridge that a boy named Ken— and Damien— were with Jason at the time. The fact that she said he was with Damien was later underlined on a police transcript of her statement.

Gail also told Ridge, "You know, Jason, he's a good boy. There has been so many times that he has baby-sat his brothers. He washes the dishes for me and everything. He takes care of his little brothers for me. He's a— they get into fights sometimes, but he ain't never killed one of them."

"I understand," Ridge said.

"And he's got a good heart. He loves animals. He never would hurt an animal."

The two then told Ridge how good an artist Jason was. He won a plaque earlier in the year, and ribbons. And he recently got an improvement card for his courses at school, they said.

Ridge then remarked that Jason wasn't speaking to the police.

" 'Cause I told him," Gail replied.

" 'Cause you told him not to speak to us."
". . . I'm scared 'cause you all put words in his mouth and make things, make a mountain out of a molehill."

"Well, that's (the reason) we got tape recorders. I'm not putting words into your mouth," Ridge said.

One reason she didn't want Jason talking to the police was because of the way the investigation was conducted, she told Ridge.

"After Damien, after the police questioned Damien, there was rumors started. People were saying that the police told them this and told them that, and I thought in my mind then, the police are trying to make him out to be the guilty one and I told him not to talk to them, to anybody. And I told him, if you hear of anybody else saying something that a policeman said, get his name, 'cause I am going to go to the police station with it."

Ridge, however, simply told Gail Grinnell: "It's like this. We've got a story that is very, very believable. It is so close to perfect that we have to believe it."

Gail's advice that Jason not speak to police became a foretelling of how later events would unfold. Standing on the Fifth Amendment, he never got his story across.

Thirteen

The Secret Order of the Undead

A long, hot summer had begun. Over the next several months, the West Memphis police would search quietly for Misskelley's cult. They would interview shadowy characters, gather reading materials on teen Satanism, and consult so-called "occult crime" experts.

Meanwhile, the public went cult-crazy.

Hysteria hit the streets the morning of June 7, when *The Commercial Appeal* published the first account of Misskelley's statement to police. By afternoon, the West Memphis *Evening Times* printed an editorial condemning Satanism and urging unspecified public action.

The town became hysterical, residents repeating and embellishing upon secondhand tales of animal sacrifices and sexual orgies. From pulpits, preachers trumpeted salvation. Parents looked at their kids and wondered if they were prone to getting caught up in the darkness they feared.

In Jonesboro, Arkansas, an hour north of West Memphis, when a group of Wiccans opened a store in an old antique-shop section of town called Old

Nettleton, there was an uproar. The shop featured charms, potions, and recipes for spells. Community leaders saw a threat and spoke to the landlord. The landlord said he'd been misled about the nature of the business and terminated the lease.

On a sunny Sunday, a small group of Wiccans marched down the main church-lined street in a Freedom of Religion rally as churchgoers and television cameras looked on. They were taunted and jeered. Steve Branch, the natural father of one victim whose accused killers would soon be tried in Jonesboro, read passages from the New Testament from the courthouse lawn.

The volume rose. Crittenden County librarian Nelda Antonetti talked to police and reporters about something she'd noticed recently— more local kids were checking out books on Satanism, the occult, and magic. One book checked out by Damien Echols, *Cotton Mather on Witchcraft* (Mather, 1663-1728, had chronicled the Salem, Massachusetts, witch trials), had a dog-eared page that listed human fat in a recipe for a potion enabling witches to fly. It also mentioned the heart of an unbaptized baby as a delicacy following a black mass.

The newspapers hinted at an even larger conspiracy. Juvenile officer Jerry Driver was quoted as saying he was himself concerned by a supposed local satanic ringleader, named by several teens only as Lucifer. "I've been looking for Lucifer for two and a half years," Driver said, but he'd never found him. One paper also noted that on the night of the arrests, police confiscated a book from Echols's home, *Never on a Broomstick* by Frank Donovan.

But even in the West Memphis area, Damien had his defenders. "He liked vampire movies and vampire books, but I do, too— so what?" Dian Teer told the Memphis newspaper. "What really scares me is the one who really (killed the boys) is still out there, and the cops are sitting there patting themselves on the back."

Ministers, too, railed against an invisible, unthinkable evil lurking in the community.

"Ladies and gentlemen, I want you to know that we live in a perverse and crooked world today," pastor Johnny Thomas told a funeral gathering in the stifling heat in nearby Wynne, Arkansas. "Don't you know we have to watch out for one another? Hold on to your children."

There was plenty of reason for fear. That June 27 funeral in Wynne was for thirteen-year-old Geneva Smith, whose decomposed body had been found a year earlier but had only recently been identified by forensic experts. It was widely reported in the media that Geneva was one of six children in eastern Arkansas, including the three West Memphis boys, to "die mysteriously" in the past two years. Geneva's body was found May 31, 1992, in the St. Francis River.

Authorities said there was no link between the West Memphis killings and the others. But not everyone was convinced. During Geneva's eulogy, Thomas said the West Memphis boys were killed by a "Satan-worshiping sorority" who "drained and drank the victims' blood in their rituals."

The flame of hysteria rose a notch when juvenile officer Driver publicly confirmed that he had sought help a year earlier from occult-crime consultants. Driver became concerned with what he called a noticeable increase in teens dabbling in the occult. His chief consultant was Steve Nawojczyk, the Pulaski County coroner in Little Rock, who ran a business on the side advising law-enforcement agencies and schools on problems posed by teen occult-dabblers. Nawojczyk visited several West Memphis sites in the summer of 1992 where authorities had found evidence of bonfires, graffiti, and animal carcasses.

His assessment: Crittenden County had a group of "self-styled" Satanists, which he defined as beyond mere dabblers. Self-styled Satanists, he said, generally were troubled youths in search of an identity through sex, drugs, and the power they believe black magic will give them. These youths tend to congregate in small, tight-knit groups of five to seven members, often headed by a charismatic, manipulative older leader, he said. The followers get involved in "fantasy role-playing stuff," he said, and sometimes "they can't turn the fantasy off."

Nawojczyk's field, the teen occult, is highly controversial. Labeled "cult cops" by critics, occult-crime consultants have emerged across the country, and many are nothing but charlatans. Most are former police officers or people in law-enforcement-related fields whose jobs have brought them in contact with unusual teenagers.

Regardless, Nawojczyk's visit was ominously prophetic. While visiting the abandoned three-story Dabbs School, Nawojczyk saw upside-down crosses spray-painted on walls and the remains of bonfires on the basement's cement floor—evidence of a Satanist ritual site, he said. The school was burned down on December 26, 1992—"the day after Jesus' birthday," as one neighbor noted.

Driver didn't acknowledge it publicly at the time, but his chief concern with teen dabblers in 1992 involved Damien Echols.

The rumors that ran wild after the June 3 arrests—that Echols drank blood, planned to sacrifice a baby, and tried to gouge out someone's eyes—were all accusations Driver had known, and had tried to confirm, months earlier.

Life got rough for Domini Teer and her mother, Dian, in the weeks following the arrests. First, their landlord threatened to evict them from their ratty Lakeshore trailer. Then, acting on complaints, the Arkansas Department of Human Services threatened to take Domini away unless they cleaned the wall-to-wall litter, including the widely reported cat feces, from the home.

"There's no money to do all this," Dian Teer told a reporter one steamy June afternoon, in what had become an almost daily impromptu press briefing on her front stoop. Even from outside, the stench was unbearable. Cat leavings baked in the heat inside the trailer. Teer stared at her visitors through narrowed eyes, magnified by thick Coke-bottle lenses. Her orange hair was flat and unwashed.

Brenda Dian Teer, forty-three at the time, had been born in Memphis, but had spent thirteen years in California, in the Upland-Ontario area, east of Los Angeles. She said she'd spent much of her youth as "a hippie." She moved back from California to West Memphis five years earlier before suffering a stroke that left one side of her body partially paralyzed. She and her husband had separated, she said, but she declined to discuss family details.

Court and police records in Memphis fill in a few gaps. Michael Nathan Teer, Domini's father, was extradited from California to Memphis in 1978 for allegedly running off with $25,000 from a convenience store he had managed, stood trial but was found not guilty. A jail mug shot from 1975, when he was twenty-three, shows a pale, blue-eyed man with long orange hair, very much resembling his daughter. "He's very upset over all of this, too," Dian said. "He's been trying to get her to come there and stay with him (at his home in Illinois), but she doesn't want to do it."

As the Teers attempted to comply with state health regulations, they cleared mounds of trash and filth from the trailer.

A reporter sifting through several boxes at curbside discovered something else about the Teers that the police had missed in the house search: an underground vampire club newsletter published by Domini's cousin in California.

The *Secret Order of the Undead— SOUND*, for short— offered readers a dark forum for horror fantasy, macabre poetry, and ghoulish fantasy fiction. The amateurish periodical, consisting of photocopied sheets bound together, was published by Domini's twenty-two-year-old cousin, Tammy Jo Teer of Upland, California. The forty-page booklet included an ink sketch of a winged demon molesting a woman, a list of thirteen songs "suitable to accompany any ritualistic murder," and a column instructing "boys and girls" in the fine art of building a homemade "landmine" from a threaded pipe and shotgun shells.

"It's poetry," said Tammy Jo Teer, a college drama student, in defense of the product. "It's a performing artist-type thing." Tammy Jo had made news in the Riverside, California, area earlier in 1993, when a small film company founded by her father, Patrick Teer, produced an offbeat motorcycle gang movie called *Showdown*. It was about a fictional town where everybody is a retired criminal. Tammy Jo Teer was listed as the owner of the film company.

Tammy Jo had other outlets, too. She was listed in a San Francisco newsletter as one of twenty-six correspondents nationwide who headed vampire societies or had interests in gothic horror, heavy metal, "occult erotica," morose literature, and other offbeat pastimes. Other contacts listed in the same publication, *Necropolis*— Greek for "city of the dead"— included someone named Drucilla Blood of Hickory Hills, Illinois; a young woman who could be reached in Salem, Massachusetts; and Countess Velvet Moon of Burbank, California. In this June 1993 issue, the publishers of *Necropolis* were raving about a new publication called *Blue Blood Magazine,* which was described as a "vampire gothic porno" publication complete with pictorials and "an easygoing attitude toward life, love and sex . . ."

SOUND and *Necropolis* were among hundreds of underground newsletters nationwide that serve all sorts of people interested in death, horror, and other macabre topics the mainstream media don't often address. They also are part of the larger phenomenon, underground magazines, now commonly called zines.

Tammy Jo Teer insisted her cousin Domini had nothing to do with *SOUND.* "Domini sent us five poems, and that was years ago," Tammy Jo said. "We never even published them."

Domini and her mother became a sideshow throughout the brutally hot summer of 1993. In one light, she was pathetic: a skinny, frail, redheaded girl, forced to quit school because she carried Damien's baby. In another, she seemed sinister. Juvenile authorities said they feared the baby might be a planned sacrifice. At least one witness placed her not far from Damien and Robin Hood on the night of the murders.

But Dian Teer insisted her daughter was home in

bed the night of the murders. And one more thing, she said, before closing the door on a reporter: "Yes, we are going to keep the baby."

Fourteen

"I'll chase you all the way to hell!"

A large mob of perhaps two hundred gathered around the police station for the arraignment in Municipal Court, a one-story add-on to the police department building. The crowd lobbed jeers and taunts as they waited for the three defendants to come out.

"I want them!" screamed Pam Hobbs, TV cameras in her face. "The same stuff they did to my kid, I want to do to all three!" She looked nearly wilted in the stifling heat. The temperature was pushing eighty-five degrees, but it didn't slow anyone down.

The rumors flew. "I heard he clawed somebody's eyes out," said Kevin Lawrence, a young teen who knew Echols from Lakeshore. "He said he was going to kill two more before he turned himself in," said Roxanne Harrison, a gray-haired woman who lived in an apartment complex by the J.W. Rich softball field where Echols often hung out.

Few people offering information to reporters actually knew Echols well. But nearly all passed on a similar account: Echols often wore a long black trench coat, even on the hottest Delta summer afternoons, and told people he worshiped the Devil. A sixteen-year-old junior at Marion High School who knew Echols before he dropped out the year before said the distant teenager seldom paid attention in class, and at times carried a cat's skull around with him. "While everyone else was working, he was just playing with that cat skull," he said.

The crowd offered kinder assessments of Baldwin and Misskelley. Several people seemed perplexed that Baldwin, the only one of the three still in school, could be involved in the murders. "He was really quiet. He was a great artist," another classmate said. "We talked about the murders in English class. He just sat there. He never said anything."

Nearly everyone who knew Misskelley made similar comments. "He was a good kid," said a neighbor from Highland. "It's hard to believe he would do something like this." Big Jessie, dressed in his blue mechanic outfit, stood amid a circle of reporters who wanted to know more about his son.

"He was scared to death of Damien," Big Jessie said, speaking in a shy half-smile. Other family members beat back reporters with loud voices, but Big Jessie seemed to enjoy the attention. "Jessie told us he (Echols) ate blood, too— human blood," Big Jessie said, telling the story about Damien and a bloody fistfight that detectives had heard of two weeks earlier. "He was wiping the blood off his nose, eating it."

Security was so tight that police patted down anyone they didn't know— even after they'd gone through the metal detectors. Pal Rainey, whose silver hair and beard looked premature on someone so young, ran a tight ship in his courtroom. In Arkansas, municipal judges for the most part handled small claims, traffic matters, and the initial appearances of felony suspects headed for the circuit court. For Rainey, today was a very different kind of case.

Echols was led into the courtroom from a dingy hallway linking the court to the city jail. Surrounded by police, he leaned smugly against the wall. Everyone was getting their first look at Damien Echols, murder defendant. He wore a powder-blue shirt, his hair long in the back but partially shaved on one side. His skin was sickly white. For a kid of eighteen, he hardly seemed scared. Defiantly, Echols tilted his head back on the wall. They were watching him—and he was watching them.

The courtroom, a small, bare-bones facility with hard wooden pews and a tile floor, was filled with a collection of overweight women in too-tight polyester blends and men in the uniforms of their employers or in T-shirts and blue jeans. There were the families and friends of the victims, some haggard, some subdued, all angry.

A large, bulky man near the back of the courtroom suddenly raced forward and lunged at Echols. Two or three cops intercepted him as he came within a few feet of the defendant and wrestled him back. "I'll chase you all the way to hell!" he screamed, pointing a finger at Echols. It was Steve Branch, the natural father of the dead boy who bore the same name. He was led away in handcuffs, but was later released.

Rainey threatened to clear the court if there were any more outbursts. Aiming to keep as many details of the case out of the public eye, Rainey told Echols that criminal complaints usually are read out loud by the judge in some detail, but said that could be waived if he liked.

"Out loud!" Echols said, shooting a look of defiance at the judge. Echols didn't get his request. Rainey clamped a seal on all records connected with the case, including the probable cause affidavits that spelled out the police case against the defendants. Each boy was given a temporary lawyer, just for the weekend, until further arrangements could be made.

Outside the courthouse, the mob waited. The defendants would be escorted to police vehicles in the parking lot, and the crowd knew it. Photographers and television cameras were lined up to get a shot of the defendants. As the three youths were led away, shackled, the crowd screamed curses at them. Baldwin looked like the scared boy he was; Misskelley kept his head bowed.

Arrangements were made to house the defendants separately and as far from West Memphis as was practicable for transport to the numerous pretrial hearings that would follow. Echols was sent to Monroe County in east-central Arkansas. Baldwin went to Jonesboro, a college town in Craighead County about sixty miles northwest of West Memphis. Misskelley was sent to Clay County, a mainly agricultural area up behind the Missouri bootheel and more than a hundred miles away.

The press coverage was extensive and sensational, and it would help contribute to what many considered to be hysteria in the community. By Monday morning, as the defendants were led into circuit court, a story in *The Commercial Appeal* of Memphis appeared under the banner headline: TEEN DESCRIBES 'CULT' TORTURE OF BOYS.

The newspaper had gotten hold of Misskelley's confession, and the story told, for the first time publicly, his lurid tale of how the victims were subdued, how Christopher Byers was sexually mutilated, and how Misskelley had chased down Michael Moore and returned him to Echols and Baldwin to die. The June 7 story caused an uproar and the newspaper's request to open the sealed files was denied later that day.

Days later, in letters to the editor, the newspaper was accused of practicing "yellow journalism" and of unfairly condemning the accused before trial.

"There's talk around town that *The Commercial Appeal* has gone tabloid," one letter-writer charged. Other news organizations, unable to confirm the report, aired the confession secondhand, attributing its details to the newspaper.

That was just the beginning of press and television accounts that would affect how the public viewed Echols, Baldwin, and Misskelley. Ultimately, many believed news media hype helped determine their fate.

The Crittenden County Courthouse, built in 1910 and 1911 with six white Ionic columns on both the north and south, would be the scene of many high-intensity hearings in the case. Tall and red, the painted-brick building was the focus of life in downtown Marion, the county seat.

Rimmed with stately old magnolias, the courthouse grounds contained plaques commemorating Confederate soldiers, dedicated, as in many courthouse squares across the South, by the United Daughters of the Confederacy. The surrounding commercial area was almost like a ghost town with several empty shops and an ancient two-story hotel that once was the pride of Marion, but now was a seedy apartment building. An inscription over the courthouse doors recited a civic paradox: Obedience To The Law Is Liberty.

The paint inside was peeling, the hallways grimy. Office staff worked amid a bad retrofit of computers and fax machines in offices where court clerks still record deeds and lawsuits by hand into large, red, leather-bound ledgers. Outside in the narrow hallways, the ubiquitous Arkansas courthouse gum machines dispense a handful for a dime.

The courthouse has two upstairs courtrooms. One is old-fashioned, with a tan wood railing separating spectators from the bench and jury box, which has surprisingly comfortable hardwood chairs. The other, where the pretrial hearings in the case would be conducted, is more modern, with gray carpet climbing up the walls to form wainscoting to shoulder height. It has no source of natural light.

Between the two courtrooms, the large, second-floor lobby contains a soft-drink machine in one corner, a couple of worn-out couches in another.

Security would be tight for all the hearings. All eyes stayed on the three defendants sitting at wooden tables up front. Misskelley, as he would at every court appearance, sat in a hunch, unable to pull his eyes from the tabletop. At times, he appeared to nearly crawl under the table. Baldwin sat stiffly, head lowered, face flushed. Echols was another story altogether.

Damien leaned deep into his chair, rocking gently. Often, he turned around and stared into the crowd. It was not a maniacal Charles Manson stare, but a sleepy, oblivious one, often accompanied by a disturbing smirk. At one hearing, Echols outraged the victims' families by blowing kisses at them. At other times Echols, arms folded, chatted amiably with security officers, a big smile on his face, as if he were

According to authorities, this abandoned cotton gin sometimes called "Stone Henge" just outside West Memphis served as a gathering place for local teens to drink, have sex, and perform rituals connected to Satanism such as animal sacrifice.
(*Courtesy, Jim Arnold/The Commercial Appeal*)

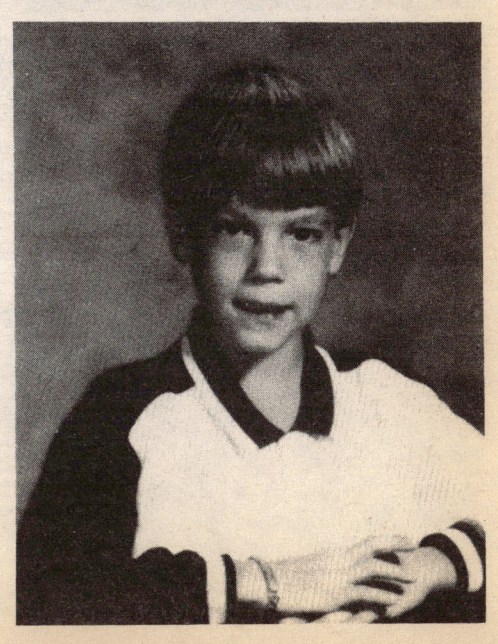

Chris Byers, 8.

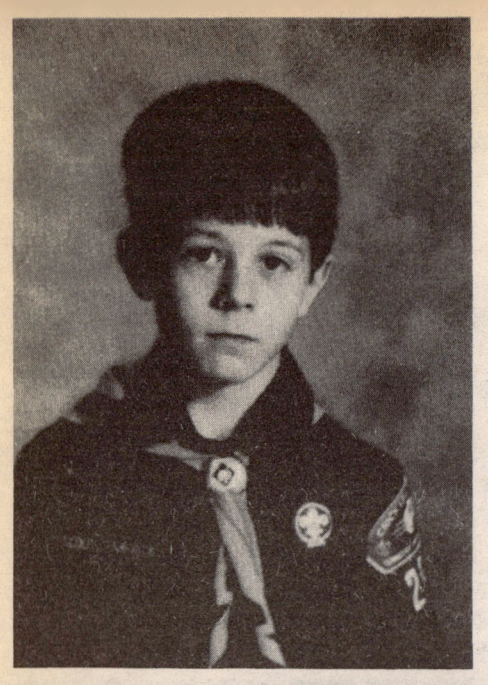

Michael Moore, 8.

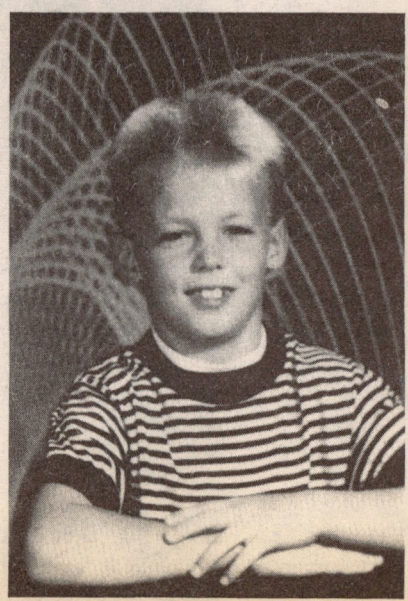

Steve Branch, 8.

The Blue Beacon Truck Wash stands near Robin Hood Hills, the heavily wooded area where the bodies of Moore, Byers, and Branch were found. *(Courtesy of Guy Reel)*

Police found a boy's shoe and a Cub Scout hat believed to have belonged to Michael Moore in the ditch where the bodies were discovered. *(Courtesy of West Memphis Arkansas Police Department)*

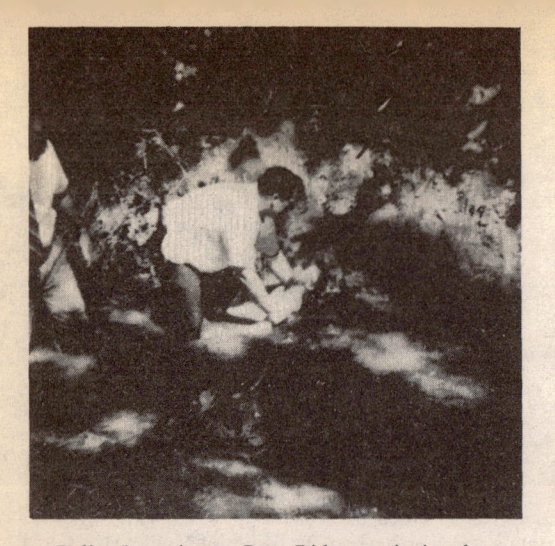

Police Investigator, Bryn Ridge, retrieving the bodies from the water.
(*Courtesy of West Memphis Arkansas Police Department*)

Cub Scout Troop 294 pray at a memorial service for the murdered boys about a year after their deaths. Michael Moore belonged to Troop 294. (*Courtesy, Richard Gardner/The Commercial Appeal*)

The entire community was stunned by the gruesome discovery. A local church posted its support for the police during the investigation. (*Courtesy of West Memphis Arkansas Police Department*)

Pam Hobbs, the mother of Steve Branch, and her husband, Terry.
(*Courtesy, Jim Arnold/The Commercial Appeal*)

John Mark Byers (center), the stepfather of Chris Byers, and Todd Moore, Michael Moore's dad (right), leave the West Memphis Police Station with Andy Taylor, a friend of Byers.
(*Courtesy of West Memphis Arkansas Police Department*)

Inspector Gary Gitchell of the West Memphis Police Department announces the arrest of three suspects at a press conference.
(Courtesy, Michael McMullan/The Commercial Appeal)

Jessie Lloyd Misskelley, Jr., 17.

Jason Baldwin, 16.

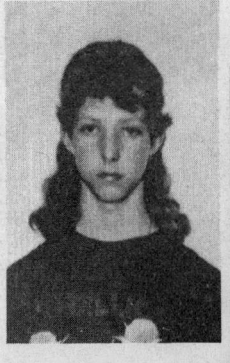

Damien Wayne Echols, 18.

One day after his arrest, Damien Echols is led from the West Memphis Courthouse by police. (*Courtesy, Steve Jones/The Commercial Appeal*)

Damien in his eighth grade yearbook. A classmate has written "devil worshoper" on the picture.

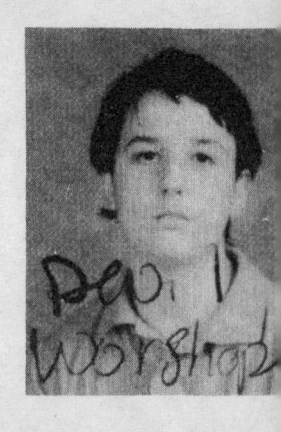

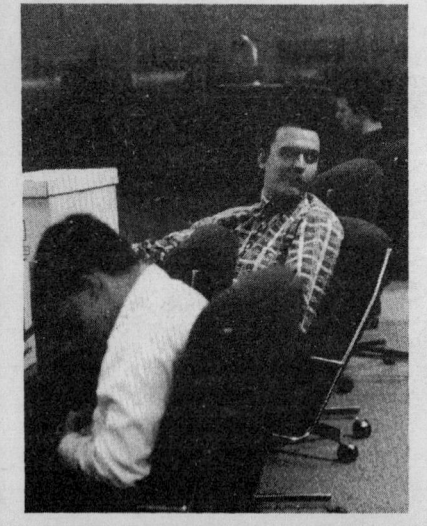

At a pre-trial hearing, Echols leers at courtroom spectators, flanked by Misskelley (foreground) and Baldwin. (*Courtesy, Lisa Waddell Buser/The Commercial Appeal*)

Damien's girlfriend, Domini Teer, 17, and their baby Seth at the trial in the Craighead County Courthouse. (*Courtesy, Lisa Waddell Buser/The Commercial Appeal*)

The trailer home of Domini Teer, where Damien often stayed. (*Courtesy of The Commercial Appeal*)

Val Price,
defense attorney for Echols.

Deputy Prosecutor
John Fogleman.

Circuit Court Judge
David Burnett.

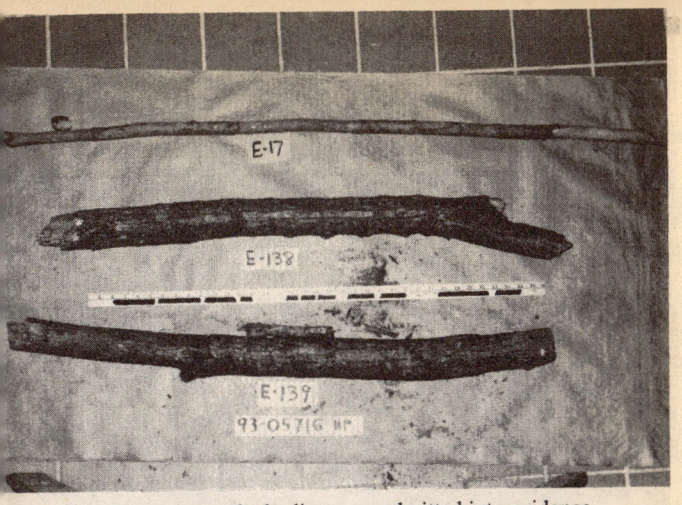

Sticks found near the bodies were admitted into evidence as the possible murder weapons.
(Courtesy of West Memphis Arkansas Police Department)

Paul Ford (left) and Robin Wadley, defense attorneys for Jason Baldwin (center), examine the clothing of one of the victims while Damien looks on.
(Courtesy, Lisa Waddell Buser/The Commercial Appeal)

Damien Echols stands to receive his death sentence.
(*Courtesy, Lisa Waddell Buser/The Commercial Appeal*)

a politician greeting members of the Police Benevolent Association.

In the drawing for public defenders, Echols got Val P. Price, tall, intense, square-jawed and very sharp; and Scott R. Davidson, more laid-back and friendly, but razor-sharp. Both were from Jonesboro. Baldwin got George Robin Wadley, a large bulldog not much inclined to accept the prosecution's early advantage, and Paul N. Ford, a dry-witted, self-confident patrician with slicked-back blond hair that hung long on his neck. Both at the time worked for the Rees Law Firm, also based in Jonesboro, although Ford worked from its far satellite office in West Memphis. Misskelley was given the firm of Daniel T. Stidham and Gregory L. Crow, of Paragould, both large, thoughtful men who, over the months, seemed increasingly troubled about what was happening to their client.

A couple of days after the lawyers got their new clients' portfolios, there was an incident that almost made the proceedings against Echols moot. The local mental health center had for some time prescribed Elavil, an antidepressant, for Echols. At about nine o'clock in the evening on June 9, Echols, held in the Monroe County Jail, received his evening's dosage of three fifty-milligram tablets. About ten minutes later, he buzzed the jailer on the intercom and admitted hoarding each evening's dosage since he'd been at the jail, and had just now taken all twelve pills at once. His eyes were dilated and he had an irregular pulse. A doctor was called, and he advised jailers to give Echols Ipecac, to induce vomiting. He was then rushed to an emergency room in nearby Stuttgart.

Searching his cell, jail officials found a suicide note,

scrawled on the inside cardboard of a Marlboro cigarette carton.

"Dear Mom & Dad," Echols printed in a childish script. "Just remember I am a Wiccan and will be reincarnated. I promise. I love you very much. Tell Domini I love her and to take care of my baby. . . . I will be back."

He survived.

The three defendants did not appear in court for another month. On August 4, they formally appeared before Judge David Burnett of Osceola to state their pleas. Each was charged with three counts of capital murder for causing the death of the three victims "against the peace and dignity of the State of Arkansas." The state requested samples of evidence from the defendants— head hair, pubic hair, saliva, blood, fingerprints, and footprints— as well as samples of handwriting. Baldwin's lawyers noted for the record that, without his consent, some of that evidence had already been taken from their client, and that they'd filed a formal objection, as well as a motion to suppress the evidence.

All three pleaded not guilty.

Now that police had their suspects, they wanted to find their cult. But searching for it was a little like chasing goblins and demons. There were plenty of shadows, but not much to grab hold of.

Cult interest grew on June 29, when a tall, lanky diesel mechanic who was incarcerated at the county jail told detectives he participated orgies with Misskelley and others out at "Stonehenge," the abandoned cotton gin east of Marion. Members of the cult, including Misskelley, Echols, and Baldwin, planned to sacrifice some young boys, he said. In-

THE BLOOD OF INNOCENTS 213

spired by a mysterious black magic book, he said the group had been sacrificing dogs and chickens.

"We would drain the blood, then we would take and cut the heart out, and put it in the center of the pentagram and set fire to it and worship the Devil," Alvis Bly told Sgt. Mike Allen in a taped interview at the Crittenden County Jail in Marion.

Police had reason to be skeptical of Bly. A jailer tipped them off to Bly after transporting the inmate to the East Arkansas Mental Health Center. Bly confessed he was "looped" on medicine, and said he was under a psychiatrist's care. On the other hand, so many people interviewed during this unusual investigation had received mental treatment, it would be impossible to ignore them all.

Bly, six feet five inches tall and thirty-six years old, loomed as a particularly intriguing character. He described in great detail rituals supposedly performed by the group. Pentagrams were drawn on the ground or on the cement floor at Stonehenge with white or blue powder chalk, he said. Cult members would cut a dog's head off, hang the carcass by its feet over the pentagram, and catch the blood in a cup to drink.

The heart, cut from the animal, would be placed in a pie pan at the center of the pentagram. After pouring a mixture of alcohol and baby oil on it, the heart would be set afire while participants "praised the Devil," Bly said.

Instructions for the ceremonies came from a "black, shiny book," he told Allen. The book, which apparently came from the library, included a picture of a dragon with a goat's body, which Bly referred to as "St. Lucifer's second son." Elucidating on the rituals, Bly asked Allen if the three young murder victims had been beaten to death.

"I can't answer that question," Allen said.

"Well," Bly said. "I understand that. But that's how we do the dogs, we beat them to death first."

"What would you beat them to death with?"

"With sticks."

"With sticks?"

"Yes, sir," Bly answered, pondering the murders. "I don't know why they didn't cut their heads off."

Allen became curious. Certainly everyone in Crittenden County knew the boys had been beaten over the head—that was reported in early news accounts. But the type of weapon was supposed to have been a secret. Police suspected the murder weapons were the tree limbs found shoved into the mud with the boys' clothes wrapped around one end. Allen pressed for more details.

"Any other body parts that they might cut off?" he queried.

"Their penis."

"How would— "

"Bite it off."

"They would bite the penis off?" Allen asked with alarm.

"Yes, sir. That's how it reads in the books to do."

It was called "Devil circumcision," Bly explained. "It said in the book that the Devil would gnash his teeth together after he circumcised them, which was biting their peter off."

The cult never performed Devil circumcision on the dogs, Bly said, because no one had "courage up" to do it. But they did cut off dog penises, he said, using an eleven-inch "gut knife" with "ripples" that Misskelley carried.

Bly told Allen the cult once had group sex with a sixteen-year-old girl at Stonehenge, and provided the detective with the girl's name. There was also a lot of "cornholing" going on there, he said. Echols, who was known in the cult as Davien rather than Damien, had sex with a ten-year-old boy at Stonehenge, Bly said.

Pushing for evidence that could link others to the May 5 murders, Allen asked Bly if there had been talk at cult meetings "about any sacrificing kids or anything."

"Yes, sir, there was. Yes, sir," Bly answered.

"What kind of talk?"

"They were trying to pick out, you know, wanting to know who we could pick out to do it." But Bly was fuzzy on details. He said he was in the process of leaving the cult because he had problems with the rape of the sixteen-year-old.

It was difficult to get a handle on Bly. When pressed, he was fuzzy on corroborating details. He said as many as twenty people attended cult meetings, but he couldn't remember their names. "It's just real hard for me to remember names," he said. "I was married to my wife for months before I could remember her name." He also described Misskelley as the leader of the cult, which seemed unlikely, given his low intelligence. He also admitted he needed mental help.

"I want to get to where I don't see the Devil no more," Bly said, noting he was in jail for "cornholing" an underage girl.

Bly told Allen he got in with the teen cult because he owned a ski boat and would take boys out to local lakes. In a May 19 interview, police asked John Mark Byers for names of anyone he might be suspicious about. Byers mentioned someone in his neighborhood who owned a ski boat, though he couldn't place the name. Bly lived five blocks from

Byers. Bly also claimed there was another adult in the neighborhood who also was in the cult.

Byers and Bly, a year or so apart, both came from the same place—Marked Tree, Arkansas. Bly also gave the names of two other adults from Marked Tree he claimed were in the cult.

Bly also gave details of several sites where the cult was to have met. In addition to Stonehenge, he mentioned an old barn and a large, abandoned house north of Lakeshore on Arkansas Highway 50. "They were planning on sacrificing them up there on Fifty at that house and leave them there," Bly said.

If police ever took seriously the psychic ponderings of the Phoenix upholsterer who said he dreamed the boys were killed near an unpainted barn, then this could confirm his story. To check Bly's story, Detective Ridge drove Bly on a tour of the sites he had talked about. Ridge's notes show Bly showed him, among other things, a vacant yellow house off Interstate 55 about ten miles north of West Memphis where he said cult rituals were performed. It's unclear whether the visits produced any evidence to aid the case.

On June 16, Ridge drove 120 miles east to Shelbyville, Tennessee, in the hills south of Nashville to interview a teenager who used to live in West Memphis and knew Echols. Ridge had hoped the teen could provide more details about the satanic cult that Misskelley talked about. Ridge did learn more about strange behavior among Echols's circle of friends, but satanism did not seem to be its driving force.

Paul Rand, a sixteen-year-old juvenile delinquent, told Ridge about drug use, animal killing, and "torture" practiced by Echols and his friends. But Rand described his former associates as more of a sadistic street gang that dabbled in the occult rather than a satanic cult.

"I knew that they were in the occult," said Rand, who at the time of the interview was confined to the Dede Wallace Wilderness Program, a program for troubled boys. Among his claims, he told Ridge the group "raped some people," built bonfires in the woods, spray-painted graffiti (including inverted crosses and pentagrams), consumed drugs (including marijuana, cocaine, alcohol, gasoline, and acid), and once cut a pig's head off and put it on someone's porch.

"That was my idea," Rand said.

The group, which included Misskelley, Baldwin, and Echols, also killed dogs and cats, he said. In agreement with Misskelley, Rand said the teens cooked dogs and ate part of the meat. "Sometimes it was initiations, and sometimes it was just done, you know," he told Ridge.

Rand described drug-induced parties where kids had sex, got into fights, or did whatever came to them.

"Sometimes it be flat-out violence, you know, getting into fights and stuff," he said. But other times, "you'll start thinking of some cartoon characters, let's say the little guys in blue."

"Smurfs?" Ridge asked.

"Yeah, Smurfs, things like that," he replied. "And the next thing you know, you be, all of a sudden somebody will be running at you, and the Smurf has a heart on his arms and he will be running at you and stuff."

The ramblings made Ridge impatient. He asked Rand if the cult members ate dogs as a ritual "to give them power," a phrase the police had picked up on from occult-crime consultants. Rand seemed confused. Ridge asked the question a second time, and Rand tried to field it.

"I guess, I would say, it was like, uh, you know, 'Let us eat this meat,' you know, right here. They would eat it and they start feeling real good," he said.

Rand blamed the dog-eating on peer pressure, not Satan. "I wanted to be with the group. I wanted people to like me," he said. If there truly was a secret satanic society, Rand apparently had not reached its inner circle.

Rand said some of the members of the group claimed to have killed someone in a local housing project a few years earlier. He knew no details of the killing, but said it was gang-related.

"The cult are Crips, you know, some cult people are Crips," he said, referring to the Los Angeles-based Crips gang that has spawned imitators throughout America. As in L.A., the West Memphis Crips have rivals, he said—the Bloods. "Bloods, Crips have attitudes about them and every time you see them, they just blow, you know, and the cult are pretty much crazy, too."

West Memphis had several youth gangs, among them the Saints and the Shorty Folks. Police encountered members of both gangs while investigating the May 5 murders, but there is little evidence they considered the murders to be gang-related rather than satanically inspired. Throughout the investigation, "cult" rather than "gang" was the operative word.

Like juvenile officer Jerry Driver, the police turned to Little Rock coroner Steve Nawojczyk and other "cult cops" to try to explain the murders.

According to Nawojczyk, kids attracted to teen Satanism often include intelligent, creative youths between ages eleven and seventeen, many of them rebellious types with low self-esteem, his seminar handouts say. Teens involved in this activity often obsess over movies with occult themes, read occult books, play fantasy role games like Dungeons & Dragons, eat raw meat, grow their fingernails long, speak to people in rhyme, and listen to "black" heavy-metal music, a brand of intense rock that pushes satanic themes.

Other by-products include grave robbery, "satanic graffiti," supremacist attitudes, and, in some cases, murder, Nawojczyk states. Teens can be recruited by "satanic cults" or "born into families who practice satanic cult rituals," he says in his seminars for schools and police departments.

Like many in his trade, he hints at a dark conspiracy, citing the surgical mutilation of cows and other large animals.

"It has not been until the past few years that law-enforcement agencies have realized that cadavers offer numerous 'tattle-tale' clues which clearly expose operating cults," says a Nawojczyk handout entitled "The Who, What, When, Where, and How of Teen Satanism." Missing blood, a lack of bullet wounds, and missing internal organs and tongues are among the clues, he says.

"Another horrifying community sign is missing children," the paper says. It cites a figure discussed frequently by satanic conspiracy theorists: There may be as many as fifty thousand to sixty thousand human sacrifices a year in the United States. "There is simply too much evidence verifying these incredible facts for anyone to flippantly approach the problem. Denial must stop. Kids are dying!"

Yet cult cops and satanic conspiracists have their critics. In his 1993 book, *Satanic Panic: The Creation of a Contemporary Legend*, Jeffrey S. Victor scoffs at the teen Satanism label, referring to it instead as "teen pseudo-Satanism." Victor doesn't deny teen interest in black magic and the occult, but he says there are sound explanations for the phenomenon.

"Explaining such behavior as being a product of religious 'cult' brainwashing and the influence of evil religious beliefs is dramatic, but entirely misleading," writes Victor, a sociology professor at the State University of New York. "The behavior of teenagers engaged in pseudo-Satanism needs to be understood in the context of what we know about juvenile delinquency."

Victor contends that much of the graffiti, cemetery vandalism, and supposed altar sites found by police actually are the remains of adolescent "legend trips," in which youths visit sites for the thrill of testing local legends about ghosts and other supernatural activity.

Though clearly there are teenagers who profess to be Satanists, most lack a sophisticated belief system revolving around Devil worship, Victor states. Instead, they are motivated by the kind of things that motivate most juvenile delinquents: the need for a peer group to justify dispositions toward aggressive hostility, a desire to gain control over their frustrated lives, or simply a thirst for attention.

Victor supports his claims of "satanic panic" by citing extensively from available research and including an appendix listing sixty-two incidents of "satanic cult rumor panics" in the United States and Canada between 1952 and 1992.

Despite differing terminology, youth interest in the occult can lead to trouble and, on rare occasions, even murder.

As far as Rand was concerned, the myriad possible explanations for Echols's circle of friends meant little. He knew only that they could be a dangerous lot.

THE BLOOD OF INNOCENTS 221

Officials at the Middle Tennessee youth camp called West Memphis police after Rand claimed he had once seen Echols and Baldwin "torture a girl with a rope" by placing a slipknot around her neck and hanging her from a tree in a woods near Marion.

In the subsequent interview, Ridge at one point tried to focus Rand's thoughts on the May 5 murders.

"You don't want to get anybody else implicated or anybody else involved, but you know . . . these three boys and know that they were part of it?" Ridge asked.

"Yes," Rand answered.

How would they kill, Ridge wanted to know. How would they do it?

"Torture. You get a thrill out of torture," Rand said. "Torture is the main thing."

Another West Memphis teenager gave authorities more puzzling tips about a shadowy cult supposedly behind the murders. During a chance encounter with juvenile officer Steve Jones four days after the arrests, the teen said a "man called Lucifer" had placed a demon inside of Echols. This demon was to kill nine people before it could become a god, the long-haired fifteen-year-old who was friends with Jason Baldwin and once dated Domini Teer said. On June 10, Jones feverishly jotted down a report for the West Memphis police:

"He was definitely sure that Lucifer was involved in the murders," he wrote. The report showed he provided several biographical details on the mysterious Lucifer: He was dating Echols's old girlfriend. He had once lived with Echols. Lucifer, it seemed, also had a sense of style, too— he sported a purple streak in his blond hair.

It's unclear if police ever seriously delved into Lucifer, who seemed to be the stuff of urban legend. Driver said he'd been looking for Lucifer for more than two years. "I've never found him," he said.

On June 11, Ridge also asked him what he knew "about these cults." The teenager said he only knew there was some guy named Lucifer.

He also said his sister was best friends with a girl at Lakeshore—a girl Misskelley had named among his list of cult members the day he confessed. That link apparently was overlooked, and Ridge asked no questions.

He remained curious on a couple of fronts. On May 19, two weeks after the murders, Sergeant Allen asked the teen if Echols had told him he'd killed the three boys. Allen was acting on a tip, but he countered it. He said he had spoken with Echols but said "Damien stated that he wishes they would catch the person who done it to keep the heat off of him."

Police had also spoken with him on May 31, three days before the arrests. He told police then that Baldwin had once invited him "to a meeting of Satan worshipers" in a building behind Lakeshore. The teen also said Echols huffed gas, smoked marijuana, and once "blacked out and was dancing with trees" he mistook for women.

Also sitting in on the May 31 interview was Murray Farris. He and Farris told police they had talked with Echols in Farris's home two weeks after the murders, where the strange teen told them some incredible stories.

Echols once placed gasoline on a cat, put a bottle rocket up its rear end, then lit it. He kept a collection of animal skulls and occult paraphernalia. He once placed a young boy in a noose until the boy turned blue and nearly passed out. But, despite the apparent inclination to sadism, he told police then he did not think Echols was guilty.

"He stated that Damien had been in a hospital four times and that he knew that he was crazy. But he stated that he didn't think that Damien had killed the boys," Ridge typed in his report.

Finally, in the June 11 interview, he said he and Farris had conducted their own investigation into Echols prior to the arrests. According to the teen, he and Farris interviewed Echols at Farris's house two weeks after the murders. The conversation was intended to discover if Echols had committed the murders, he said.

"We were trying to trick him," he told Ridge. "Not really tricking, but trying to get him to confess, just say he did it. 'Cause me and Murray both were tired of being questioned and we wanted to find out who had done it."

In an interview with *The Commercial Appeal* on June 23, Farris elaborated on his "investigation" of Echols. "I told him, 'I feel like you're hiding something from me,'" Farris said. "He danced around it a lot. He said, 'No, I didn't do anything. I didn't do anything.' He said, 'Man, they're just screwing around with me because I'm from out of town, and they didn't like me when I left.'"

Farris said Echols also attended a meeting at his house before the murders, but said Echols was never initiated into Farris's coven of white witches, The Order of the Divine Light. "His orientation wasn't right," Farris said. "I shook his hand once and I shivered."

Fifteen

"What are the undead?"

Even with three defendants in jail, there seemed to be plenty of holes in the police investigation. Deputy prosecutor Fogleman made it no secret he was upset police had missed the *SOUND* vampire magazine during the house raids, despite search warrants that empowered the officers to seek and remove "cult materials" and "satanic materials." Police also had missed Damien's black trench coat. In the coat, a witness told them, Damien generally concealed a knife. Echols would later testify the coat was lying in the open on the bedroom floor the night he was arrested.

The state had no knife. They had no murder weapons at all.

The prosecution did have the stout tree branches found at the crime scene, and they were fully prepared to suggest these wooden limbs had caused the boys' head injuries. Yet the crime lab never could precisely match the branches to the boys' injuries. No tree bark or wood splinters were found in the wounds. And, because the police bungled, leaving evidence at the crime scene for a time, the crime lab didn't get all the sticks.

It would get worse. Over time, more information would surface that strongly indicated police had missed potential pieces of evidence.

Later that winter, a newspaper reporter and a new tenant living at Echols's former trailer found a thirty-six-inch homemade club with a red stain and hairs stuck to one end. A photographer for *The Commercial Appeal* took pictures. The club was resting in a cavity in a bedroom closet. Police apparently had missed that in the search, too. When the state tenant called the police, a detective swung by to pick up the club. He didn't bag it as evidence. He picked it up by his bare hand, tossed it into his undercover Lincoln, and drove off. It was later sent to the crime lab, but could not be linked to the murders.

There were other problems.

The bloody, muddy black man with an arm cast who had stumbled into the Bojangles restaurant the night of the murders also remained an unresolved mystery. After police lost the blood scraped from the bathroom wall, they made a feeble attempt nearly two months after the May 5 murders— weeks after the June 3 arrests— to locate him. Police interviewed a couple of black men with injured arms in June, took pictures of them in their casts, then released them.

Despite the public show of strength— taking fingerprints and blood, hair, saliva and other samples from suspects— the truth was the police had virtually no evidence to match those items against.

Lacking solid evidence to round out his case, Fogleman launched his own investigation. Operating on a hunch, Fogleman asked Arkansas State Police scuba divers in November to search the lake behind

Jason Baldwin's trailer. They found a twelve-inch survivalist's knife that later would be introduced into evidence.

Before that, in September, Fogleman quietly subpoenaed several witnesses to his office to testify about events surrounding the murders. Under Arkansas law, prosecutors have power to demand the presence of individuals for questioning. Fogleman solicited testimony from Pam and Joe Hutchison, and Domini Teer, among others.

Here, out of the public eye, Fogleman searched for answers.

On September 10, 1993, Fogleman interviewed Damien Echols's parents under oath. In the presence of police inspector Gitchell and a hastily appointed attorney, Gerald Coleman, who represented the rights of the interviewees, Fogleman grilled Joe and Pam Hutchison about their son's whereabouts the day of the murders. The prosecutor also probed into Damien's dabbling in witchcraft, his mental problems, and his fascination with knives.

First up was Pam, sworn in at 10:16 A.M. Fogleman started slowly at first, asking the short, plump woman with the jet-black hair about the family's background. The interview covered some of her and her husband's multitude of marriages and divorces. Then, the conversation quickly turned to Damien.

Pam Hutchison said her son had been hospitalized at least three times for mental and emotional troubles, twice in Little Rock and once during his brief stay in Oregon. It had been hard on Damien there, she explained. He was very depressed. He cried a lot. He wouldn't come out of his room. It got so bad, Pam and Joe sent Damien back to Arkansas by himself on a bus in September 1992. Damien lived for a while again with his ex-stepdad, Jack Echols,

THE BLOOD OF INNOCENTS

also staying at times with the Teers. When Pam and Joe returned to Arkansas the following February, Damien was subsisting on his disability checks.

Soon, the talk turned to witchcraft. It was clear that Fogleman, the police— even Damien's parents— didn't have a firm handle on the precise nature of the moody teen's interests.

"Now I understand that Damien says that he's a Wicca," Fogleman asked, misapplying the name of the religion for the term denoting one of its practitioners.

"Yes, sir," Pam answered.

"When did he first become interested, to your knowledge, in this witchcraft, or the occult, or whatever it is? When were you first aware of it?"

About a year and a half ago, she answered. Fogleman pressed for a better understanding.

"Do you know how he got started in it?" This question was potentially vital, given Jerry Driver's assertions that several "cults" operated in Crittenden County, some with adult members, and that Damien may have been schooled in the occult by "an older woman." The question had further importance in that Misskelley had said in his confession that pictures of the three boys had been passed around at cult meetings prior to the murders, implying that others could have been involved in the killings.

But Pam Hutchison said she didn't "know for a fact" who started her son in it, but said "my understanding is that the young lady he was seeing at the time" was responsible. That was the girl Damien had been arrested with in the abandoned trailer.

Eventually, Fogleman asked Mrs. Hutchison about her son's writings, focusing on those "where he talks about being on the dark side." Had she ever asked Damien about those, Fogleman asked.

"I understand a lot of what he writes," Pam answered. "I try to get him to explain some of it to me. But it always seems to be because he's in such a state of depression. That's why he writes like he does."

Fogleman asked about reports that Damien was seen walking through Lakeshore with dog intestines wrapped around his neck, and that he carried cat skulls to school. Pam knew nothing of the canine bowels, she said. There was no cat skull, she added, but Damien did have a dog skull that he had found along a road.

Fogleman took Pam back to May 5, walking her through the day. Pam repeated the account she had told to Detective Ridge on May 15, explaining that she took Damien to the doctor that day, then took him to Marion to fill a prescription. She dropped her son off at Lakeshore about one P.M., then picked up Damien and Domini at a laundromat in West Memphis around four P.M. After dropping Domini off at Lakeshore, Pam took Damien home. The Hutchison family—Damien included—visited the home of some friends later that night. But other than that, Damien didn't leave the trailer, and he talked on the phone with friends from about 7:30 until 10:45 P.M. before going to bed, Pam said.

Curiously, Pam Hutchison changed her story about her sudden breakup with Joe. Ten days after the murders, she had told Ridge that she and Joe separated May 4, the day before the murders. In that account, she said Damien was crying, upset because his father had deserted him again. But now she told Fogleman the sudden breakup happened May 9, four days after the murders. She remembered it clearly now, she said. It was May 9, she

THE BLOOD OF INNOCENTS

said, because that's Joe's birthday. She remembered his cake sitting on the table, she said.

The point was not dissected during this interview, but the implications were obvious. Pam may have been fabricating an alibi for her son. In her account about picking up Damien and Domini at the laundry, Joe and Michelle were also in the car. Joe also went with Pam and the kids that night to visit friends. Is this the behavior of a man who only the night before had walked out on his wife and moved back home with his mother? And when Damien and Domini gave initial statements to the police, they mentioned only Damien's mother picking them up at the laundry. At any rate, the couple was separated just two weeks, Pam said, and now she and her husband were back together.

Fogleman had one other important point to cover with Pam.

"If you remember, what was Domini wearing that day?" This was crucial on two counts. In his statement, Misskelley said Jason Baldwin was wearing blue jeans with holes in the knees. The only three people Misskelley mentioned being present at the crime scene were himself, Jason, and Damien. But Narlene Hollingsworth and her family claimed they spotted Damien and Domini walking away from Robin Hood Hills that night. Were they confusing Domini with Jason? The Hollingsworths said Domini had on jeans patterned with "white flowers." The jeans had holes in the knees, they said. Yet Domini and Jason looked alike, both thin with long, light-colored hair. This point was essential not only to solidify the case against Baldwin, but to clear up lingering suspicions about Domini.

Pam couldn't recall exactly, but said she thinks

Domini wore a "multicolored T-shirt and a pair of jeans."

"Do you remember anything about the jeans?" Fogleman pried.

"No, I don't," Pam answered. "I'm not positive that's what she was wearing, but that's what she wears most of the time."

Eddie Joe Hutchison was sworn in at 11:33 A.M. His dark eyes stared from behind his large, bumped nose. Like the hair of his wife and son, his hair was pitch-black. Called Joe by most who knew him, Hutchison, thirty-seven, provided a brief biography: He had been working the past five months at a Petro gas station in West Memphis since returning from Oregon in the spring. He told how the family had just come back from Oregon three months before the murders. Before reuniting with Pam, Joe had lived several years outside Portland, working in gas stations and living in cheap apartments. Most recently, Joe had been a manager at a BP service station, he said.

Fogleman quickly zeroed in on the September 1992 fight between Joe and Damien. Joe confirmed the incident and told how Damien had shouted, "I'll eat you alive," then strapped three knives on his body. Fogleman was curious about the knives, and Hutchison told him they were straight knives, not folding ones. Joe downplayed the incident, emphasizing that there was no physical confrontation.

"Was that when he threatened to kill you?" Fogleman asked.

"He never threatened to kill me," Joe answered.

"Are you sure about that?" Fogleman pried.

"I'm sure about that."

Joe told Fogleman he didn't "picture Damien as hurting other people . . . his self maybe. I would believe that more than I would him hurting other people."

"Have your ever seen him try to hurt himself?" Fogleman asked.

"No, nothing, you know, I've seen him beat his head on a wall."

Joe provided the same basic alibi, telling how he'd picked up Damien and Domini that day at the laundry, then went to their friends' house that night.

Fogleman asked Joe about his sudden separation from his wife. When was it?

"The middle of May, something like that," Joe answered.

"It wasn't anything in particular about any time that made you remember when it was?" Fogleman asked without stating the obvious: Was it May 4, the day before the murders, or May 9, your birthday?

"No," Joe answered, nothing in particular had made him remember.

By 2:30 P.M. it was Domini Teer's turn to answer questions. Now Fogleman was dealing with a potential suspect whom eyewitnesses had placed near the crime scene the night of the murders. With Domini's mother, Dian, present, Fogleman launched a meticulous inquiry.

In a soft, shy voice, Domini told how she'd dropped out of the tenth grade at Marion at age sixteen when she learned she was pregnant. She had lived her first twelve years in Ontario, California, near Upland, with her mom and dad, who had since broken up. She'd bounced around a bit since then, living for a while with her father and his girlfriend in Illinois.

Fogleman saw an opening.

"Did your dad or his girlfriend practice any witchcraft or—"

"No, sir," Domini shot back before Fogleman could finish.

". . . engage in any occult—"

"No, sir," she said, cutting him off again.

". . . -type behavior. They did not?"

"No, sir."

"Tell me about SOUND, that organization," he queried.

"It's something my cousin does just to take up time," Domini said.

"Okay. What does SOUND stand for?"

"Secret Order of the Undead. It's like a little club."

"All right. And they publish a little magazine, though, right?"

"Flyers."

"Okay. And what are the undead?" he asked. "Are those like zombies?"

"No, it's just like vampires and stuff," Domini said.

Fogleman pushed for details on Domini's cousin, Tammy Jo Teer. Domini testified that her cousin practiced witchcraft with "a group of friends," but indicated it was harmless stuff. "They just burned candles. That's really about it."

Contrary to Jerry Driver's assertions, Domini denied knowing anything about blood-drinking. And contrary to Vicki Hutcheson's account, she said she had no idea what an esbat was. She agreed that Damien practiced Wicca, but denied he attended meetings with other "witches." Damien did like horror movies, she agreed at one point.

Domini then turned her attention to Damien's previous girlfriend, calling her a "kook" who is "the one that's obviously involved in witchcraft." Domini said Damien and the girl would "read books and crap" on witchcraft.

Eventually, the talk turned to May 5. Domini explained that she, Damien, and some friends had planned to get together that day to hang out. Jason Baldwin and a neighbor boy— who she knew only as "Ken"— had planned to skip school, she said. But Jason wound up going to school that day, and the teens waited for him. Eventually, Ken, Damien, Domini, and Jason met up about 3:25 that afternoon at her trailer in Lakeshore, she said. The four of them then walked to Jason's uncle's house in West Memphis, arriving about four P.M. There, they watched Jason mow the lawn. Damien and Domini then left and went to the laundromat where Damien's mom, sister, and dad picked them up around five or 5:30 P.M., she said.

Pam Hutchison had said that happened around 3:45 or four P.M.

Domini said the Hutchisons dropped her off at Lakeshore about 5:45 or six P.M.. She promptly walked her dog.

"And I took a shower," she said, " 'cause Mom had told me what happened (on) *Time Trax*," the television show, which had just come on when she came in, she said. The show aired at seven P.M. that night. Domini's times seemed slightly amended from what she had told police on May 10, when she said the Hutchisons had picked her and Damien up at the laundry "just before it got dark."

Fogleman asked where Jessie Misskelley was that day. Domini said she didn't see Jessie that day. In fact, she said, she didn't see him until after the murders, and, prior to that, hadn't seen him in a year.

"All of a sudden Jessie comes showing up, and

this is the first time we've seen Jessie since the year before that," she said. Jessie came over to Jason's trailer one day, wanting Damien to accompany him to Blockbuser Video, she said.

On the night the boys disappeared, Domini lay in bed until Damien called about ten, she said. The young couple quarreled, she said, because Damien recently had been paying attention to another girl.

Finally, Fogleman reached the central issue. Where was Domini that night? Those in the room grew tense with anticipation.

"There is a person who says that they saw you and Damien walking on the service road that night," away from Robin Hood Hills, he said.

"We never walked on the service road. Ever."

"Y'all walked on the interstate?"

"Yeah."

"All right, you were not with him," Fogleman decided. "Has he told you that he was with Jason walking around that night?"

"I don't know. Number one, he doesn't walk on the service road, whether he's with Jason or he's with me. He just doesn't walk on the service road because it's quicker to go over the interstate."

"Okay. Did he tell you that he went walking with Jason anywhere that night?"

There was a pause. Fogleman seized the moment.

"You quit looking at me," Fogleman said, sensing a lie. "He didn't tell you that?"

"No . . . He didn't tell me he was walking with Jason anywhere at night, 'cause usually Jason has to be in the house. 'Cause Jason's mom is strict."

"She's strict," Fogleman said, testing her.

"Yeah."

"Okay. Strict about what?"

"Strict about Jason coming in. Because usually

she's at work and she wants him to take care of his little brothers. . . . He usually doesn't go anywhere at night."

Domini said she couldn't remember what she wore that day. She couldn't remember what Jason wore either.

"Did you ever see Jason wear any blue jeans with the knees torn out of them? With holes in the knees?"

"He's got some jeans with holes in them. . . ."

"And you had some too, right?"

"What? Jeans with holes in the knees?"

"Uh-huh," Fogleman said, sensing her discomfort. "The ones Jason had, what color were they?"

"What? The ones Jason had with the holes in the knees?"

"Uh-huh."

"He had a pair of gray ones."

"Any other colors?"

"I can't tell you. I don't even know. Those are the only ones I ever saw with holes in them."

Domini had succeeded in changing the color of Jason's pants from blue to gray. She also had successfully defended herself against insinuations she may have had something to do with the murders. But she had convinced no one that her boyfriend and Jason weren't there that night.

Despite the ongoing investigation, there were serious doubts, even in authorities' minds, that they had truly solved the case. Fogleman never said publicly there could be other suspects at large, but he didn't toe the police line on the investigation, either. On the day of the arrests, Gitchell said he expected no additional arrests. Fogleman, though, said there might be more.

On September 2, Fogleman questioned L.G. Hollingsworth, who remained the most tangible link between the charged and uncharged. No one remained a bigger target in the ongoing police investigation than L.G., the West Memphis teen who was questioned days after the murders when his Aunt Narlene fingered him as a suspect. Nagging at them was L.G.'s supposed furtive visit to the laundromat with dirty clothes, and his possession of a "stinky box" immediately following the killings.

The pursuit of Hollingsworth showcased the great difficulties police faced while investigating the May 5 murders. At times it seemed the police simply failed to capitalize on solid tips; at other times it seemed there was just nothing there.

On June 16, Det. Bill Durham had driven down to Horn Lake, Mississippi, to check a tip—received five weeks earlier—suggesting Hollingsworth may have played a role in the murders. On May 11, five days after the bodies were found, Horn Lake schoolteacher Robin Taylor phoned West Memphis police, telling them a girl in her fourth-grade class had just told her a startling story.

A young relative of L.G.'s breathlessly told Taylor about visiting relatives over the weekend in West Memphis. There, she overheard adults talking about L.G. and the murders.

"This date a student told her that she needed to talk to her about the murders in West Memphis," Lieutenant James Sudbury typed in a May 11 report about his phone conversation with Taylor. "The student said that [L.G. Hollingsworth] came home . . . and that he had blood on his clothes and himself. That [L.G.] had something concealed in a box and put it in his car and told his family that if they even went near the car he would kill them."

"[The young student] told me over and over again that if anyone in the family found out, it would [mean a] whipping," Taylor, the teacher, later said. "[The child] was never the kind of little [kid] that made something up."

It remains unclear why police waited five weeks to check out the child's story. According to his report, Durham visited the Hollingsworth residence in Horn Lake on June 16, but, finding nobody home, left his business card and departed. The child's parents would later say the police returned to Mississippi after June 16 with a video camera to interview the child, but, they said, their daughter told the officers she knew nothing.

Durham's trip to Mississippi seemed poorly timed for other reasons. Following two days of police questioning on May 10 and 11, L.G. left the state with a middle-aged friend on a trip that landed him in more trouble. On May 16, police reports show West Memphis police received a call from Sheriff Jim Dorrah of Princeton, Kentucky, who said authorities there had had some trouble with L.G. and his friend, forty-nine-year-old Richard Simpson, the City of West Memphis building inspector.

According to Dorrah, the pair had checked into separate rooms in a motel there. Deputies found L.G. with a teenage girl in his room. The girl had recently been living in West Memphis and was best friends with Domini Teer. The girl's uncle and aunt called deputies after Hollingsworth and Simpson showed up at their home outside Princeton and took the girl with them.

The purpose of the pair's trip to Kentucky remains a mystery. The girl and her mother had moved from West Memphis shortly before the May 5 murders. The girl's mother fled town with her daughter because she feared the circle of teens that her daughter was hanging out with, a relative said. The teens included Damien and Domini. "They were Devil worshipers," the relative said. "(She) said at different times they liked to catch cats and take their skins off."

After initial questioning at the motel, Sheriff Dorrah said he told Hollingsworth and Simpson to get back to West Memphis, where police had more questions for them. Police had already interviewed Simpson on May 13, when he told detectives that L.G. was over at his house the evening of the murders. But, armed with fresh concerns, police interviewed Simpson again on May 26, when Durham hooked him up to his polygraph:

"Have you told the truth about L.G. being at your house on Wednesday, May fifth, 1993?"

"Yes," Simpson answered.

"Was L.G. at your house from approximately six-thirty to nine-fifteen P.M. on Wednesday, May fifth, 1993?"

"Yes."

"Did L.G. ask you to say he was with you on Wednesday, May fifth, 1993?"

"No."

"Did L.G. ask you to lie for him?"

"No."

Durham noted deception on each question, his report showed, and Simpson changed his story. "Richard stated that he did spend Thursday night through the weekend with him but that L.G. didn't come over on 5-5-93, Wednesday," Ridge put in his report. Simpson also told Ridge that he and L.G.

had visited Beale Street in Memphis over the weekend following the murders. There, seventeen-year-old L.G. had drunk a beer and a margarita, Simpson said. "I seriously question his motives for being friendly with the much younger L.G. and feel that he has been responsible for the possible delinquency of L.G.," Ridge wrote. However, other city officials said Simpson, who in his spare time served as a nondenominational preacher, had met Hollingsworth through his ministry.

That same day, May 26, police took hair and blood samples from Hollingsworth, and this time asked him to detail his May 5 whereabouts in a three-page written account. He stuck to his story, saying again he was at Simpson's house from about six until 9:30 that night. But the next day, May 27, police interviewed Laszlo Benyo, a forty-five-year-old Hungarian architect who was visiting the United States through an exchange program that had him working temporarily with City of West Memphis officials. Benyo, who was staying at Simpson's house, said he didn't recall seeing Hollingsworth there the night of May 5.

The issue finally came to a head in September, when Fogleman grilled Hollingsworth under oath for more than forty minutes, asking him again to detail his whereabouts on May 5.

L.G. testified he visited his aunt Narlene Hollingsworth that day in Lakeshore and saw Echols and Domini Teer arguing there about 4:30 P.M. "Domini went her way," Hollingsworth testified, leaving Echols, dressed in black from head to toe, standing outside waiting for his mother to come pick him up. Hollingsworth, who said he got a ride home to West Memphis from his aunt Narlene, said he last saw Echols standing on a street in Lakeshore about five P.M. as they rode by.

L.G.'s account contradicts the Hutchison family alibi. Pam and Joe said they picked Damien and Domini up at the laundromat shortly before four P.M., dropped Domini off, then drove back home to West Memphis.

But L.G.'s testimony also seemed to contradict his own earlier stories. He told Fogleman he was at home in West Memphis about 7:30 or 8:30 P.M., although he had earlier told the police he was at Simpson's house at that time.

Hollingsworth told Fogleman that he later went to Simpson's house that night. He said he and Simpson then went to the Flash Market laundromat in Simpson's 1979 yellow Ford LTD. Hollingsworth said his aunt, Dixie Hubbard, gave him Domini Teer's phone number, then he left.

But Hubbard had told police that L.G. came to the laundry that night in a small car— not Simpson's vehicle— which she said she recognized.

"Now, L.G., this is where we're going to start getting into some problems," Fogleman told the teen. "Richard says that he saw you that night and it was just for a few minutes, and that he didn't go with you to the laundromat."

"Yeah, he did," Hollingsworth replied.

"And your aunt says that she knows Richard's car, and the car you came in wasn't Richard's."

"Yes, it was."

"Why did your aunt say that it wasn't and Richard say that it wasn't?"

"I don't know. I have no idea."

"You're going to stick with that?"

"Yes, sir."

Fogleman moved onto the "stinky" box. Hollingsworth said it contained nothing but test papers that Simpson was grading for a class he was teaching at

THE BLOOD OF INNOCENTS

the local vocational-technical school. Fogleman came back to the car.

"I really feel like you're not telling us everything that you know, L.G.," he said. "And it could be bad for you."

At one point, Fogleman asked the teen point-blank: "Were you around the woods that night?"

"No, sir, I was not."

Fogleman pressed on, asking L.G. if he had told people, "I'm the next one that's going to be arrested. Tell me why you said that."

"The reason why I said that is, see, the police went over there and got Damien first."

"Uh-huh," Fogleman prompted.

"And they talked about, and then they come and talked to me, and then they went and talked to whoever else, and all I said was, well, you know . . ."

"Come on, L.G."

"I'm serious, I was at my mom's house when somebody called me."

"But you told that you were going to be the next one that they came to arrest."

"Yes, sir, it was . . ."

"Who all did you tell that to?"

"My mom. And I think my aunt heard it over the phone. I don't know, and whoever else, she could have told anybody. She tells anything and everything," L.G. droned on.

Fogleman, seemingly in frustration, cut him off, asking one last time if there was "anything else that you want to tell us."

"The only thing I want to say is everything I told is true," L.G. said.

Over the months to come, Hollingsworth would insist he was a victim of false and wild claims by his aunt Narlene Hollingsworth, whose testimony the prosecution was counting on to place Damien near the crime scene. As disturbing as the L.G. inquiry had been—the bizarre trip to Kentucky, the contradictory alibi, the police failure to act quickly on the schoolteacher's tip—something else was equally disturbing. The police had nothing on L.G. And if Narlene Hollingsworth had been wrong about L.G., and wrong about Domini, then couldn't she be wrong about Damien, too?

Sixteen

Speedy Trial

Arkansas law requires prosecutors to try cases where defendants are incarcerated within nine months unless the defendant waives his right to a speedy trial. There would be no waivers in this case.

Circuit judge David Burnett, fifty-two, knew the press coverage of the trials was going to be exceptional, but he was determined it would not taint the process. A former prosecuting attorney before he became a judge in 1974, he had a reputation as a straight-shooter, and often spoke his mind from the bench. He could be witty and folksy. A Vietnam veteran, hunter, competitive grower of champion hybrid tea roses, and active in the Boy Scouts, Burnett had been on the bench almost twenty years. He appeared comfortable with the unusual case and its plethora of legal and other issues. He said once that there was "too much commotion, too much hullabaloo about it," but in the same breath added, "but I can handle it."

Burnett's home court was at Osceola, Arkansas, the southernmost of two courthouses serving Mississippi County in the northeast corner of the state.

The Second Judicial District, in which the case would have to be tried, was made up of six counties, a sprawling Delta of proud farmers and mostly conservative Democrats. Several of the counties were large enough to need dual courthouses.

Burnett's courtroom was high-ceilinged and airy. His second-floor office on the quaint courthouse square across the street still had a plaque that read David Burnett— Attorney-At-Law on the door. Self-effacing and unpretentious, Burnett answered reporters' questions carefully and fully, offering backup reading or the names of experts to clarify nuances in the law. He wore his black judge's robe in court but, at the end of a hearing, unzipped the formal symbol of his authority and chatted with reporters in shirtsleeves, the robe slung over his arm. His office shared a hallway with the local Juvenile Services office next door, which picked up his phone when he wasn't in.

The trim, red-haired jurist grew up in Blytheville, Arkansas, just south of the Missouri bootheel on Interstate 55. The son of a successful tire retailer, he attended public schools, became an Eagle Scout, went to the University of Arkansas in Fayetteville, and later attended its law school. He served in Vietnam as a military policeman.

When he returned home from the war, he and former U.S. congressman Bill Alexander and Osceola lawyer Henry J. Swift went into a largely civil practice. Alexander, first elected to Congress in 1968, was tossed out by voters in 1992 after it was widely reported he'd bounced 487 checks on the now-defunct House Bank.

Burnett ended his private practice rather quickly, running for and winning the 1974 race for prosecuting attorney for the six-county northeast Arkansas

THE BLOOD OF INNOCENTS 245

judicial district. He came to the prosecutor's office on a crusade to clean up a still-evident system of petty organized crime in his jurisdiction. He went after the tough vice lords of Poinsett County, known locally as the Hillbilly Mafia, and later against dogfight organizers in the same rural backwater. He won some success and statewide headlines. Asked about some unusual cases he took pride in, Burnett pointed out his prosecution in a murder case in which there was no corpus delicti—no body.

A practical joker, Burnett told a group of reporters that, just for laughs, he once sent sheriff's deputies to break up a poker game he would normally have been attending himself.

At the same time, Burnett was a studious jurist. He was working on a judicial master's degree at the time of the trials. His master's thesis touched on a subject matter that comes before judges more and more these days. It was, as he put it in an interview prior to the trial: "that psychologists and psychiatrists are no more capable of predicting future violent behavior than laymen, and yet we use them as experts."

While Burnett went to public schools, he appeared comfortable with the dove-hunting plutocrats in the Delta, a place where planters will put in tens of thousands of acres in cotton and soybeans and milo in the rich alluvial loam, and let an army of laborers keep track of the crops. The judge occupied an especially lofty social status in eastern Arkansas, but he retained a common touch that made him both likeable and popular. His wife, Sonja, was an English teacher; at the time of the trial, they had a daughter in high school and a son in college.

Colleagues and friends said he was an excellent choice when his fellow judges sat down after the arrests and decided who should take the case. Burnett said the case was like any other except for the "nuisance and annoyance" of news media interest.

For some, Burnett is the picture of a man the public would want as a judge. The Arkansas Trial Lawyers Association gave him their highest rating, but it was no secret that many defense attorneys believed he was sympathetic to the prosecution. The defense, in fact, would spend much of their time fighting Burnett rulings that they believed hurt their cases.

The youthful man who would prosecute the case, deputy prosecutor John N. Fogleman, was something of a patrician, with the appearance of a man distracted by what was happening around the corner or in the next room. He could trace his family's roots— and extensive land ownership— well back into the nineteenth century. But outside the courtroom, he could be friendly or even solicitous. As the case developed, it became clear that behind his sky-blue eyes was a brilliant tactician who knew his case and how to make it.

The nephew of an Arkansas Supreme Court chief justice, Fogleman was not all that confident of his abilities going into law school. For one thing, his undergraduate degree from Arkansas State University was in physical education. But that soon changed. He made up for his lack of confidence with long hours of work. And it paid off. He was invited to join the Law Review but declined because his wife, Nancy, whom he married in 1976 while a sophomore in college, had just had the first of their two sons.

Fogleman's slow, Southern speech was set several

THE BLOOD OF INNOCENTS 247

gears slower than his reasoning. Rapier-thin, he was known to coach fifth- and sixth-grade basketball and had recently entered and completed a marathon in Memphis. He was thirty-eight, but looked younger, and had been a deputy prosecutor for ten years.

On the wall in the lobby of Fogleman's law office, over a table piled high with University of Arkansas alumni magazines, is a picture of the steamboat *Sultana*.

At the end of the Civil War and just days after Lincoln's assassination, hundreds of Union soldiers from the northern Midwest who had been held as prisoners of war in the South— including some from the concentration camp at Andersonville— boarded the *Sultana* at Vicksburg, Mississippi. On the night of April 27, 1865, just above Memphis, the boat exploded, throwing the sick and exhausted men into the churning current. According to Civil War historian James M. McPherson, there were more lives lost in that disaster than when the *Titanic* went down a few decades later. Estimates place the minimum number killed or missing in the *Sultana* disaster at 1,600, making it the worst maritime disaster in American history.

The men who survived swam ashore at Fogleman's Landing, and were treated on the broad front porch of the local ferryman, Capt. John Fogleman, the prosecutor's great-great-grandfather.

Fogleman's partner in the case was Brent Davis, thirty-seven, who was, by contrast, a bulldog man of the people. Smart and self-assured, he wore boxy suits to fit his compact body and he spoke with the flat Arkansas accent of the Delta. He also had a sense of the dramatic and, while his role was minor compared to Fogleman's, he was well-versed in the issues and witness testimony he'd carved out for himself.

Fogleman's methodical, thorough, and even at times icy precision won crucial points for the state, but it was Davis who made the case for retribution with some snappy courtroom showmanship and a palpable contempt for the accused. This case would be a career builder, and both Fogleman and Davis worked hundreds of hours to present the fruits of the sometimes confused police investigation. They were critical of the news barrage, but in the end they lifted their early objections to having the trials televised.

The case prompted some unusual legal maneuvers as well as efforts to disguise them from the public. Baldwin's lawyers' attempts to seal the court file in the case were fought by *The Commercial Appeal,* with some moral support from the American Civil Liberties Union and others. The sealing of legal arguments and the motions they supported would have been almost unprecedented. Evidence is often sealed against its later revelation, but not the very legal arguments in a public prosecution. One professor of law from Loyola University Law School in Chicago said all future pretrial proceedings from that point would turn Kafkaesque if the underlying basis for the arguments being made in open court weren't available for review by the press and public.

The files remained open.

Misskelley's lawyer Gregory L. Crow next made the argument for a change of venue—outside eastern Arkansas.

"The Memphis *Commercial Appeal* has gone as far as to print the alleged confession—alleged statement—of Mr. Misskelley. That was published out all

THE BLOOD OF INNOCENTS 249

through Crittenden County, and we will later argue was also published all through the second judicial district," Crow said. He also told the court that, in his effort to get people to sign affidavits in the six counties to establish the pervasive coverage, he ran into people who told him, "They can't get a fair trial but I'm not going to sign (the affidavit) because I want the blankety-blank to fry."

His attorney Dan Stidham told the court that, in Crittenden County, his client's family had received death threats and that, elsewhere in the district, "people I have met . . . say, 'We don't need to have a trial. We just need a lynching.' "

Burnett made his ruling. "Certainly a defendant is not entitled to have a jury that is totally ignorant and unaware of things that are happening in the community," he said. "However, the defendant is entitled to a fair trial by a jury that is unbiased. While I agree with certain statements made by the state . . . I think from the record and from my personal knowledge of this area, and the circumstances, that a change of venue is appropriate."

Paul Ford and Robin Wadley, in behalf of Baldwin, wanted to try their case separate from Echols, whom they argued the news media had already characterized as the mastermind behind the murders.

Although Burnett had not technically ruled that Misskelley would be tried separately because of his statement, it looked likely. Ford said his and Echols's defenses in the case were antagonistic, good grounds for separate— meaning three— trials.

Ford asked the court to consider the mechanics of jury selection in a trial with two defendants with antagonistic interests, then launched into the problem of perceptions.

"From what I read in the paper, Damien is a nickname and that nickname has been associated with a movie by the name of *The Omen*, where the main character in that movie, Damien, is the Antichrist."

Ford made the first in-court reference to Domini Teer. In open court, he called her "a third party, uncharged, at the scene of the crime."

After a lengthy argument by lawyers for both Echols and Baldwin, Burnett ruled that their cases would be tried together and specifically found that "there's no reason that either defendant would be unduly jeopardized by a joint trial, and that it is not necessary to sever them."

Burnett suggested at the same hearing that Misskelley would probably have to be tried separately because of his statement to police.

On October 11, Misskelley's lawyers filed a motion arguing that their client's statement to police on June 3 should be ruled inadmissible. It was a complicated argument and at the same time simple: He'd made the whole thing up. They'd been working with the theory that possibly their client gave a false confession and were putting together evidence that Misskelley was not just stupid, but inordinately susceptible to suggestions by the police. In short, he'd implicated himself and the others because, out of earshot of the microphones that captured his words, police detectives had told him what to say.

A ruling on the request to suppress the statement was postponed to within five days of the jury selection in his trial. In the end, after hearing arguments January 13, 1994, the defense arguments were rejected. The statement would be allowed.

The January 13 hearing also produced testimony from a Miami, Florida, polygraph expert, Warren D.

Holmes, who said his reading of Misskelley's reactions as measured by the lie-detecting machine showed that Misskelley wasn't lying when he said he was not involved in the killings. In fact, he said, the statement showed no sign of deception except when Misskelley was asked whether he had ever smoked marijuana.

Holmes, a former Miami Police Department detective, had worked on elements of the John F. Kennedy assassination, the Boston Strangler case, Watergate, Martin Luther King's killing in Memphis, and the William Kennedy Smith date-rape case in Florida.

Holmes's report had been filed days before the hearing and had infuriated prosecutor Davis. The headline in the January 9 *Arkansas Democrat-Gazette*— LAWYER SAYS POLICE LIED FOR CONFESSION IN THREE BOYS' DEATHS— led to furious phone calls after Stidham was quoted saying police "were preying on a retarded kid" to make their case.

Also present at the hearing was Richard J. Ofshe, a professor of sociology at the University of California at Berkeley. Ofshe, whose bushy salt-and-pepper beard and intense expression made him all the more professorial, listened to police explanations of the confession but did not testify. He would later testify at the trial that he believed the statement was coerced, that the whole story was made up.

Ofshe had worked on previous cases in which defendants had been accused of being part of satanic cult conspiracies. The best-known was his effort to prove that a sheriff's deputy in Washington state had falsely implicated himself in the molestation of his two daughters. Ofshe's role, described in the critically acclaimed 1994 book *Remembering Satan*, initially was to evaluate the Washington state defendant for the prosecution. Later, Ofshe became convinced the man had been psychologically overwhelmed by his jailing and had convinced himself that his daughters' claims were true.

Ultimately, Burnett decided Misskelley's trial, which would be held first, would be in Corning, a tiny, conservative town of 3,200 in northeast Arkansas, just miles from the Missouri line. It would get under way in late January.

On November 6, Baldwin's lawyers permitted him to give a jailhouse interview to Creative Thinking International of New York, a team of documentary film makers that had been covering the case for Home Box Office since the arrests.

The film company's young principals, Joe Berlinger and Bruce Sinofsky, had released their critically acclaimed documentary entitled *Brother's Keeper* the year before. The film explored the reactions of the residents of a small rural town in New York when an old man was arrested and tried for murder of one of his three elderly brothers. Along with the pool of cameras operated by other technicians from TV stations in Little Rock, Memphis and Jonesboro, the Creative Thinking crew was allowed to film the entire proceedings of both trials.

Despite the fact that their interview with Baldwin included only biographical details and self-serving opinions, the prosecutors demanded access to the audio portion of the taped interview. Creative Thinking sought protection of the First Amendment rights and fought the prosecutor's supoena. After the hearing was postponed due to snow, the courts sided with the film makers.

* * *

THE BLOOD OF INNOCENTS

Burnett and the lawyers had a gentlemen's agreement not to let the case spoil the Christmas holidays, but a nagging issue—Misskelley's mental status—needed to be resolved.

The hearing opened on a frigid December 21 in Osceola, in the beautiful bronze-domed courthouse that can be seen on a clear day from Interstate 55. Misskelley's lawyers wanted to prove that their client was simply too stupid, as a matter of law, to be sentenced to death in the event he was found guilty of murder.

During the hearing, a crack appeared in the until-then wholly sympathetic portrait of the victims' grieving families.

Jackie Hicks, Jr., Pam Hobbs's brother and the uncle of victim Stevie Branch, confronted Hobbs's former husband, the senior Steve Branch.

He accused Branch of capitalizing on the case's notoriety. Branch, Hicks said, never cared about his son until he was dead. They began fighting. Mississippi county sheriff's captain Jim Stovall had to break it up.

It was an ugly incident, but just the first of many as the victims' families tried to maintain an air of civility while the world crashed down around them.

Upstairs in the courthouse, meanwhile, the hearing went forward. In Arkansas, a defendant is presumed mentally retarded if he has an IQ of sixty-five or lower, and the law prohibits imposition of the death penalty for such people. Stidham and Crow were trying to make sure their client's worst fate was life in prison.

But Misskelley had an overall IQ of seventy-two—borderline retarded—and seven points too high to escape death automatically. Misskelley's expert witness told Judge Burnett the defendant—the product of a broken home, drug abuse, and a dysfunctional family—"lives in a kind of schizoid world."

Burnett wasn't interested in the psychologist's apologia. "He's not mentally retarded," Burnett ruled. "He is right above that level."

Misskelley, if convicted, could be sentenced to die.

Seventeen

A Monkey Jump in Corning

Corning, Arkansas, was until January 1994 best known for its thirty-nine-year tradition of raffling off a new Cadillac at the annual Independence Day festivities. Before the Misskelley trial, the town's biggest brush with national fame occurred when the hometown newspaper publisher's daughter, Angela Rockwell, won the Miss Arkansas USA contest in 1991, then appeared on national television from the competition in Wichita.

For Misskelley, being tried in Corning would be a mixed blessing. The town was more than a hundred miles from the intense publicity of the case, but it was also full of residents who took a hard-line attitude toward accused lawbreakers. The residents of Clay County in Corning were products of a hardscrabble town. There was no tolerance for shirkers; everyone had a job.

Like its neighboring towns, with the exception of perhaps Paragould and Jonesboro, Corning has a decaying downtown. Strip shopping centers bring modern conveniences and their attendant ugliness to the city's outskirts. Much of the downtown commercial property has been abandoned. Across the street from the Corning courthouse, a house, which must have been a handsome structure thirty years earlier, stands windowless and abandoned.

Corning retains a defensive, old-fashioned attitude toward big-city values. One politician went out of his way to point out to a reporter that there were no black people in his town, nor in the county. (He was mistaken, according to the U.S. Census for 1990. There were six black residents of the county that year.) The remark was made in a context suggesting the politician was of the mistaken view Misskelley was black.

There was a good share of Memphis-bashing in Corning, with strong racial overtones.

"We'd probably be better off without that kind of publicity," Mayor Bob Cochran said of the expected frenzy a week before the satellite dishes began arriving. "Most people are wondering why they picked Corning."

Despite the residents' distrust of Memphis, the big city was a dominant influence in Corning. Although it's 120 miles away, Memphis is Corning's shopping center and its media market, except for those who get their news from across the bordering towns of Springfield or Cape Girardeau, Missouri.

Corning also is "dry," a fact readily apparent to the out-of-town reporters and support crews who came for the trial. Missouri's boundary-line liquor store and twenty-four-hour truck stop diner, twelve miles north, saw an uptick in business during the trial, despite dense fog and icy roads.

The week before jurors convened was cold, but Sheriff Darwin Stow had the forethought to have the courthouse grounds spruced up by jail trusties. They raked and swept. But an ice storm destroyed any plans to showcase Corning's scenic charms. Old trees lost their limbs and littered the area around the courthouse, limiting the space for television reporter stand-ups as satellite trucks began to line the building's south side.

The one-story plain brick courthouse was the judicial center of a poor county. The courtroom walls were made of cinder blocks, and the courtroom had cheap tile floors and hard wooden benches. The building also housed the sheriff's office and the offices of other county officials, including the county clerk and county extension agent.

As the trial date approached, Police Chief Ronnie Stewart, a handsome, young man with a well-trimmed black moustache, made it clear that his eight-member force would keep order in town. Sheriff Darwin Stow threatened to "monkey jump" any reporter who got out of line. Asked for an explanation of the threatened tactic, Stow volunteered he once jumped over his own officers to pin a suspect to the ground after the offender had offered one of his officers an indignity. The impressive dexterity came to be known as Stow's "monkey jump."

Jury selection, scheduled to begin the Tuesday after the Dr. Martin Luther King, Jr., national holiday—which coincides with the officially observed Jefferson Davis birthday in Arkansas—was postponed because of an ice storm and snowstorm that blacked out most of the town and the courthouse. The ice was so bad, a reporter from the *Arkansas Democrat-Gazette* in Little Rock flipped his truck on the icy roads and had to hitchhike to the courthouse.

The jury call had been low-key, but most of the

western half of Clay County knew who made the jury pool weeks before the group convened in the courtroom. The need for three hundred prospective jurors was the third most important story in the January 6 edition of the weekly *Clay County Courier*, after a notice that no first baby of the year had yet been born and a brief account of a local Air Force lieutenant commended for "technical competence" in Florida.

Security was tight but makeshift and imaginative. The single courtroom's front doors were held closed with handcuffs as lawyers assembled inside, and thereafter during lengthy recesses. Spectators were at first checked out with a handheld metal detector, and later walked through a freestanding unit sent from Little Rock. On the first day of jury selection, John Mark Byers had the metal detector pushed down into his snakeskin cowboy boots before he was allowed access to the courtroom.

On the first day of jury selection on January 19, a city clerk said that, without electricity for several days, her fish tank had frozen solid. It was that kind of bone cold, with temperatures in the teens and a stiff wind making breathing painful. The high hit twenty-two degrees that day.

Nonetheless, most of the prospective jurors made the 9:30 A.M. roll call. Of the first hundred called for day one, only eleven were no-shows.

Lawyers had asked and Burnett had agreed to ask jurors only the broadest questions about conflicts of interest and knowledge of the parties or participants in open court. Burnett asked them how they felt about the case coming to them from a change of venue. He told them the state had the burden of proof. When he asked them if they had any "strong religious beliefs or . . . moral scruples" that made them oppose the death penalty, no one raised a hand.

With occasional fair warnings from Burnett that prospective jurors should have brought their knitting or a good book to pass the hours of pure tedium—and one assurance that the trial should be finished before planting season—a jury of seven women and five men plus two male alternates was seated.

Jurors ranged in age from twenty-three to sixty-five and included a Wal-Mart cashier, a bank loan officer, the town's postmaster, an official from the store-shelf manufacturer, a worker from a local shock-absorber factory, and a housekeeper. All were white.

As the lawyers and townsfolk and reporters assembled for the start of the legal battle of *State of Arkansas* v. *Jessie Misskelley, Jr.*, Gitchell and Byers were convening a meeting that, to an outside observer, could certainly raise questions about how sure the police were about their theory of the case.

Gitchell told Byers they needed to talk about a knife that had recently been forwarded to police. It was a knife that Byers had given to a member of the documentary film crew. Byers was read his rights.

The difficulty Gitchell had in confronting Byers is obvious from the official police question-and-answer transcript.

"I've got to ask you point-blank," Gitchell said, warming up. "Were you around or (did you) participate in the deaths of these boys?"

Byers said no.

Byers said he had never cut himself with the knife and didn't know why bloodstains with factors identical to both his and his stepson's appeared on the blade.

He said he'd used the knife to cut up venison jerky. "I have no idea. I have no idea how it could have any human blood on it," Byers told police. "I don't even remember nicking myself with it cutting the deer meat, or anything."

The morning's heavy fog turned to drizzle as a stream of farmers filed into the courtroom. They wore overalls and baseball caps and, respectfully, sat in the last of eight rows of pews. The long winter had left them staring at idle rice, bean, milo, wheat and cotton fields. They were ready for the excitement the trial would bring.

County employees, townsfolk, and news reporters pressed closer to the front.

Eight microphones rested atop the judge's bench, pointing toward Judge Burnett. The Creative Thinking camera was stationed next to the jury box, along with a news-pool camera that fed into a nearby media room. There, several television monitors sat in a row on a table, carrying live pictures from the courtroom. Cameramen and extra reporters lounged on several rows of benches.

On any given day, there would be thirty or forty media people in and around the courthouse. The accommodations were adequate but somewhat less sophisticated than those in most high-profile trials. A portable phone bank with wheels was stationed outside the courthouse door, while television satellite trucks lined the street.

Minutes earlier, there had been a mad rush of feet as cameramen and reporters surrounded deputies escorting Jessie Misskelley into the building.

Across the building, Big Jessie pulled up in his beat-up Chevy pickup, the one he'd used to fetch his son for the police the day he confessed. A blue-and-white campertop now stood over the truck's bed. Lacking money for a hotel room, Big Jessie and his family planned to sleep in it. A local church, in a show of Christian magnanimity, soon offered the family its parking lot and an extension cord for electricity.

The victims' families had taken their place near the front of the courtroom, sitting in a tight group. Collectively, they looked more polished than before. Steve Branch sported a pair of new blue jeans and white tennis shoes.

The jury stood, raised right hands and took the oath to "well and truly try this case now before the court and a true verdict render." The jury was given paper and pencils; the courthouse's new nonsmoking policy was noted. Burnett made a final announcement, cautioning the audience not to make any noise. Burnett would also make it clear he'd brook no public criticism of his rulings. His no-nonsense style grated on some lawyers, whom he chided publicly for violating traditional court decorum, such as speaking at the same time the judge was making a point.

As the trial got under way, Misskelley's lawyers tried to rein in one of Burnett's techniques on the bench even before he had a chance to exercise it. Stidham asked Burnett not to question witnesses.

"I'm going to ask any question that I think is pertinent," Burnett responded, denying the request.

After the first of dozens of bench conferences out of earshot of the jury and audience, Burnett told prosecutors, "State your case."

Fogleman began matter-of-factly, giving the jury a primer on what the state needed to prove. He then started with the state's version of the facts.

"If you would, I want you to think back to May

fifth, 1993. On May the fifth, 1993, Michael Moore, Stevie Branch, and Chris Byers went to school at Weaver Elementary School, in the second grade. All of them eight years old."

He told how they got together after school, the three on two bikes, Chris Byers riding double on Stevie's new red-and-black Renegade. He told how Mrs. Moore saw the three riding north toward Robin Hood woods. He described a "frantic night" of searching for the boys. "They searched and searched and searched but they don't find their children."

As Fogleman talked, John Mark Byers quietly came through the courtroom door. Moustache drooping, eyes bleary, Byers seemed to be listing to one side as he crept down the aisle in cowboy boots and a brown leather jacket. Gingerly, he found a seat among the victims' families.

In his slow, Southern drawl, Fogleman described Sgt. Mike W. Allen's search the next day. Allen, trying to jump the narrow slough where the bodies were later found, fell in. "He lifted up his foot and Michael Moore's body comes up.

"He's nude. He's tied hand to foot with shoestrings out of shoes. . . . One of the officers has to get down and inch by inch go through that creek. And they find a Cub Scout hat. Michael was a Cub Scout and liked to wear his uniform a whole lot. He'd been wearing his Cub Scout shirt that day."

Fogleman noted that police found boys' pants, turned completely inside out but still snapped at the waist. Still reciting this information methodically and without much emotion, he said police searched the muddy water and next found Steve Branch. Further downstream, they found Christopher Byers.

Moore and Branch, he said forensic evidence

would later prove, died of drowning. Byers, his sexual organs severed, bled to death.

In the weeks after the murders, a woman who had an eight-year-old son "played detective" to find out more about the case, Fogleman said. "Ultimately, Victoria Hutcheson would lead police to Misskelley, and Misskelley would confess."

Fogleman said that not all of Misskelley's statements were true—that, in fact, Misskelley tried to minimize his participation in the crime. But Fogleman insisted that certain elements of the statements bore too close a resemblance to the facts of the case to be mere coincidence: One of the boys had been cut in the face, one had been sexually mutilated, and all had been beaten mercilessly.

"I submit, ladies and gentlemen, that the proof is going to show that this defendant was an accomplice of Damien Echols and Jason Baldwin in the commission of these horrifying murders," Fogleman stated, reaching his conclusion. "And I submit that at the appropriate time, after all the evidence is in, after all the witnesses have testified, and all the exhibits are in, after Judge Burnett has instructed you as to the law, that we will come back before you and we will ask to return your verdict of guilty of three counts of capital murder."

Misskelley's lawyer, Daniel Stidham, was on his feet before Fogleman sat down. He introduced his client as simply "Jessie," then pointed out others at the defense table.

Misskelley, missing the cue or failing to catch his lawyers' invitation, did not stand, but sat, head bowed, chewing gum. It would become a familiar posture for the jury.

"It's not often that I agree with the prosecutor about anything," said Stidham. "But I do have to agree that this is a horrible and a senseless crime. Nobody can change that. But that's not why we're here today. The purpose for why we're here today is for truth and justice."

Stidham, a hand stuffed at times in his suit jacket pocket, said the evidence would show that his client had nothing to do with the crime. He reminded jurors about Misskelley's right to be presumed innocent and he mentioned the state's obligation to find him guilty beyond a reasonable doubt.

"Ladies and gentlemen, this whole case is a sad, sad story," he said. "But what's even sadder is the way the West Memphis Police Department decided to investigate this crime."

Stidham told the jury about Gitchell's comment that the case had been the most difficult of his career; Stidham noted that Gitchell had been forced to conduct daily news conferences that yielded nothing.

"Ladies and gentlemen, there was a public outcry. The public was demanding that someone be arrested for this crime, and the police department (was) trying to respond to this tremendous amount of pressure. In addition to the public outcry, there was a reward."

Stidham's points were emphatic, but his voice remained calm as he stared into the jury box. He said that, besides the pressure and the reward money for tips, the police had what he called "Damien Echols tunnel vision . . . They had Damien Echols picked out as the person responsible for this crime from day one."

Stidham said Misskelley's second defense would be that the statement he gave to police was "a false story." Stidham noted that the statement was "factually incorrect in many, many important areas. . . . The police knew it, but they kept right on interrogating. . . . They didn't care that what he was telling them was wrong."

Stidham next ridiculed the idea that only Misskelley knew what had happened to the victims almost a month after they'd been found. The whole town knew, and some with the precision of eyewitnesses.

He said his client had been railroaded into making a confession, that "psychological police tactics" forced his suggestible client to incriminate himself and the two other boys, who remained a chimerical but oft-mentioned presence throughout the trial.

"They broke his will. They scared him beyond all measure," said Stidham, and he sat down.

Mrs. Moore, the Cub Scout's mother, was the first to testify. Her long red hair drawn into a ponytail, her face pale but poised, she said she watched her son on his own bike and Byers on Branch's riding toward the woods. It was late enough to call him in to dinner. Her daughter was dispatched but never caught up.

"I went back home and waited for him," she said. "He didn't come back."

Next, Melissa Byers said she last saw her son in the carport of their home about 5:45 P.M. Nothing about the earlier beating at the hands of John Mark Byers was revealed, although Misskelley's lawyers knew about it.

"I went outside hollering for him," said Mrs. Byers, with dark circles under her eyes and a look of exhaustion. "He was gone."

The prosecution did not call any of the victims' fathers, but they did introduce the boys' bicycles that were dumped in the bayou, and the small bikes would remain off to the side, in the front of the courtroom, throughout the trial, serving as a constant reminder of the boys who'd never ride them again.

Then, Detective Ridge told how he blindly felt for evidence, running his hands through the mud of the streambed, and how he pulled the boys' bodies from the ditch. He testified like a cop, matter-of-factly, keen on science and evidence. But Ridge, perhaps more than any police witness, betrayed real humanity. This case got to him.

"I was raking my hands from one bank of the water to where it came out on the other side along the bottom all the way," he said. "That's what I did until I made my way to that body."

He fought tears, then succumbed, as he described pulling the three blanched bodies from the debris-strewn stream.

Polaroid pictures helped jurors imagine the gruesome sight.

Prosecutors asked Ridge to identify, and recite details, of another forty photographs from the crime scene. As he did, the front two rows of victims' family members raced from the courtroom. Later, Moore's father, Todd, returned and sat down, all by himself in the front row.

Eighteen

"Nobody knows what happened but me."

It was left to the unemotional Dr. Frank Peretti of Little Rock, the state's forensic pathologist, to give the horrifying details of the boys' deaths. On the trial's second day he testified matter-of-factly that all three boys had suffered fractured skulls from blunt objects, that Branch had received a serious wound to the lower left part of his face and that Byers had been sexually mutilated. Moore and Branch were still breathing when they were thrown into the muddy water.

But Chris Byers did not drown, Peretti noted coldly. He bled to death.

Methodically, Peretti rattled off the multiple injuries to the Byers boy.

"They consisted of the multiple facial contusions, abrasions, lacerations, the contusions and abrasions of the ears, the left parietal scalp lacerations, the fracturing of the base of the skull, the subarachnoid hemorrhage and contusions of the brain, the abrasions that were situated in the front of the neck. We have the genital mutilation with absence of the scrotal sac, testes, skin, and head of the penis with multiple surrounding gouging and cutting wounds.

"We also have the dilated anus, the bindings of the ankles behind the back in hog-tied fashion, the multiple contusions, abrasions, and lacerations of the torso and extremities, terminal aspiration of gastric contents. There was no evidence of disease that would have contributed to his death."

Peretti could offer no precise time of death for the three boys.

Burnett allowed prosecutors to show the jury pictures taken of the victims as they lay nude and bound with shoelaces, resting on examining tables prior to their autopsies in Little Rock. Peretti testified that the boys' injuries were consistent with blows that could be administered with clubs or with the stout branches found at the scene already introduced into evidence.

Under cross-examination by Stidham, Peretti said none of the victims appeared to have been choked to death and that, although each received injuries to the anus, there was no physical evidence of sodomy. The testimony contradicted Misskelley's police statement that he watched as Echols used a club to choke one victim into unconsciousness and that he'd seen both Echols and Baldwin "screwing" two of them.

It never came out in trial, but a convicted child molester, once a top suspect in the case, told police two weeks after the murders there was a plausible explanation for a rape with no apparent evidence. For some reason this pervert knew experienced molesters "don't want to have anal sex with them because it leaves too much scarring and evidence," the Marion man, then thirty-three, told police May 19,

THE BLOOD OF INNOCENTS   269

1993. Instead, a molester may simply rub himself between the buttocks, he told police.

Of the parents, only John Mark Byers and his wife sat through Peretti's testimony. The other parents tried to listen, but they departed when Peretti testified—over strenuous objections from Stidham—that injuries to the boys' ears were consistent with their having been forced to perform oral sex.

During a recess, the victims' families huddled in a circle outside the courthouse. Throughout the trial, it would become routine: They smoked cigarettes and discussed developments in nods and hushed voices. This morning, though, Pam Hobbs was crying.

"We hope those boys get what they deserve," said Terry Hobbs, talking for his wife. "There are some sick people out there."

Back in court, Ridge was recalled to tell how police got Misskelley to confess. Ridge went through the details but deferred to Gitchell when it came to the first true confession. It was left to Gitchell to explain how the statement was obtained. Finally, the public would get an inside look at how the case was broken.

Once sworn in, Gitchell proudly gave the jury his qualifications: nineteen and a half years with the West Memphis Police Department, where he now is inspector of criminal investigations. Gitchell said while interrogating Misskelley on June 3 before any tape recorder was turned on, he left the small detective's office and retrieved a microcasette tape. Gitchell said he then played one snippet of a tape on the handheld recorder.

Again, just as he had done with Misskelley, Gitchell snapped on the tape. He held it up to the witness microphone, and a small boy's voice was heard saying, "Nobody knows what happened but me." And again, just as he had done in the interrogation room with Misskelley, Gitchell quickly snapped it off.

Gitchell had played the same snippet at a pretrial hearing less than a month earlier, stirring wide speculation about its meaning. Television reporter Paul Morrison had reported as early as July that a fourth boy also had witnessed something strange in the woods. Rumors had it the boy narrowly missed getting killed himself.

But once again, the mystery remained a mystery. Some reporters demanded to know whose voice was on the tape and what the statement meant in some kind of context. But there was no demand by defense attorneys to play the tape in its entirety for the jury, no offer by the prosecution to reveal anything more than six words spoken in an eerie, high-pitched voice.

The tape had a profound effect on Misskelley, Gitchell testified. Immediately, he was willing to come clean. After a few emotional moments in which Misskelley was overcome, then tried to compose himself, the defendant confessed, Gitchell said.

Before the statement was read in court, Stidham had cross-examined Ridge on circumstances leading up to Misskelley's statement. "Was there anything found at the crime scene that would indicate this was a cult killing?" he asked. "Any upside-down crosses, carvings on the trees of six-six-six? Anything that would make it look like a cult killing?"

"Sir, I'm not an expert on the cult-type killings," Ridge answered.

"Didn't the police department receive some anonymous tips through *America's Most Wanted* or other tips anonymously that this was a cult killing?" Stidham pressed.

Yes, Ridge answered. Stidham was working on his theory that the police investigation was built on baseless claims about cult involvement. But he kept getting the wrong answers from the state's witnesses.

"Did you find any confirmation whatsoever that there was a cult or Jessie was involved in a cult?"

"Yes, sir."

"What is that?"

"A young man by the name of Paul Rand in another state that is separated from the group," he answered.

Ridge also named another teen who supposedly had attended a cult meeting near Turrell, Arkansas. Police had been unable to find the youth, a resident of Memphis, whose last known address was a trailer park in a seedy commercial strip of Summer Avenue.

Ridge noted that several people Misskelley had named as fellow cult members had denied any cult participation.

The Misskelley confession tape was introduced into evidence. The lengthy pretrial efforts to keep it out were noted for the record. Following along with typed transcripts, the jury listened to the thirty-four minutes of confused but incriminating testimony.

"This is Detective Bryn Ridge of the West Memphis Police Department, currently in the detective division of the West Memphis Police Department, conducting an investigation of the triple homicide, Case No. 93-05-0666," the tape began, echoing through the courtroom in a hollow, distant quality.

At the defendant's table, Misskelley stared into his

lap. He did not look at the jury. Fourteen sets of eyes—twelve jurors and two alternates—focused on the cringing accused.

The tape picked up the police interrogators, detectives Ridge and Gitchell, and Misskelley's polite "yes, sirs" to the technicalities—did he understand his rights, were these his initials on the waiver-of-rights form?

Ridge asked the first substantive question. "Okay, Jessie, let's go straight to that date, five-five-ninety-three, Wednesday, early in the morning. You received a phone call, is that correct?"

The question, like many in the session, provided the answer in its phrasing. The leading questions would form the basis for Misskelley's defense.

"Yes, I did."

"And who made that phone call?"

"Jason Baldwin."

"All right, what occurred, what did he talk about?"

"He called me and asked me if I could go to West Memphis with him, and I told him, no, I had to work and stuff. He told me he had to go to West Memphis so . . ."

"All right, when did you go with them?"

"That morning."

"Nine o'clock in the morning?"

"Yes, I did."

Ridge asked him about where he and Echols and Baldwin had gone in West Memphis, and how. Misskelley said they'd gone to "Robin Hood" and went by foot.

"Okay," Ridge raced forward, "what occurred while you were there?" There was no setup for this question. About who else was with him or how long it took him to get there.

Neither detective asked for the physical location

except what is, by legal description, four and more acres of dense woods. But Misskelley was nevertheless obliging.

For the next several minutes, Misskelley's flat, monotone voice filled the courtroom. He described how Jason and Damien viciously beat the boys, how one was sexually mutilated. When Michael Moore tried to run off, Misskelley said he chased him down and brought him back.

Out in the gallery, Steve Branch sighed deeply. Throughout the courtroom, everyone—the defendant's family, the victims' families, reporters, the farmers, county employees—stared at the little black microcassette recorder sitting in front of Gitchell.

Misskelley said it was after he saw "them" cutting on Byers "and I saw some blood" that he "took off." This was Misskelley's fourth reference to heading home before the others had completed their grisly act.

Eventually, Ridge asked if Echols had prior contact with the three boys.

"Had Damien seen these boys before?"

"Yes."

"Has he done things with them before? Or had he just been watching them?"

"He had been watching them."

Next came a section of the interrogation that was never fully explained, involving the photos of the boys described by Misskelley as being used in cult activities prior to the murders.

Ridge next wanted to clarify the time.

Misskelley said it was nine o'clock Wednesday morning when he met with his pals in the woods.

After another confusing exchange about Jessie's ability to keep track of time in general, Ridge introduced an entirely different scenario.

Ridge: "So your time period may not be exactly right is what you're saying?"

"Right."

"It was like earlier in the day but you don't know exactly what time. Okay. 'Cause I've got some real confusion with the times that you're telling me. But now, this nine o'clock in the evening call you got, explain that to me."

This is the first reference in the interview to a nine P.M. phone call or about anything that would clearly have occurred after dark. It's clearly something that's been discussed earlier, however, and Misskelley's answer to this question helps push the whole murder event back to what Ridge and Gitchell assume is its more likely sequence.

Misskelley: "Well, after all of this stuff happened that night that they done it, I went home about noon. Then they called me at nine o'clock that night. They called me."

"And what did they tell you on the telephone?"

"They asked me how come I left so early and stuff, and I told them that I couldn't stay there and watch that stuff no more so I had to do something to get out of there."

"Okay, who called you?"

"Jason."

"And you mentioned that you heard some voice in the background?"

"I heard some dingling—"

"And what else? I think you said that he made the call from his house?"

"He made the call from his house and Damien was hollering in the background, saying, 'We done it. We done it. What are we going to do if somebody saw us? What are we going to do?'"

"Okay, the knives," Ridge said, without further

elaboration on the phone call. "Was it one knife? Two knives? Was your knife there?"

Misskelley said no to the first question, then said he didn't know what happened to the knife Baldwin was using because he left early.

"He didn't tell you that he hid it somewhere?" Ridge asked. But before Misskelley could answer, Gitchell again stepped in. "I've got this feeling here you're not quite telling me everything," he said. "Now you know we're recording everything, so this is very, very important to tell us the entire truth. If you were there the whole time, then tell us you were there the whole time; don't leave anything out. This is very, very important. Now just tell us the truth."

Now, more than halfway through the tape, the jury sat in rapt attention, flipping pages as it followed Little Jessie's lurid details about the murders, and the murder weapons.

Misskelley said he ran from the scene but denied he had any blood on him. "I didn't have no blood. I didn't get close to them."

Wrapping up, Ridge needed to know what kind of clothes Echols and Baldwin were wearing that night. He said Baldwin was wearing a Megadeth T-shirt, or perhaps a Metallica, and Echols was wearing black— all black. Baldwin's blue jeans had holes in the knees. Misskelley said he, too, was wearing blue jeans and "a regular old greasy-up T-shirt," plain white.

Misskelley had on Adidas sneakers subsequently lent to a friend. Both Baldwin and Echols wore lace-up black boots.

"Okay," Ridge asked, "has Jason and Damien talked to you since this happened?"

"No," he said, then: "You know, Damien keeps

asking me how come I left and stuff and hadn't anybody said anything to me about it."

Ridge, now ready to conclude the session, wanted to know one more thing from this thug sitting before him, this vacuous tough guy droning on about his and his friends' role in a crime the police department had just solved.

"What do you think ought to be done to them for killing these boys?"

"They need to be put away for a while."

"Put away awhile," Ridge repeats. "Do you think they are sick or just mean?"

"I think they are sick."

"Is there anything else that you want to add to this statement?"

"No."

It was nearing four, on what had already been a long day, and Stidham asked to wait for the morning to begin his cross-examination of Gitchell. It was evident that the man who said a tape-recorded snippet led to the so-called confession was a key to the case. Gitchell had appeared shaky at times. When asked the sequence of events leading to Misskelley's confession, he said at one point, "I hope this is right." At another, he conceded, "It does get a little confusing, even for me."

Because everyone knew how important the cross-examination would be, the next day's events would prove inexplicable.

Nineteen

"I was really there."

The assembled news media dutifully took up their positions behind snowdrifts Friday morning to watch Misskelley, wearing handcuffs, walk the short distance from a plowed parking lot to the courthouse's back entrance. The glassy branches of the tall elms still shimmered in the early morning light, while fat red cardinals chirped in the cold.

As was his habit, the now-short-haired kid with the beady eyes kept his head down as Sheriff Darwin Stow led him past reporters shouting questions about his taped statement. He said nothing.

Before the jury was ushered back to the courtroom, Burnett began the day by announcing to the assembled newspeople that he was considering a "substantial fine" and a contempt of court citation against some unnamed newspaper that had printed a picture the day before in which members of the jury could plainly be seen. The *Paragould Daily Press* from the next county acknowledged it had missed the ground rules and the issue died.

In fact, even if Burnett still believed the jury was anonymous, there were few people in Corning who did not know everyone on the panel. *The Commercial Appeal* had already described them by age and occupation before the trial began. Burnett went on to assure the jury that the television camera operators were under strict instructions not to focus on their faces.

Still photographers were also under strict instructions that their shooting would be silent or they'd find themselves outside. In response, one reporter wrapped her 35-millimeter in a checkered dish towel. The photographer for the *Arkansas Democrat-Gazette*, Rick McFarland, complied by designing a camera holder consisting of a Tupperware cake box loaded with foam plastic ripped from the backseat of his car. Silence prevailed.

Gitchell was still on the stand. Stidham started his cross-examination with an accusatory question.

"Inspector Gitchell, you heard the tape yesterday of Jessie's statement. I want to ask you, did you and Detective Ridge rehearse Jessie's story before you turned the tape recorder on?"

"No, sir. We did not," Gitchell answered. Strike one.

Stidham made the useful point that much of the statement appeared to refer to a conversation that had already taken place before the taped statement began, but wanted more.

"Let's talk about the things that Jessie told you that are just absolutely incorrect," Stidham said. Baldwin's early morning call to Misskelley suggesting a rendezvous, Stidham suggested, couldn't have taken place as Misskelley described it because Baldwin was at school at that hour.

It may have been a trial technique or it could have

been Gitchell's real confusion but he asked Stidham to repeat his question, then asked Stidham to show him where in the statement Misskelley said the call occurred at nine A.M. "Is it in there? Could you show me?" Gitchell asked.

Stidham leafed through the statement for a minute before acknowledging, "I stand corrected, Officer Gitchell; that was something Mr. Misskelley told Detective Ridge prior to the tape recorder being turned on."

On his second question, Stidham was apologizing to the witness who would make or break his case. It would get worse. One of Stidham's questions involved a liberal misreading of the Misskelley statement. Misskelley had said he headed for the service road after the beatings began, and Stidham wanted Gitchell to acknowledge that it would have been impossible for the defendant to see the beatings from the road.

Nonetheless, Gitchell said he couldn't recall anything in the statement that made such a suggestion, and said so.

When the cross-examination resumed, Stidham referred to page three of the statement and Misskelley's reference to the defendants gathering in the woods at nine A.M. Stidham reiterated his earlier point: Baldwin was in school at that hour, and the police had verified it. The statement was in error in this detail, Gitchell acknowledged, but it was like pulling teeth to get it in the record.

Stidham got going with the obvious discrepancies. Could the victims have been killed at noon, as Misskelley said? No, Gitchell said, they were still in school. Did the victims skip school, as Misskelley had asserted? No, they didn't, Gitchell acknowledged.

"And you knew that that was incorrect when Jessie told you that?"

"Yes, sir."

Gitchell was asked how the boys were tied when they were pulled from the ditch. With shoestrings, Gitchell said. In Misskelley's second statement, played for the jury the day before, Misskelley said they'd been tied with a brown rope.

"These seem to be pretty important issues with regard to his statement," Stidham said. "Did at any time when he made these statements you knew were incorrect—did it ever occur to you that what he was telling you was false, that his entire story was false?"

Gitchell answered with a long explanation. There's a time in any defendant's questioning where he may give police a version of the truth but with an explanation that lessens his role in the wrongdoing, he said.

Stidham pressed on. Is it common, he asked, for police to ignore obvious untruths?

"It's easy to ignore the part about the boys skipping school because we simply knew that's not true. Jessie simply got confused, that's all," Gitchell answered. Gitchell said that he wanted Misskelley to keep talking, not intimidate him into silence with nit-picking.

Stidham asked next about all the witness statements and news accounts before the arrests that indicated a lot of people knew about the crime scene, and that his client was not revealing "top secret" information when he said one had been mutilated.

An Associated Press dispatch was entered into the record that said the victims, plural, had been castrated, along with the statements of two witnesses questioned in the case. One as early as May 12 had told police he'd heard they had been sexually mutilated.

Gitchell pointed out that the press had reported that all the victims had been sexually mutilated, "which in fact was not true." Misskelley had said only one was castrated, and he'd pointed to the right one, he said.

It never came out in trial but, despite the press reports, others in the community discovered early on that not all the boys had been castrated. Notes from a May 27 police interview show that Bob Loomis, then a sixteen-year-old junior at West Memphis High School, was told by an adult the day the bodies were found that "at least" one boy had been castrated.

Fogleman later would resurrect the rope issue, asking Gitchell if there was "any evidence that would indicate that there had been some sort of binding other than the shoestrings?" Gitchell was prepared to say that a wound on one boy had indicated to him that the boys could have been tied with rope at one point. Stidham objected.

"I think that calls for pure, unadulterated speculation on the part of a witness who is not qualified to render such an opinion," Stidham said.

Judge Burnett allowed the testimony, saying Gitchell could testify about the wound he observed, but could not "speculate as to the cause."

"I observed this bruising," Gitchell testified. "I believe it was on the left leg stretching approximately three and a half inches of the leg." Fogleman asked Gitchell if he observed a pattern to the bruise, and asked him to draw it on a piece of paper.

Stidham and partner Greg Crow again objected, contending the jury should view the photograph, rather than the artistic renderings of a police witness. "They are trying to pass him off as an expert in pathology," Stidham argued in a bench conference. "That could have been caused by a stick. That could have been caused by anything."

But Burnett overruled him. Gitchell was allowed to draw his picture of a rope burn. Just as the problem with the times had been plugged, now Misskelley's discrepancies about the manner of binding had been addressed.

The prosecution never said in so many words that it would present the alleged motivation for the killings. Then it called Vicki Hutcheson.

The courtroom door opened, and a slender woman, her red hair drawn in a bun, walked up the aisle toward the witness stand. The audience craned to watch the witness who was the subject of so much out-of-court speculation. Even Misskelley temporarily broke from his hunched stupor. His eyes seem to bulge at the sight of her.

Stidham immediately asked for a bench conference outside earshot of the jury. He knew what was coming: Hutcheson was going to tell her tale about a satanic esbat meeting she claimed she attended with Misskelley and Echols two weeks after the murders.

"Just because he was somewhere drinking and carrying on with somebody doesn't mean he's satanic," Stidham said. A heated discussion was brewing.

"Well, ladies and gentlemen, I've got another tough one," Burnett announced to the jury as the attorneys retired to his chambers.

"The theory of relevance is that the defendant in his confession stated that he had been engaged in cult activities with Damien Echols," Fogleman argued behind closed doors. "And there were orgies that took place, and the defense has taken the position that we would not be able to prove any of these cult activities or any connection with any cult.

"And this is offered to corroborate what the defendant said as far as his involvement in these activities, which the defendant in his statement relates to the murders by his statement that there was a photograph of the little boys that was passed around at one of these meetings," he pleaded.

Stidham and Crow countered. Crow, noting the supposed esbat occurred two weeks after the murders, said it lacked relevance to the homicides.

"The prejudicial effect of this type testimony in front of your average American juror is obvious," he said. "Jessie doesn't say in his statement it was a cult killing. There's no physical evidence, to my knowledge, on the scene making it cult-related."

Stidham jumped in.

"That's why they are wanting to hang this boy and that is why the newspapers have been splashing this cult stuff and that's why everybody's got their mind made up about his guilt or innocence because they are so petrified and horrified by this cult stuff," he said.

Burnett reached a compromise. Victoria M. Hutcheson could testify about going to the witches' meeting, but she wouldn't be allowed "to go into all the circumstances of what was seen."

In the courtroom, composed and deliberate, Hutcheson told her story of how she "played detective" after the murders, convincing Misskelley to introduce her to Echols after hearing rumors about him. She described, within Burnett's narrow parameters, attending the meeting at night in an open field where "ten to twelve, maybe fifteen" people were gathered.

It was an esbat, she said. "I had to look it up, but it was in one of the witch books and it's an occult satanic meeting," she told the jury.

"Those boys, I loved. And I wanted their killers caught," she testified, explaining her motives. Strangely, she never suspected Misskelley and said he had slept inside her trailer the night before his arrest—to protect her from prowlers. She didn't elaborate.

Her eight-year-old son Aaron was the voice on Gitchell's tape, she said, confirming widespread speculation about the "nobody knows" statement. Again, she didn't elaborate. She said only that Aaron was a classmate of the victims at Weaver and "a really, really good friend of Chris's and Mike's." Michael Moore's father, she recalled, was the leader of the boys' Cub Scout troop.

She said she lured Echols to her trailer with "satanic books" she checked out from the local library with help from a Marion police detective, Don Bray. She didn't bother to volunteer that she knew the Marion police detective because he was investigating a complaint of credit card fraud that occurred while she had been at work.

But she did testify that she never bothered to inform the West Memphis police about her sleuthing. They'd come to her.

Fogleman asked a final time whether Hutcheson had considered Misskelley a suspect when she asked him to introduce her to Echols. "No," she testified, breaking into sobs.

Stidham was quickly on his feet. How did she even know the Marion detective, Don Bray? Through an incident, she said, at the Delta convenience store in Marion, where she had worked as a clerk.

"I'm not going to elaborate on it," she said.

"I want you to elaborate on it," Stidham insisted.

Hutcheson mentioned what she called a "credit card mess-up," adding, "I don't really know the particulars . . . All the charges were dropped." She didn't mention it, but the incident prompted her employer to fire her, two weeks after she had started.

Stidham asked her if she had been convicted for writing "hot checks," a fact she acknowledged.

Later, Stidham raised other questions about Hutcheson. He asked her whether a roughly $30,000 reward being offered in the case had motivated her, and she said it hadn't. Stidham eventually attempted to call a witness to say Hutcheson had expressed interest in the reward money. But the issue was dropped after Judge Burnett said he didn't recall Hutcheson denying any interest in the reward.

The taped voice of Aaron Hutcheson remains at least a partial mystery. While it was important for the prosecution to explain that there was a connection between Misskelley and Aaron, for some reason, Stidham never explored it.

On New Year's Eve, Fogleman interviewed Aaron on videotape. Aaron said Misskelley raped him on the day of the murders, and tried to get him to join their "club." Aaron said Misskelley threatened to hurt his mother if he told.

Fogleman, appearing skeptical, asked, "Aaron, can you look at me? Were you *really* there or are you just trying to help your friends?"

"I was really there," Aaron assured him.

Finally, as the prosecution prepared to rest in Corning, Aaron's tale advanced again in another closed-door interview with Bray. Aaron said Misskelley forced him to participate in the murders, putting a knife in Aaron's hand and guiding it to castrate Chris Byers.

"He made me . . . cut his private spot off," Aaron told Bray. He also said a black man, also present during the murders, held a gun to his head. "He said I say anything about this he will kill me right now."

Aaron Hutcheson was never called to testify.

Vicki Hutcheson's curious relationship with Echols and her contention that she "played detective" led to other questions. Domini Teer had offered an alternative explanation of her involvement while testifying in Fogleman's office under a prosecutor's subpoena on September 10, 1993. Domini claimed Hutcheson bragged she had slept with Echols six times. Echols had other girlfriends at the time, too, she said. Although there was an apparent rivalry between Domini and Vicki, the teen told Fogleman that Hutcheson's claims of sexual conquest "were impossible, unless she crawled in bed with me and him, and I know she sure didn't."

Melissa Byers was called again. She was going to tell about something her son had told her. But before she could, Stidham wanted a hearing on the admissibility of her testimony. Courtroom observers noted the evident satisfaction Burnett's ruling gave the victims' families. She would be allowed to testify about statements made by Christopher under an exception to the hearsay rules.

Mrs. Byers testified that around mid-March, six weeks before the murders, she and her husband had gone to the corner grocery store to buy cigarettes. When they returned, Christopher told them that a man dressed in black had parked his green car in the driveway, gotten out and snapped his picture, then driven away.

Because it gave credence to the stalking theory, the story had an ominous ring.

The prosecution also introduced more evidence implying the crimes were related to the occult, including the book *Never on a Broomstick*, collected on the night of the raids. Echols's and Baldwin's black boots also were introduced to bolster Misskelley's description from the taped statement.

Twenty witnesses had been called by prosecutors by the end of the third day. Evidence technicians from Little Rock were called to describe the shoelace knots used to hog-tie the victims. Lisa Sakevicius from the crime lab testified that some of the fibers found on the victims were microscopically similar to fibers found on a shirt at Echols's house and to other clothing found in a closet in Baldwin's.

Under cross-examination, Sakevicius noted that a "Negroid hair fragment" had been found inside the sheet used to wrap Byers when he was transported from the crime scene to the lab. At the time, few knew the significance of the evidence. Anticipating the defense's strategy, *The Commercial Appeal* told the public for the first time about the bloody man who stumbled into the Bojangles restaurant the night of the murders. Based on interviews the previous fall with restaurant manager Marty King, the newspaper told King's story of the mysterious black man who staggered into the ladies restroom, where he smeared blood on the walls. The defense later called King, who told the jury the same tale from the witness stand.

Yet the defense never advanced beyond the mere suggestion that the Negroid hair fragment might be connected to the man at Bojangles. Fogleman would dismiss the notion as a "Mr. Bojangles" defense theory.

Twenty

"Michael Moore doesn't get to go home."

The day the state rested its case, Jerry Driver finally got to tell the jury his tale of seeing Misskelley in the company of Echols and Baldwin, when they were walking together, dressed in black, carrying "staffs." Driver was the last witness for the state—but that hadn't been the plan.

The prosecution had intended to call one more: a Lakeshore teen who told police eight days before the arrests that Echols had confessed to him.

Now, the prosecution learned, William Winford had recanted.

Fogleman and Davis asked for a hearing in chambers, where they alleged an investigator for the defense had been improperly interfering with witnesses. Ronald L. Lax, a Memphis private investigator, videotaped Jones the day before saying, "I just up and said something that I didn't know nothing about."

He said he had only heard the rumors about Echols's involvement, but had made false claims to his mother that Echols had confessed to him. When his mother called police, Jones said he was forced to then lie to them, too.

But the prosecution suggested a less innocent explanation.

"Your Honor, there's some information to indicate that this Lax may be intimidating witnesses and, frankly, I have never had this come up in a trial," Fogleman told Burnett. The Arkansas State Police was asked to investigate Lax's actions and subsequently cleared him of any wrongdoing. But the threat cast a cloud over further defense investigation.

A staunch death penalty opponent, the professional, well-dressed Lax was working for Echols's lawyers, but much of what he found was made available to all three defense teams. At least two key witnesses recanted after Lax spotted apparent inconsistencies in their police statements, then interviewed them.

One was a sixteen-year-old at the time of the murders, who skipped school on May 5, 1993, and spent the day with Domini Teer. He told police on Sept. 16, 1993, that Echols had told him days after the murders "that he knows who killed the little kids, 'cause he was there, with a couple people."

But when Lax interviewed him at his new home in Memphis months later, he said police had accused him of lying, then intimidated him into making a false statement.

Fogleman vented venom at Lax, noting "there are plenty of private investigators who don't drive a Mercedes or BMW." Lax, who lived well and whose colorful ties drew envious looks, wasn't the run-of-the-mill private eye. His offices in downtown Memphis featured polished-tile floors, Oriental rugs, antique artwork, and a top-notch case file and video library. When filmmakers came to town to shoot *The*

Firm, the legal thriller based on John Grisham's book, they took one look around Lax's office and left. It didn't fit the stereotype of the seedy private eye office they were seeking.

Defense witnesses appeared in the courthouse that Monday morning wearing yellow ribbons printed with the words "Jessie, Jr." In short order, eleven people were called to the witness stand to provide alibi testimony, or to say that they had seen Misskelley during some part of the day the murders occurred.

But no eyewitnesses to his whereabouts between the critical hours of 7:15 P.M. and eleven P.M. were called, although several witnesses said Misskelley had left to go wrestling in Dyess, Arkansas, about forty miles northwest of West Memphis, during that period.

The defense hoped the sheer number of alibi witnesses would be convincing. Misskelley's girlfriend said she saw him that afternoon. A sixteen-year-old girl said Misskelley had baby-sat her child and she had seen him at 6:30 that evening. Big Jessie said he saw his son when he drove home—on a suspended license—from drunk-driving class at about 7:15. (A state's rebuttal witness would testify later that the DWI class hadn't ended until nearly eight.) A neighbor said he had seen Little Jessie that night, getting ready to go to Dyess to wrestle, carrying his black wrestling headgear.

The wrestling alibi would be pinned for the count, but a group of strong, strapping young men, products of the amateur wrestling scene that forms the minor leagues of professional wrestling, put on a dismal display. One of them, a fifteen-year-old by the name of Dennis Carter, testified that a group had left for wrestling at about seven that night.

They were headed for a converted movie theater, which had been made into a wrestling ring.

But Davis had a statement Carter had given to police on June 9, just after Misskelley's arrest, in which he had made no mention of being with the defendant that night. Then Davis asked him to read a statement he'd made on June 22.

"I went to Dyess one or two times but it was after the three little boys was murdered," Carter read slowly. "I have never went with Jessie to Dyess." Davis asked him to account for the statement in light of his earlier testimony.

"I wasn't thinking," he said.

"Rowdy Rebel" Fred Revelle, another wrestler with an aspiration to join the big-time professional ranks, testified he had gone to the police to offer Misskelley's alibi as early as June 9. He had been with Misskelley in Dyess and had signed a contract with the owner of the wrestling ring that night. He had the receipt to prove it.

"I later found out that was false," Revelle acknowledged. "I might have jumped the gun."

Davis had a copy of the receipt. "What date does that receipt show?" he asked.

"April 27," Revelle said.

Revelle and Carter not only destroyed any credible Misskelley alibi, but made all his alibi witnesses look like liars.

Next, Marty King, the Bojangles restaurant manager, testified about the mysterious man in the women's rest room. Prosecutors would let the testimony stand unquestioned, preferring to argue later that the same person who sanitized the crime scene would not then make a public spectacle of himself.

THE BLOOD OF INNOCENTS

The defense's expert witness testimony would prove spotty, then disastrous. Perhaps the most beneficial for Misskelley was Warren D. Holmes. He had already submitted a widely reported analysis of the lie-detector test on June 3.

"It's extremely difficult for the average person to believe that someone would confess to a crime he did not commit," Holmes told the jury. But he said that, while he did not want to impugn the integrity of the investigating officers, "in a case of this importance and national significance, they (the police) had a vested interest" in using the confession despite the discrepancies between Misskelley's version and the known facts.

Holmes said one telltale sign of a false confession is that the person being interrogated doesn't add anything new to what police already know.

On cross-examination, Holmes said he had analyzed hundreds of confessions and that, in his experience, ninety-nine percent of those who recant their confessions are in fact guilty.

Also testifying was Richard J. Ofshe, who had appeared at a preliminary hearing. He came to Corning as an expert on cults. He had shared a 1979 Pulitzer Prize for a series of stories in *The Point Reyes (California) Light* newspaper that explored the Synanon cult. But he also arrived with some baggage: He claimed an expertise in detecting false confessions. Prosecutors said that expertise wasn't recognized by Arkansas courts, and asked for a ruling.

Ofshe's connection with the book *Remembering Satan: A Case of Recovered Memory and the Shattering of an American Family*, was known to many observers as a result of his appearance at a preliminary hearing.

Ofshe assumed a scholarly tone as he testified outside the presence of the jury. He had talked to Jessie and said that during his June 3 police interrogation, the defendant had adopted a strategy of "simply parroting back to police what they told him in order not to displease them and not be subject to additional pressure."

Burnett ruled that any mention of what Misskelley told him would be inadmissible, especially any conclusion about Misskelley's motives.

The bearded professor said Misskelley thought he was telling police vital information and didn't understand the consequences of appearing to confirm what police already knew. Ofshe also volunteered that he saw no evidence of an occult connection in the case and attributed the police allegations to "satanic hysteria."

With the jury back in, Stidham began by asking about the police interview technique—was it overly suggestive?

"Yes, and . . . the contents of that statement were shaped by those techniques," he testified.

That was all Stidham could get. Ofshe's testimony was limited to the police interrogation techniques.

On cross-examination, Davis asked about Ofshe's assistance in the Washington state case. Wasn't it true that the court had accepted Ingram's guilty plea and had refused to overturn his conviction despite Ofshe's theory? It was.

Earlier in the day, the defense called Jonesboro psychologist William E. Wilkins, but before he got a chance to discuss his patient, an effort was made to impeach his credibility. Davis wanted to explore whether Wilkins was qualified to give evidence as an expert. Davis asked for an explanation of disciplinary actions that had led recently to Wilkins being placed on probation by the Arkansas Board of Examiners in Psychology.

The ambush triggered a rise from Gitchell, who was watching the developments on a television screen in the media room.

"Bingo!" Gitchell yelled, turning the heads of several reporters. Technically, witnesses who were expected to provide additional testimony, as Gitchell was, were not allowed to go into the courtroom or listen to the ongoing testimony. But Gitchell floated in and out of the courtroom and the media room.

Prepared to describe Misskelley's state of mind, Wilkins was instead defending himself. Davis introduced documents that showed Wilkins was required to practice only under supervision and that he had only the week before written to the psychology board declaring his intent to practice forensic psychology.

Wilkins underwent the attack on his credibility as Stidham and Crow looked on helplessly. Finally, he was permitted to describe nineteen hours of examinations and tests that, he said, showed Misskelley could not tell fantasy from reality and that he was highly "suggestible."

Outside the presence of the jury, Wilkins struggled to justify the conclusions of the soft science of psychology. He tried to explain the research of an academic psychologist, Gisli Gudjonson, who had devised something Wilkins called a "suggestibility scale." Wilkins had used the scale on Misskelley before the trial.

But this sort of thing didn't sit well in Corning, Arkansas. The state objected, Davis saying it sounded like "some hocus-pocus test" to him.

Pointing to the empty jury box, Davis argued his common-sense theory to a common-sense judge. "The state doesn't believe there's an expert on the face of the earth who can give any kind of test that can tell you anything about 'suggestibility' better than the people sitting right there."

After Wilkins admitted he'd never used the suggestibility test on anyone except Misskelley, Burnett ruled that the test either lacked a scientific basis or, if it had one, that Wilkins was not qualified to administer it.

However, Wilkins was allowed to testify about some of the tests he had given Misskelley, including sketches he'd asked Jessie to make of a house, a tree, and a person. They amounted to amateurish line drawings. The psychologist said the drawings allowed him to render certain conclusions about Misskelley's thinking.

Davis, on his cross-examination, asked to see the drawings. He then made fun of the conclusions.

"From these pictures," Davis asked, reading from Wilkins's report with sarcasm, "did you determine that he was of abnormal or low levels of inferiority, insecurity, a tendency to low self-assurance, low self-concept, a modest withdrawal, an overconcern with interpersonal warmth, a need to demonstrate masculinity, a marked pattern of very weak and inadequate strength, sexual immaturity, and some preoccupation with phallic symbols?"

"Yes," said Wilkins, suddenly at a loss for words.

Fogleman had a cold on the day of closing arguments. His voice was raspy, his throat raw. He was sucking on cough drops.

The courtroom was jammed. The spectators had been waiting for the climax for days. In Corning, a trial like this was high entertainment. There was silence as Fogleman stood, approached the jury box, and began.

As any good prosecutor would do, Fogleman put the defense witnesses on trial. He particularly went after experts Wilkins, Ofshe, and Holmes. Standing before the jury, Fogleman dismissed Ofshe as "an expert at testifying" whose Pulitzer, he said, was about as relevant as the Heisman Trophy.

"What scientific basis could he give you that that statement was coerced?" he asked. "He didn't give you any."

Holmes had testified that Misskelley hadn't provided any new information they didn't already know. But Fogleman pointed to examples in the statement where Misskelley had in fact challenged his interrogators on certain points. And he noted that Misskelley had described the injuries to victims correctly, and had identified them correctly.

"The most significant details of the crime he gets right," Fogleman insisted. Despite his hacking cough, Fogleman talked for an hour. It was a careful, calculated summation. Just the facts.

Stidham was next. He wanted to concentrate on what he said were twelve reasonable doubts the jury should consider in its deliberations. He called the confession a "wild story" at odds with the physical evidence. He mentioned Misskelley's assertion that the murders occurred at noon, that the victims were tied with rope, that they were choked.

Stidham said that he had presented five witnesses who placed Misskelley forty miles from West Memphis at a wrestling match the night of the crime. He said police never attempted to account for the man at Bojangles. And he said there was never any evidence the case involved the occult. He ignored the state's rebuttal witnesses who poked holes in Big Jessie's claims about coming home from drunk-driving class and seeing his son.

"My client, Jessie Misskelley, is an innocent man," he said, as he prepared to sit down. "I would ask you to bring back a verdict you can live with for the rest of your lives."

When Stidham sat down, Davis got up— and he stole the show.

Throughout the trial, he gave the impression that he was fighting to confine a raging fury. Now he let go. His contempt for the defendant, his disgust at the crime, the pitiful sadness of the victims' families— he struck each chord.

Although references to the dog-eating cult were there in black-and-white in the statement, not a lot had been made of the motivation for the crime.

"I don't know what the definition of a cult is. I don't know if it has to mean that they go once a week and worship the Devil, or what," Davis said, voice and intent blue eyes projecting cynicism. "But when the evidence is that all three of them are involved in this type of activity— that's a cult in my book."

If Stidham disagreed, Davis suggested, "Maybe he ought to move to Berkeley, California, with Mr. Ofshe."

He said the defense had tried to suggest that the police had duped Misskelley into making the incriminating statement, had risked their integrity to solve the crime. But he said that if the jury looked at pictures of Misskelley at the time of the crime, with shaved head and braided topknot, and the clean-cut kid before them now, "Please tell me who it is that's the deceptive party."

Davis pulled out a large color portrait of Michael Moore in his Cub Scout uniform.

"See this picture? This defendant—who won't look up, won't look at you—but this defendant's action, if you think about it, if this defendant does not chase down Michael Moore, if he does not run through the woods and bring him back, Michael Moore lives. Michael Moore gets to go home that night and his parents get to be with him. But because of what Jessie Lloyd Misskelley, Jr., did, and what he told you about in his taped statement, Michael Moore doesn't get to go home."

If Misskelley had let Moore escape, perhaps the others, too, could have been saved, Davis said. "Maybe it's just a kidnapping or battery. Maybe they're just seriously hurt. But ladies and gentlemen, we'll never know, for Jessie Misskelley, Jr., didn't let Michael Moore get away."

He suddenly streaked across the courtroom and held Michael's color portrait over the defendant's head.

"He chased him down like an animal and brought him back and, as a result of his actions, Michael Moore is dead, Stevie Branch is dead, and Chris Byers is dead."

Burnett sent the jurors to the jury room at 4:17 P.M., and told reporters he planned to let them deliberate late into the night, as late as they wanted. Reporters ordered pizza. A clerk from one of the offices brought in home-baked cookies. The lawyers loosened their ties. Burnett, casting off the black robe, was surrounded by reporters and got quizzed by reporters about gardening, other cases, his interest in cooking.

The Creative Thinking crew, always on the lookout for the human interest angle in the proceedings, captured the lively exchange on film.

At 10:57 P.M., the jury asked to replay a two-minute tape of Tabitha Hollingsworth, the blond-haired seventeen-year-old daughter of Narlene Hollingsworth. The girl had testified she and her family saw Echols and Domini Teer walking near the truck stop west of Robin Hood the night the murders occurred. Curiously, the prosecution never called Narlene, but left her sitting in the hallway for two days.

In her testimony, Tabitha described Damien and Domini, both wearing dark, muddy clothes. Domini had black pants with holes in the knees and "white flowers," a detail the jury may have wanted to reconcile with the notion that it was Baldwin who was walking on the service road. In his closing arguments, Fogleman had asked the jury to consider several points that corroborated Misskelley's statement. One point involved the bruised ears that Gitchell said Misskelley had described. Another was the black pants with holes that Misskelley said Jason Baldwin wore that night.

The Hollingsworths simply had mixed up Domini with Jason, he had argued. After listening to the tape again, the jury returned to deliberations.

At ten minutes after midnight, the jury asked a bailiff to let them out. There would be no verdict that night.

The jury returned in the morning.

Prosecutors were nervous after seven hours and fifty-three minutes of deliberations Thursday night. Now there would be more waiting.

The victims' families huddled near the front door or went outside into the freezing air to compare thoughts, or smoke cigarettes. They had nothing to say.

Back behind the courtroom, in a cramped sixteen- by fourteen-foot room, seven women and five men discussed Misskelley's fate. Tall racks of law books surrounded them on three sides; a green metal safe in the corner further limited elbowroom. Three narrow windows provided a view of a piece of Corning.

Sitting in folding chairs around a dark oak table, they considered the various angles in the case. Early on, two jurors said they thought Misskelley might have given a false confession. That's what the case boiled down to— the confession. Jury member Lloyd Champion later recalled the jury had to decide if Misskelley was "trying to make up a story" or if he was telling the truth. Champion, a squat ex-Marine and the postmaster of Corning, who looked considerably older than his thirty-eight years, said the jury came to focus solely on this concern.

Their other focus— what it meant if Damien and Domini were on the service road— was dismissed as an aside. "Like a hound dog on a trail, we just tried all the trails at first," he said.

The case boiled down to Misskelley's taped statement, and the jury played it over. It wasn't long into the tape before the jury stopped it, then replayed it.

Misskelley described chasing down Michael Moore. No one was badgering him. No one was suggesting that to him. He'd volunteered it.

Suddenly, while television reporters were phoning their desks that they'd have nothing but an update on the extended deliberations for the noon news, the jury announced that it was ready to pronounce Misskelley's fate. It was 11:54 A.M.

The jury was led in and Burnett said his piece

for civility. "I am acutely aware that your feelings are on edge," he addressed everyone in the courtroom. "There's a great deal of emotion involved, but the court cannot tolerate and will not tolerate any verbal outburst, any display of emotion whatsoever."

The verdict was handed to the judge, and Burnett read it live for television audiences in Memphis, Little Rock, and Jonesboro.

Misskelley was guilty of first-degree murder in the death of Michael Moore and second-degree murder in the deaths of Christopher Byers and Steve Branch.

Jessie kept his head bowed.

Under Arkansas law, for both the first-degree conviction and the lesser, second-degree felonies, the jury was required to return to the jury room to recommend sentences. Since jurors did not return with a verdict of capital murder, they could not consider the death penalty.

Prosecutors were again permitted to make oral arguments to argue for stiff penalties, and defense lawyers were allowed to counter them.

Davis asked for the maximum sentences on all three convictions. He used the classic argument of retribution. The jury would want to forget photographs and testimony in the case as soon as they could be free of the courthouse, he said, but he asked them to think just one last time of the agony the victims had gone through that day.

The defense asked the jury to consider the mitigating factors. Crow said Misskelley was seventeen when the crimes occurred but that, mentally, he was much younger. He asked them to consider Misskelley's family background. He said he would trust their judgment, then sat down.

"What we're talking about is responsibility," said

Fogleman, in the final argument of the trial. Speaking even more slowly than usual and looking both weary and sad, he reviewed salient points, then stopped himself, knowing the recitation didn't matter. The boys were dead.

"They won't grow up. Their lives are gone." The guilty verdict wouldn't bring them back and neither would the harshest available punishment.

"Honestly, when you look at it, nothing you do is going to make the families feel all that much better," he said, his sincerity and the state's position almost at odds. "It might make them feel good for a minute if you gave him the maximum, but it's not— in the long term, it's not going to make much difference.

"But what can your verdict do? It can stop these kids doing these sick, stupid, crazy things and it can put an end to it. And that's what we're asking you to do."

The jury was out just twenty-six minutes this time. It returned with the maximum it could recommend— life in prison plus two twenty-year sentences. In Arkansas, that sentence meant life in prison. Only some future governor could commute the sentence to a term of years and the possibility of parole— highly unlikely in the case of a convicted child-killer.

Burnett imposed the twenty-year sentences to run consecutively. Misskelley would be out of prison only in death.

Misskelley showed no emotion when Burnett read the sentences, then asked him for comment or questions. He cocked his head to the left and said, "No, sir."

Outside the courtroom, going through interviews in the biting cold, the families expressed every emotion from grief to rage, anger-tinged happiness to silent thankfulness.

"He took a life, he should give a life," said John Mark Byers. "I hope he never sees sunlight again. Life plus forty—that's fine with me. That means Cummins keeps his dead ass forty years after he dies," he said, referring to the notorious Arkansas prison unit near Pine Bluff. "The only way he should come out of Cummins is feet first in a box!"

Todd and Diane Moore, reserved and decent throughout, declined comment after the sentencing. When a television reporter asked Todd Moore whether he was "relieved" at the outcome, he answered, "What do you think?"

Pam Hobbs, Steve Branch's mother, said she hoped life in prison would be tough on Misskelley, that a long life of torment would be worse than an easy death by lethal injection.

"The healing process will go on forever," she said. "Even though the guy was found guilty, that won't bring Stevie back."

Pam Hobbs's father, Jackie Hicks, was already looking forward. There would be another trial. This bull of a man who'd spent the night of May 5 and the morning of the next day ripping through the tangled undergrowth searching for the little grandson to whom he'd just given that shiny new bicycle, said he was glad of the sentence. But he said he still wondered whether even the next trial would deal with all those involved in the killings.

Stidham, now finished with his first capital case, said he was glad the jury had rejected capital murder and the possibility of a death sentence. He and Crow declined further comment, knowing they'd appeal.

Burnett said that while it had been a long and

THE BLOOD OF INNOCENTS

complicated trial, he was "well pleased" with the way it had been handled by the news media. He put it this way: "It was a little extra nuisance, but it worked out."

Misskelley was placed in the custody of Sheriff Darwin Stow and ordered sent to the Department of Correction diagnostic unit near Pine Bluff, the first processing center for new inmates.

Before leaving, he met with Big Jessie in the vault of the circuit clerk's office across the hall from the courtroom.

"I'll never make it down there," said Little Jessie.

"You're stronger than that," the father replied. "You're stronger than me."

It's a long ride from Corning to Pine Bluff— about 175 miles, little of it by interstate—and, according to reports that quickly made their way back to prosecutors and the press, Misskelley got into a conversation with the two officers who were transporting him. What he told them was astonishing—so much so that the deputies, Jon Moody and James Lindsey, immediately faxed a report to prosecutors after the ride.

After Misskelley was assured that nothing he said could be used against him, he told them what had happened on May 5. Baldwin had called and suggested they go to West Memphis to "get some girls," Misskelley told them. Misskelley was smoking marijuana and drinking whiskey that Vicki Hutcheson had bought him, he told them.

They went to the woods and Echols and Baldwin went into the muddy creek; Misskelley didn't go in because of his broken eardrum. When they saw the three boys come into the woods, they hid. Echols grabbed Michael Moore and, when Christopher and Steve came to his rescue "hitting Damien, trying to help their friend," Misskelley and Baldwin joined the fray.

The cops reported that they asked Misskelley how the boys were kept under control. "They were like puppies," he told them. "When you whoop a puppy and tell it to stay, it will."

In his flat drawl, Misskelley then described the removal of Chris Byers's sexual organs, saying he was about a "car-length away" when Baldwin started cutting with a buck-type locking knife.

"Blood went everywhere," he said. The boy was still alive.

The testicles, penis, and scrotum were thrown into the weeds.

Little Chris was "still squirming around in the water" when Misskelley ran away, the officers reported.

It was Friday, February 4, eighteen days before the second trial was to begin.

Misskelley's conviction was a very helpful first step for prosecutors. Anyone in Arkansas with a newspaper subscription or access to television or radio knew one of the three suspects had been convicted. But the state couldn't use Misskelley's damning statement implicating Echols and Baldwin in their trial. The U.S. Supreme Court's *Bruton* decision had settled that.

But if he testified from the witness stand about what he saw and did that day in the woods, the defendants' right to face and question their accuser would be intact.

There was already public speculation about what evidence the state could present at the second trial that would identify anyone involved in the crime.

THE BLOOD OF INNOCENTS

Misskelley's trial had produced no physical evidence that he had been present— no fingerprints, no weapons, nothing left behind by murderers fleeing in haste.

Misskelley's own words had convicted Misskelley. And unless he testified, his words couldn't be used against Baldwin and Echols.

Prosecutors let it be known that Jessie hadn't necessarily seen his last day in court. Despite his conviction, they noted, the sentence Burnett had imposed could be modified anytime within 120 days.

The state was prepared to make a deal.

Exactly what happened on the road to Pine Bluff isn't clear, but within days, Fogleman and Stidham were dispatched to the warden's office, where Misskelley joined them in his prison-issue white jumpsuit.

Stidham was adamant that his client would not turn state's evidence at the Echols and Baldwin trial, where his only useful testimony would be self-incriminating. So Fogleman asked for anything, short of trial testimony, that might be useful. Among other things, the session yielded the potentially corroborative story about the Evan Williams whiskey bottle broken on the bridge abutment.

Misskelley, already locked in an isolation cell and looking forward to being shipped to the state's Varner unit for young burglars and dope-sellers, where child-killers are the lowest of the low, had begun considering his options.

For thirteen days, Misskelley stewed.

Meanwhile, Baldwin's lawyers were still trying to get their client tried separately from Echols. In a hearing in Osceola on February 9, they argued Baldwin's defense theory was harmed by Echols's increasing notoriety, if nothing else.

Another ice storm, this one of tremendous proportions, hit the Mid-South as the hearing started and Burnett took the issue under advisement. He decided to think it through while rabbit hunting in North Mississippi but, when he couldn't get home because of the paralyzing storm, he called lawyers and a handful of reporters with his ruling Friday evening.

The two would be tried together.

The following Wednesday, as lawyers gathered in Jonesboro for a final pretrial hearing, Echols's lawyers decided to drop a few bombshells. If public opinion and the potential jury pool were already against them, they'd play to the cheap seats and raise— some said "create"— fairly plausible, even reasonable doubts about the state's case.

At the hearing, Echols's lawyer, Val Price, said a witness known to the police had told detectives that John Mark Byers— the stepfather, the police informant— was in the woods the day the murders occurred.

Byers would later call the statement "a bald-faced lie."

At the same hearing in Jonesboro, Echols's other lawyer, Scott Davidson, asked Burnett to require the documentary film crew working on the case to turn over segments of an interview with Byers. The film, Davidson asserted, "will show Mr. Byers at the crime scene talking about being accosted when he was eighteen or nineteen years old, tied up, sodomized, and thrown into a ditch."

Davidson also revealed at the hearing that someone from the Creative Thinking film crew had delivered a knife to West Memphis police, and that the film crew member had gotten it from Byers.

This was the first public reference to what became known as "the John Mark Byers knife."

Vicki Hutcheson said Byers called, asking for her son, shortly after the Jonesboro hearing ended. She wouldn't allow him to talk to Aaron. She told reporters she had asked for help from West Memphis police— witness protection, or something.

"I'm scared to death," she said. "I'm getting ready to get the hell out of town."

Besides the high drama, something else was taking place in the Jonesboro courtroom that afternoon, something the crowd of reporters couldn't see. Burnett signed an order calling Misskelley out of prison. It did not make the next day's headlines, but shortly would.

On Thursday afternoon, February 17, Misskelley was picked up by Craighead County officials for the trip back north.

Misskelley had been taken to Clay County deputy prosecutor C. Joseph Calvin's office in Rector, where Davis was waiting. Stidham and Crow learned about their client's sudden change of location when he arrived at Rector Thursday night. And they were furious.

They'd already notified the state he would not testify. The order transferring him from prison was made without their knowledge, without their argument against it in court, and clearly without their consent.

In a hearing a few days later, they would call the maneuver an egregious example of prosecutorial misconduct.

Stidham and Crow raced to Rector but Misskelley already had made up his mind to give another statement. They called Burnett at home in Osceola asking the judge to head off any questioning. They also asked for Misskelley to be given a psychiatric evaluation before talking to prosecutors.

But Burnett would not interfere. Misskelley had already made a postconviction admission of guilt. After Burnett had told prosecutors they could offer him "use immunity" for his testimony, he talked. The immunity meant his statements, which incriminated Echols and Baldwin, couldn't be used against him in an appeal or second trial. At 8:02 P.M., the statement was taken as Calvin, Stidham, Crow, Brent Davis, and Misskelley crowded around a tape recorder.

"Do you realize that once you make this statement there is no turning back?" Stidham asked him, according to a transcription of the statement.

"I know there is no turning back," he answered.

Misskelley repeated what he'd told police days before on the way to Pine Bluff. The boys were jumped and badly beaten. Misskelley says he grabbed the boy with the "Boy Scout" uniform, which would have been Michael Moore. Baldwin cut one boy in the face with his knife and Echols "stuck his finger on his cheek and licked the blood off of it."

Misskelley said he was perhaps ten yards away from where Baldwin was sitting on one victim, "swinging his knife at his legs."

Davis asked: "Could you, did you ever see one of the boys get cut with the knife?"

"After he got through I noticed what he had done."

"What did you see?"

"I saw the boy was missing everything . . . When he was doing that, I seen blood fly."

After that, Baldwin came over to where Misskelley had subdued Michael Moore. "He wanted to do to him the same way and I would not let him," Misskelley said.

Davis asked: "What did Jason do?"

"He looked at me real weird, showed me that knife and he just walked off." Misskelley said it was a folding knife, nothing like the commando-style knife Arkansas State Police divers had pulled from the lake behind Baldwin's trailer.

Davis wanted to know about Misskelley's original statement. Why had he told police the boys were tied with ropes?

Misskelley said he did it "to get them off tract (sic)." Misskelley said he helped pull the shoestrings out of the boys' shoes and handed them to Echols and Baldwin. He also said he watched as they were thrown in the water, something he'd never admitted before. One of the boys was still "moving around," he said, later describing him as "moving like a worm."

Misskelley said that at that point, he was preparing to leave. Davis asked why. "Because I was going to wrestling," he said, holding on to his discredited alibi. He left first, walking along the interstate back to the trailer park, and broke the whiskey bottle after throwing up. It was "close to dark" when he left the woods.

He went home, got his black wrestler's gear, and did go to Dyess that night to wrestle.

For the record, Stidham wanted Misskelley to acknowledge that he'd refused to talk with his lawyers prior to making the statement but understood they had advised him against doing so. Stidham also said he believed Misskelley had perjured himself.

Davis, in follow-up, asked if what Misskelley had just said was the truth. "Yes, sir," he answered.

"And if asked to testify to that in court, would

you and could you testify truthfully to those same things?"

"Yes, sir." The statement was over at 8:45 P.M.

Misskelley's lawyers knew how an admission of guilt in open court might play in the court of public opinion, or with any appellate judge in the habit of reading the morning paper over breakfast. And Burnett, who would stand for reelection in the fall, retained sole discretion over whether Misskelley's testimony, even if offered, would earn a reduction in sentence.

The statement at Rector was taken to establish what Jessie might be willing to say, and it was every bit as horrible as everyone expected. But as prospective jurors answered the call to duty the following Tuesday after President's Day, Misskelley's status as a state witness was very much up in the air.

Twenty-one

Fort God

Town histories call Jonesboro, Arkansas, "Fort God." The quaint city of 46,500 is home to more than a hundred churches. The home of Arkansas State University, with 8,500 students, it is the county seat of Craighead County and a bastion of conservatism and Protestant fundamentalism. In the weeks before the Echols-Baldwin trial, a local preacher had organized a seminar on Satanism at the downtown civic Forum Building. It was a sellout.

Like an increasing number of small towns across the country, there had been rumors of occult activity in and around Jonesboro prior to the trial. Police reports indicated several instances in which the Keller's Chapel south of town had been broken into and desecrated. Police reports called these incidents malicious mischief. Most residents knew nothing of them.

A local sociology professor wondered aloud how Jonesboro could provide an objective jury panel— or whether such a place existed anywhere in the country.

Burnett began to answer that question on February 22.

But before the first prospective juror had been questioned, a tense session got under way in the judge's chambers. Stidham was making his case for prosecutorial misconduct, backed by lawyers for Echols and Baldwin. Stidham argued that he had notified the state that Misskelley would not testify and that, before he had been taken from Pine Bluff, his lawyers had told prosecutors that, if called to the stand, he would declare his Fifth Amendment rights.

"Under Arkansas law, the prosecution can't even call Mr. Misskelley once they've been notified that he would assert his Fifth Amendment privilege," Stidham told Burnett. "They had no right whatsoever to pick him up at the Department of Correction and transport him anyplace, much less the prosecuting attorney's office in Rector."

Stidham was particularly offended at the conduct of a deputy who, he alleged, had "strong-armed him into believing it was in his best interests to testify."

Stidham went on. "They even promised to bring his girlfriend"—a fifteen-year-old girl—"to see him at the jail, Judge. I think that is the most abhorrent, ridiculous, flagrant violation of my client's rights that I have ever seen."

He said he heard that his client was at Calvin's office at 6:15 P.M., when his partner, Crow, got a call from Calvin in Rector. Crow and Stidham then raced to Rector, a good half hour's drive, but, by then, Misskelley "was very reluctant to talk to us."

Stidham and Crow were in an unenviable position. Although their client wanted to talk and perhaps see the light of day by his old age, they advised patience and, especially, silence. They would appeal. There were a lot of errors in the first case that could get him a fairer second trial, they argued. Give them time.

Fifteen minutes into discussing Misskelley's options, Stidham said, "Mr. Davis and Mr. Calvin burst into the room and announced that they were tired of waiting, that they were going to take a statement from our client irregardless of what we thought or believed and irregardless of the situation."

Misskelley announced that he was going to talk. And he also talked to the prosecution on Thursday, Friday, Saturday, and Sunday, the final three interviews without his lawyers being informed, Stidham told Burnett.

"I think that it is absolutely abhorrent and a mockery of justice for these prosecutors to allege that by the offer of use immunity and the circumstances that it was granted that, therefore, they can do whatever they want to with our client."

Davis said Misskelley had willingly talked to the cops on the way to Pine Bluff. When he heard what Misskelley had said, Davis called Stidham asking about a postconviction plea bargain. Davis said he and Stidham drove to Pine Bluff the Tuesday after the Friday afternoon conviction and were met there by Gitchell and Fogleman.

Stidham asked his client to swear on a Bible that he was telling the truth. Misskelley did. Over a period of hours, Misskelley finally told his lawyer of his involvement.

But Stidham wanted to see if any part of the statement could be corroborated. That's when the whiskey bottle came up again.

The four men drove back to West Memphis and, in Davis's words, "(It's) ten o'clock in the evening (but) we proceed, the four of us, to roam underneath the overpasses of West Memphis and, lo and behold, find a broken bottle in the location indicated by his client."

He told again how they spent the better part of the next hour examining liquor bottles in a nearby liquor store for comparison, Davis said. "Lo and behold," he repeated, "it matches." The broken bottle neck matched a bottle of Evan Williams Kentucky Bourbon, seven years old, the kind Misskelley claimed he'd been drinking that day.

Davis said Stidham said that wasn't good enough.

Davis said from then on he decided to deal with Crow. "I make no bones to the court: I was dealing with Mr. Crow because I thought Mr. Stidham had lost his objectivity as to what was in his client's best interest, what actually to do in order to get to the bottom of the truth."

Davis said he had asked for the order to get Misskelley out of prison and had done it many other times before, in other cases, without notifying defense lawyers.

After Misskelley gave his statement, Davis said he called two respected defense lawyers and asked them whether he'd done anything wrong. They told him, Davis said, that he would have been derelict in his duty if he hadn't tried to get Misskelley to testify.

There were three different tape recorders going when Misskelley made his Rector statement, Calvin, the local prosecutor, told Burnett later. One recording wasn't audible, so they had to get another tape and retape from it. While the retaping was proceeding, Calvin said Stidham and Crow and he were "very cordial," drinking beer and what Stidham called "cheap bourbon." Misskelley had been returned to the Clay County Jail.

For the record in court five days later, Stidham accused prosecutors of kidnapping his client and said no court should condone what they did. Prosecutors said Stidham was in the position of trying to protect his client's rights while "his wishes and his client's wishes are no longer consistent."

Burnett said he was inclined to appoint an independent lawyer to evaluate whether Misskelley in fact wanted to testify, someone with no interest in the outcome, who could explain all the pros and cons. He suggested appointing Bobby R. McDaniel, the respected Jonesboro lawyer who was that week on the front pages of half the newspapers in the country as the lawyer representing Susan McDougal, the wife of James McDougal and a partner in the failed Whitewater real estate deal that continued to plague President Clinton and First Lady Hillary.

But McDaniel was one of the lawyers Davis had consulted the day after Misskelley gave his statement in Rector, and at least one of the defense teams had also sought his advice.

Someone then suggested the dean of the University of Arkansas Law School at Little Rock, Howard Eisenberg. Fogleman objected to that, saying he didn't try cases. In the end, Burnett appointed Phillip Wells of Jonesboro.

The judge also said he would not find that the state had engaged in misconduct. Burnett said it was clear that the state could not subpoena Misskelley to testify if prosecutors had been informed that he would invoke his Fifth Amendment right against self-incrimination. But Burnett said Stidham and Crow appeared to have given the state "mixed signals," so their efforts to get him to testify were not improper.

Burnett said that the police officers who told Misskelley nothing could be used against him and asked him about the case on the ride to Pine Bluff may have engaged in misconduct, but that the officers' testimony was clearly inadmissible.

Wells met with Misskelley in jail. Wells would later say that he believed the prospective star witness understood the concept of use immunity and the consequences of his decision about testifying. Wells said he had advised Misskelley to get a specific offer for a reduced sentence before he made his decision.

Only sixty-two of the first 150 jurors called for Tuesday showed up. They sat patiently in the courtroom or milled around the courthouse while the session continued behind closed doors. By late afternoon, most reporters had seen a copy of the joint defense motions.

When the lawyers emerged from the hearing, prosecutors were barraged with questions about one of its allegations— Fogleman had told Misskelley's father that the state would seek a reduced sentence of forty years in exchange for his son's testimony. A reduction to a term of years would make him eligible for parole, unlike his life sentence.

After Burnett made his ruling in chambers, Davis asked to file a transcript of the ruling in the court file so that he could continue his policy of not commenting to the throng of reporters.

Burnett said he'd do better than that. He went out into the courtroom and declared from the bench that there had been no misconduct in bringing Misskelley to Rector. Then, in partial answer to the question on everyone's mind, Burnett said that Misskelley would "be permitted to testify if he chooses to do so."

Twenty-two

Did the Devil Make Them Do It?

Before the second trial got under way, Geraldo Rivera invited some principals in the case to New York City to appear on his tabloid television show. But it wasn't until March 23 that the program aired nationwide.

By perhaps unfortunate coincidence, the show appeared on television in Jonesboro in the last week of the trial, during a daylong continuance. Jurors had been ordered to avoid commentary or press accounts on the case, but they were home the day the incendiary accusations flew on *Geraldo*.

Employees at the Craighead County Courthouse gathered around the basement television in a conference room while at least one person who had served as a juror in Corning watched the program with a reporter.

Viewers were treated to the spectacle of Geraldo Rivera trumpeting the satanic aspect of the murders. Joining Geraldo in New York were Pam and Terry Hobbs, mother and stepfather of Steve Branch, looking solemn and forlorn; Jackie Hicks, his grandfather, and Paul Morrison, formerly with Channel 5 in Memphis. Via satellite was Jessie Misskelley, Sr., who was flanked by several unidentified supporters. The name of the program: "Kids Who Kill: Did the Devil Make Them Do It?"

The show only demonstrated how much attention this case had received.

The entire state was focused on it. The crowds were bigger. The story was bigger. The courtroom was, too. A stately second-floor chamber with twenty-five-feet-high ceilings, marbled walls, and tall windows facing south, it seated three hundred people and often was full.

Burnett told jurors he understood they'd probably rather be somewhere else. Many spectators in the courtroom looked at the trial as cheap theater.

Many in the audience were familiar faces— the victims' families, the defendants' families— but there were also college students attending the trial for class credit. Unlike in Corning, there were other young adults with shaved heads, dressed in black, and wearing pentagrams. Two pale women from Memphis sat through many of the sessions. They said they were friendly with the defendants and were adamantly opposed to the death penalty.

Also attending the trial was Damien's newborn son, Seth, with his mother, Domini.

The infant smiled at all. Eyes beaming over a toothless grin, he bounced on his mother's knee. Reporters circled them during court recesses, intrigued by the child whom Jerry Driver feared would be a sacrifice.

Domini proudly explained her son's name: Damian Seth Azariah Teer. The name "Damian," spelled differently than his father's, was in honor of the biblical

Adam's "third son," she said. Azariah was a prophet from the Salem Temple.

"Seth" she didn't explain.

Sitting next to them, Dian Teer, decked out in a polyester jogging suit, shook her head. "It's the Salem witch trials all over again," she said. She was disgusted with everything— the insinuations, the finger-pointing. She called herself just "an old hippie" and nothing more. "The only cult I've been a member of is the *Rocky Horror Picture Show*," she said.

During recesses, Echols stared toward the audience. His lawyers had tried to rein in his antics and had him dressed in dark blue trousers and a white, gray-striped button-down shirt that he buttoned to his neck. But he sometimes couldn't restrain himself. His dark, dull eyes would scan the gallery, stopping on people he either recognized or wanted to intimidate. At times, his head swayed slowly, and he smiled. Not far from where he sat were the boys' two bicycles, introduced into evidence and, as in the first trial, left in the front of the courtroom throughout the proceedings.

Baldwin, for the most part, kept his head bowed, but not like Misskelley. Baldwin was cowed by the attention but tried to project an air of confidence. He wore a blue button-down shirt and dark-blue pants. He was alert, and often smiled politely while talking with his lawyers.

The Commercial Appeal filed a lawsuit demanding that the jury be questioned in public for the second trial. When Burnett denied the request, the newspaper's lawyers appealed to the Arkansas Supreme Court.

"It's amazing," he announced to an assembled throng after the lawsuit was filed. "I, for one judge out of about seventy in the state, am probably the most liberal in allowing access to the press, and I'm being challenged on this issue.

"To ask lay people to come in from their work, their homes, their normal pursuits, and to be bombarded by very sensitive questions to where they have to verbalize their innermost feelings, in front of a few hundred people, the eyes of the cameras, the eyes of the world—to me, that's unreasonable."

But the newspaper argued that it was simply seeking the same right to observe a public process in a public forum as, it argued, everyone in the courtroom had. The secret sessions denied everyone that right.

The high court agreed to hear the appeal on an expedited basis and scheduled a hearing for the following week. It ultimately ruled with the paper, and new law was created in Arkansas. But the ruling wasn't made in time to affect the voir dire process in Jonesboro. A jury of eight women and four men were interviewed, selected and sworn in behind the closed doors of the court.

Fogleman made the state's opening argument, predicting that the defendants' own words would convict them. But this time, there was no talk of a helpful neighbor "playing detective" and helping to solve the case. Vicki Hutcheson wouldn't take the stand in Jonesboro.

Fogleman went over the disappearance on May 5, the frantic search by parents, the calls to the police, the discovery in the woods. He explained that there would be very little physical evidence. Their words would convict them as accomplices in murder. He didn't mention Misskelley.

The stylish, golden-haired Ford, in his opening

statement on behalf of Baldwin, asked the jury to consider the police investigation as a whole, as well as the state's original theory of the case. He said police started from scratch, without clues and without useful physical evidence. Police sought people with military experience, hunters, transients in homeless shelters, known sex offenders. They asked for the fuel records from nearby truck stops.

"They weren't looking for a sixteen-year-old boy," he said. "Pressure began to build. The public wanted someone. The press wanted someone. Suddenly, an arrest is made."

Davidson, taking on a folksy, friendly manner, told jurors Echols, too, had been railroaded into jail by what he called "police ineptitude."

"What you'll see is sloppy police work, things the police decided not to do, evidence they decided not to send to the crime lab, leads they decided not to follow." When they couldn't find a suspect among the kinds of people they knew must have committed the crime, they switched to Plan B and got what Davidson called "Damien Echols tunnel vision."

"Our client, Damien Echols—I'll be honest with you—he's not the All-American Boy," Davidson said to muffled laughter in the courtroom. "He's kind of weird. He's not the same as you and I might be."

But being weird is not illegal, he said, and the state had no evidence that Echols committed murder.

The state's first witnesses were the same as in Corning. The mothers of the three slain boys testified about the last time they'd seen their sons. Pam Hobbs, just back from taping *Geraldo*, told of meeting with the police at the restaurant where she worked. Melissa Byers, under cross-examination, added to her earlier testimony that, yes, her husband had beaten Christopher with a belt just hours before he disappeared from the carport.

The first major change in the state's case was testimony from witness Bryan Woody, not offered in Corning, that he'd seen four boys— not just three— together that day near Robin Hood Hills. Two of them were on bicycles, one was carrying a skateboard, and one was walking. The testimony appeared to be preparing the way for Aaron Hutcheson who, along with Misskelley, was considered another likely ace for prosecutors in the second trial.

The trial went over ground that was familiar to most observers. Det. Mike Allen retold his tale, and he testified into the trial's second day. During cross-examination by Val Price, Allen acknowledged that police had left at least one of the club-like sticks at the crime scene after recovering the bodies. He said he went back out to the woods to retrieve one stick on July 1, 1993, nearly two months after the murder. But in his answer, he mentioned the until-then unmentionable, and tempers stormed.

Price's question was intended to raise further doubts about police competency. "You all did not take this stick into evidence at the time you recovered the bodies?" he asked.

"No, sir," Ridge answered. "I didn't take this stick into evidence until the statement of Jessie Misskelley."

"I move for mistrial," Price shouted, as Allen's lips hardened and the jury was quickly ushered from the room. "The question I asked the officer did not call for him blurting out the fact that Jessie Misskelley gave a confession. The whole purpose for our trial being separated from Mr. Misskelley's trial in the first place was the confession of Jessie Misskelley."

Burnett ruled there would be no mistrial, but said the detective shouldn't have "volunteered" the helpful detail. "I suggest, gentlemen, that there isn't a soul up on that jury or in this courtroom that doesn't know Mr. Misskelley gave a statement." When they were recalled, he told jurors to ignore the comment.

Reporters gathered around Echols later that day, asking him questions across the railing that separated the audience from the defense table. In his soft-spoken yet blunt manner, he said he didn't really want Burnett to stop the show. "I don't want a mistrial because I want to hurry up and get this over with."

The role of the occult in the slayings continued to be a dominant influence at the trial. In a hearing on the issue outside the presence of the jury, Price said that Detective Ridge had written a report in which he took down the statement of a witness who'd seen two black men and a white man coming out of the woods at about six P.M. on May 5. Then Ridge noted on the report, "Has been mentioned that during cult activities, some members blacken their faces."

The observation, not related to the witness's statement, seemed to be an attempt to tie the killings to the occult. Where did this observation come from, in a report written on May 8, Price wanted to know. "It's our conviction that police from day one were alleging this was a cult-related killing, but there's no evidence it was a cult-related killing," he said.

Burnett said he would not allow Ridge to answer that question in front of the jury unless the state decided it would attempt to prove an occult motive.

Fogleman said that decision hadn't been made. There was a cult expert on the state's witness list, but he was never called.

With the jury back in, Ridge was asked about the bloodied black man at the Bojangles restaurant. Ridge said he'd taken scrapings from the bathroom wall after the sun went down on the crime scene on May 6.

"What was the date that you sent the blood samples off to the crime lab to be analyzed?" Price asked.

"They were never sent."

Price paused, pretending to be shocked.

"Where are the blood samples at this time?"

"I don't know . . . If they were blood, they were lost. That's my mistake. I lost a piece of evidence."

The police ineptitude theory seemed to be working.

The knives in the case also were admitted into evidence on the second day. Peretti, from the state crime lab, testified that the serrated pattern on some of the wounds were consistent with the survivalist's knife pulled from the lake behind Baldwin's house on November 17.

Under questioning by Price, Peretti said that injuries were also consistent with what Price wanted to call "the John Mark Byers knife," the folding knife sent to police by the documentary film crew member.

A sixteen-year-old trailer-park resident and snitch, who had been assigned very briefly to Baldwin's row of cells at the Craighead County Juvenile Detention Center, took the stand the next day. The prosecution tried to make him look like a good kid who'd just made a minor mistake.

Michael Roy Carson offered what would be the most damning evidence against Jason Baldwin. He testified that, while playing spades with Baldwin and two others on the third day of Carson's stay at the detention center in August of 1993, he'd asked the defendant whether he'd killed the three boys. Baldwin said no.

But the next time the group met to play cards, Carson took Baldwin aside. "I asked him, 'Just between you and me, did you do it?'"

The conversation took place over two minutes.

"He told me how he'd dismembered the kids," Carson said matter-of-factly. "He sucked the blood from the penis and scrotum and put the balls in his mouth."

Carson said he had kept it to himself for six months.

"I didn't really want to get involved in it. I'd just gotten out of jail," he said. But as he watched coverage of the first trial, he began to feel sorry for the victims' parents. That's when he decided to come forward.

"I got a soft heart," said the youth, who'd just recently burglarized his grandparents' cabin and admitted other burglaries in search of firearms. "I couldn't take it."

Carson also gave prosecutors another present. He claimed Baldwin also had commented on Misskelley and his confession. "He said he was going to kick his ass," Carson said. "He said he'd messed everything up."

Baldwin also predicted, said Carson, that "he was going scot-free."

The circumstances of Carson's testimony are curious, but were not given to the jury. Carson had told police his story on February 2. Sixteen days later, a twenty-nine-year-old adolescent treatment worker who was employed where Carson had been counseled spoke with Davis. The treatment counselor, who also contacted Paul Ford, was concerned about the veracity of Carson's claims. The counselor said he feared Carson was just parroting back rumors and tales that he had heard—from the counselor himself.

A transcript prepared by someone with Misskelley's spelling skills captured the essence of the interview.

The jury never got to hear the treatment counselor's account.

There was more crucial testimony that day. Under questioning by Paul Ford, Dr. Peretti, the forensic pathologist, said there was no evidence the victims had been tied up with a rope, countering Gitchell's testimony and artwork in Corning. Peretti also acknowledged that, with each victim carrying several pints of blood in their systems, it would have been difficult to clean such a "big mess" from the forest floor. Ford got Peretti to say there were three possible places where the boys had been killed: in the water, on the bank, or "somewhere else."

"It would be difficult to have injuries of this nature without having blood," Peretti said, "unless it was done in the water or some other place."

The possibility that the murders had taken place at a different site—contrary to the prosecution's version of the case—had been raised. Peretti also said the unusual injuries to Chris Byers—the skillful removal of the testes and the severance of the head of the penis—was no crude castration. It could have been done by someone with "medical experience" and indicated some knowledge of anatomy. The procedure would have taken him, a skilled pathologist, several minutes under prime conditions, with scalpels and bright lights, indoors.

But Ford wasn't done. He raised more doubts about the prosecution's case when he got Peretti to cite an estimated time of death that conflicted entirely with the known facts of the case.

Peretti said he didn't have the best evidence to work with since the local coroner had failed to make what would have been useful measurements such as body temperature.

Peretti hesitated, and Ford had to ask the question a couple of times. Finally, Peretti said, with the available evidence he had to perform the autopsies on May 7, the boys probably died between one and five A.M. on May 6.

For Misskelley's confession to be accurate, the murders would have to have happened between about six and nine P.M. on May 5.

As Ford took his seat, the prosecutors were clearly rattled. Fogleman and Davis, masters of the courtroom poker face, were infuriated. Questioning Peretti, Davis focused on the limited information available to estimate time of death.

But when Ford questioned Peretti again on redirect, the pathologist said his estimated time of death was based on his experience of having performed more than five hundred autopsies, the air temperature when the bodies were found, the time the boys disappeared and the time they were found, and the cause of death.

Ford asked if Peretti consulted two colleagues.

Yes, the pathologist answered. "They're in agreement."

"Pass the witness," Ford announced, returning to the defense table.

The significance of Peretti's time-of-death testimony was most likely lost on the Jonesboro jury, but was critical to Misskelley's lawyers. When Stidham heard it, he announced he'd be seeking a retrial. Peretti, who could not offer an estimated time of death in Corning but now could, had changed his testimony.

During brief recesses, reporters, encamped in a hallway converted to a miniature newsroom for the press and sophisticated video editing, tried to anticipate the state's next move. They learned in calls late that Wednesday to the state Department of Correction that it appeared unlikely Misskelley would take the stand. He'd checked back into his cell at Pine Bluff that afternoon.

Twenty-three

The Devil on Trial

By the time the second trial began, there was so much public speculation about Christopher Byers's stepfather and the knife he gave to the film crew that it was obvious the state needed to confront it.

When Gitchell took the stand, Price wanted to get Byers's interview with him into the record. But Burnett said that, with Gitchell, he could only ask whether the questions in the police transcript of the January 26 interview in Corning had in fact been asked by the detective.

The awkward procedure nonetheless introduced testimony showing Gitchell had found it hard to confront the undercover informant.

Byers sat stone-faced in the second row of the courtroom while the questions he was asked were read but left unanswered.

Gitchell testified that when Byers was questioned on January 26, he was a suspect. Blood found on the knife matched Christopher's factors. But, it also matched the stepfather's, despite the fact the two bore no blood relationship.

Also that Thursday, defense lawyers asked Burnett

to allow the jury to see a list of people the police considered suspects before the arrests of Misskelley, Echols, and Baldwin. The top three listed included Echols and John Mark Byers. The third was the nineteen-year-old former West Memphis ice cream truck driver who had known the victims and told Oceanside, California, police some crazy statement in more than fifteen hours of videotaped interview, including: "Maybe I freaked out, blacked out and killed three little boys."

He had previously and subsequently denied any role in the murders and he was ultimately released by the police, uncharged.

Fogleman said it was "new to me" that the ice cream man had confessed, as the defense lawyers claimed. The ice cream man, by trial time a Memphis car wash employee, would later be called to testify outside the presence of the jury.

The jury did get to hear the testimony placing Damien— and Domini— near the crime scene on the night of the murders.

Narlene Hollingsworth and her son Anthony both told their tale again about riding in a Ford Escort station wagon that night on the service road near the Blue Beacon truck wash. There were at least five people in the car, maybe seven, but Narlene and Anthony saw Damien and Domini clearly, walking on the side of the road, and almost stopped to pick up Teer because of the hour. Narlene said that was about 9:30 P.M. Anthony suggested it was about an hour later.

Narlene was also asked about a statement she had supposedly made to investigators that, when she saw the two on the service road, she had felt sick to her stomach. By implication, defense lawyers were trying to show that Narlene believed she felt sick because she had a premonition that something bad had happened in the woods. She once told an investigator that she was "born to know things."

Anthony told the jury that the person walking with Echols had hair that hit her "about middle waist." Even Arkansas native Fogleman couldn't translate that reference. "What do you mean?" he asked.

"It ain't real long but it ain't short neither," he said.

During her testimony, Narlene Hollingsworth was asked about another prospective witness in the case, L.G. Hollingsworth.

Narlene said L.G. was her nephew by marriage.

Davidson wanted to know how that worked. However, Burnett decided that he'd heard enough about a fairly untrimmed family tree. "Let's not try to sort it out," he said, to peals of laughter.

Court wasn't in session that Friday, allowing Burnett and some of the lawyers in the case to attend a conference in Fayetteville. By the time they came back, the state had made up its mind about whether it was going to pursue the occult motive. As a front-page headline in the Little Rock tabloid *Arkansas Times* would shout, they were going to try to put THE DEVIL ON TRIAL.

Presenting experts in the occult required prosecutors to preplay the testimony for Burnett while jurors remained behind closed doors. In testimony so offered on Tuesday, the trial's sixth day, they called retired police officer Dale W. Griffis of Tiffin, Ohio, to the stand as an expert in the occult.

Defense lawyers challenged both his expertise and qualifications.

Outside the presence of the jury, and later in front of it, they asked about Griffis's master's degree and PhD from Columbia Pacific University, which Ford called "a mail-order college."

They elicited testimony that Griffis, fifty-seven, a gray-haired man with deliberate speech, was a full-time police officer while he obtained the degrees by correspondence. He'd been allowed to testify in only one earlier case as an expert in the occult. But he'd appeared on ABC television's *20/20* as an expert. He also had a reputation in some circles for stirring trouble with his claims. Rumors of Satanism raged in 1989 in Manchester, New Hampshire, following a three-day police conference on "satanic cult crime" where Griffis was quoted as saying "some satanic cults are criminal cartels." Griffis was featured in the 1988 book *Cults that Kill* by Larry Kahaner, which said he had sometimes received mail addressed only to "Cult Cop, Ohio."

Griffis also participated in an excavation in 1985 of a garbage site in Holland, Ohio, where the local sheriff had claimed a satanic cult had sacrificed as many as fifty or more victims. The dig turned up little, but Griffis maintained that some items, including two knives and a headless doll, were "relics" of occult ritualism.

Burnett said he would be allowed to testify.

Griffis had an opinion about the case based in part on Carson's bloodsucking testimony, and in part on physical evidence that the police had seized from Damien's bedroom on May 21, 1992, almost a year before the murders.

Probably the most damaging evidence was a framed picture—a print—of a robed figure, standing above a crowd of cowering creatures, part animal and part human. The figure held two torches above its own goat's head. Crittenden County sheriff's investigator John L. Murray testified he found the picture on Echols's bedroom wall.

Other items seized, and now placed in evidence, were a dog's skull and a handwritten book adorned with upside-down crosses and a pentagram. The book, a funeral home guest registry, contained various spells, potions, and prayers to various goddesses.

Griffis told the jury that a number of factors told him this was an occult murder. One was the full moon of May 5, which cleared the horizon at 7:41 that evening in West Memphis, eight minutes before the sun set.

He said the victims had been subjected to "overkill" and torture, which he associated with the occult. And he testified the deaths occurred near two dates of special significance in occult circles. April 30 is Walpurgisnacht, the greatest of the pagan festivals, and May 1 is Beltane, another important festival.

Fogleman asked about signs of an interest in the occult among teenagers. Griffis mentioned their black T-shirts, tattoos, and candles. A trace-evidence expert had already testified that one spot on a victim's shirt showed evidence of something consistent with candle wax.

Defense lawyers questioned Griffis about the crime scene. There were no pentagrams, no bodies laid out in a pattern, no rocks in a circle. But Griffis said the bodies were found near water, another indication, for him, of the occult motivation.

The seventh day of testimony began with two young softball players and one of their mothers.

"I heard Damien Echols say that he killed the

three little boys and, before he turned himself in, that he was going to kill two more, and already had one all picked out," said fifteen-year-old Jody Medford. The pretty brunette calmly told the jury she overheard Echols's claims at a small softball field behind the Belvedere Apartments, where Echols frequently hung out.

Jody's mother backed her up. She said her daughter had mentioned the incident as they drove home after the game. Mrs. Medford knew who her daughter was talking about when she described Echols, a distinctive figure with long black hair and shaved sideburns.

Another twelve-year-old girl testified to overhearing the same conversation.

Fogleman rested the state's case after asking Burnett for permission to read to the jury a poem from Echols's writings. Slowly, with drama in his voice, he read the earnest musings of an adolescent poet:

"I have always been in the black and in the wrong. I tried to get into the white but almost destroyed it because the black tried to follow me. This time I won't let it. I will be in the middle."

The defense called its first witness at 10:52 A.M. Echols's mother, Pamela, and sister, Michelle, provided alibi testimony. They said Echols was home at the time the murders occurred.

Then, Echols himself was called as a surprise third witness. The supposed Satan worshiper appeared almost wholesome in his white button-down shirt and slicked-back hair that now appeared much shorter than when it had hung loose in a stylish surfer cut. In his awkward gait, he made his way up the raised witness-box next to Burnett.

Now on a pedestal before an audience of three hundred, he seemed to relax. The serious and in-

THE BLOOD OF INNOCENTS

tense Price lobbed him a series of questions. One question needed to be asked and answered fast, and Price knew it.

"I'm not a Satanist. I don't believe in human sacrifice, or anything like that," Echols said.

Echols had testified earlier, outside the presence of the jury, about the circumstances of his early interrogation during the police investigation. He said police had advised him against asking for a lawyer during the lengthy May 10 questioning. But the jury never heard that.

Now, with the jury present, Price asked him:

"On May fifth, did you kill Michael Moore?"

"No, I did not."

"On May fifth, did you kill Steve Branch?"

"No, I did not."

"On May fifth, did you kill Chris Byers?"

"No, I did not."

Echols shook his head back and forth with each answer. The final time he looked out into the crowd to his mother and father, Pam and Joe Hutchison, and shook his head to assure them of his innocence.

In the quiet, packed courtroom, his testimony continued for almost an hour and a half. Unflustered, speaking in calm sentences, often ending with what seemed like a pause, as if he were about to add more, he would touch on a wide range of bizarre topics. His voice was eerily flat. His manner was relaxed, yet defiant. He seemed in full control.

Price asked him to tell the jury about Wicca.

"It acknowledges a goddess in a higher regard as a god because people always said we are 'all God's children,' and men can't have children," he said. "It's basically like a close involvement with nature."

* * *

Echols, about the right age for a college sophomore, displayed the confident manner of a university student when it came to the topic of world religions.

"I've read about all different types of religions because I've always wondered, like, how do we know we've got the right one? How do we know we're not messing up?" he asked with a tone of boyish sincerity. Damien's curiosity and his interest in magic, witchcraft, and religions would be a crucial part of his testimony. Clearly, Price knew he had to address the things about Damien that most people in Jonesboro, Arkansas, would consider strange. So he went through each issue one by one, staring intently at his client as he gave his answers.

First, Echols was asked to explain his name change—from Michael Hutchison to Damien Echols

Next, Price asked him about Satanism. There was widespread speculation about the motive for the crime: What did he think about Satanists?

"Some things I might have in common, like they say some Satanists may be arrogant, conceited, self-important. Things like that. I might be that. But I'm not a Satanist. I don't believe in human sacrifice, or anything like that."

What about the journal of his writings? Price asked In some of the writings he was just jotting down lyrics from songs and authors, Echols explained. He quietly read several entries to the rapt audience.

Echols said the "In the Middle" poem Fogleman had read was written "in one of my manic-depressive phases," and so were some of the others. "These were wrote a year or two before any of that ever happened."

Then Price showed him state's exhibit 116, an animal skull owned by Damien.

"Are you familiar with this?" Price asked him.

THE BLOOD OF INNOCENTS 339

"Yes, I am."

"Now what is that?"

"It was a skull that me and my stepdad Jack Echols had found. I just thought it was kinda cool. Before he gave it to me he bleached it out and everything to make sure there weren't any germs or anything on it. It was a decoration in my room."

"Did that skull have any type of satanic meaning?"

"No, it did not."

"Or, did it have any type of cult meaning?"

"No, it did not."

"Did it have any type of occult meaning?"

"No, and we did not kill this, it was like that when we found it."

Another state's exhibit was an ominous picture by an artist called Puss-Head, which had appeared in *Thrasher* magazine, a skateboarding magazine that he read. Despite the prosecution's suggestion, Damien said, it had no religious or cult significance.

Price asked about the notes on potions and incantations contained in the funeral registry book ornamented with upside-down crosses.

The "cure for worms," Damien said, came from something he'd read on the Salem witches' persecution era. He got the other incantations from various books and sources, he said. The symbol at the front of the book, a gold skull with wings, was a Harley-Davidson necklace. But he broke the clasp, "so I just stuck it to the front of the book." On the cover of the book was a pentagram pointing up, he said.

Price then asked if he'd read any items that pointed out the difference between pentagrams pointing up and those pointing down.

"The one that points up is from the Wicca religion; the one that points down is from Satanism. The one that points up symbolizes a man or a woman with arms and legs outstretched; Satanism pointing down would be a goat's head."

"Did you ever practice any of these spells?"

"Not that I know of."

"Did you ever use any of that material to conjure up any evil, or anything like that?"

"No."

Price turned his attention to *Never on a Broomstick*, which Damien said he'd bought at the Crittenden County Library at a used-book sale for a dime. "I just thought it was interesting."

Price noted that there was underlining of some of the book's passages pertaining to the Devil. Damien explained, "That was done when I got it. I think it was because somebody had a report to do or something because there's little notes, and dates like from the sixteen hundreds, in the outside margins."

Damien described the book as a chronicling of the phases of witchcraft and other religions over the centuries. He noted the torture of accused witches until they confessed; following the confession, the accused witches were killed. The book also had passages about Satanism and modern-day witches, he said.

Price asked him the difference between Wicca and witchcraft.

"Wicca is also called witchcraft. The word 'Wicca' was bastardized; it originally meant 'wise one.' "

He also admitted to having a book on magic, noting that just about all religions— such as Hinduism, Buddhism, even Christianity, what with its exorcisms and other ritualistic exercises— have magical traditions.

THE BLOOD OF INNOCENTS

The strategy of explaining himself continued. Price next asked Damien to tell the jury about his tattoos. Price asked him about one that he called "a circle with a stick man."

"It's an Egyptian ankh and I do have it on my chest."

"What is an ankh? What's that stand for?"

"It symbolizes eternal life. . . . I just thought it was cool at the time."

He also said he had a pentagram tattoo, also because he thought it was cool. The tattoos, he said, he made himself, using razor blades, a needle, and India ink.

He had a cross tattooed in the webbing of his hand ("A lot of people at school were getting them," he said.), and Price asked him about the letters *E-V-I-L* tattooed across his fingers.

"I had this T-shirt, it had a hand holdin' a hammer. It was for the *Injustice for All* tape. And across the hand, some of the groups of Metallica, they had things like *HATE, FEAR, EVIL*, things like that, and that was on one of my T-shirts. And I just thought it was cool, so I did that."

In one of the few times he revealed any of his formative experiences, Damien testified that he wasn't very popular in school. He was always different from the other kids. He had never been into sports or other activities that interested other people. So, he said, he acted strange as a defense mechanism— and it worked. "It kept people away."

Later, prosecutors would attack this simple statement as a lie. And they would question another claim he made under his direct examination— that he had never been in the woods of Robin Hood Hills.

Echols also said he regularly dressed in black because he had been told he "looked good in black."

"I was real conscious of the way I dressed," he explained. "If I'm not dressed the way I like it, I get a headache because I worry about it all the time." But when he dressed in black, "I didn't have to worry about it, 'cause I always looked the same."

After he had put aside the issues of Damien's dress, writings, and beliefs, Price turned to Damien's reactions upon becoming a target of the police investigation. He asked him about the visit from Sudbury and Jones. Damien said the officers told him a couple of crucial facts about the murders—and that he merely repeated those facts during police interrogations.

"Did they tell you any other details about what happened to the bodies, or how they died, or the condition the bodies were in?"

"I'd heard mutilated, but when I heard mutilated, I thought it was like all chopped up or something. I figured there wouldn't be like a whole body or anything."

Price asked him about Ridge's questioning of Damien, none of which was recorded on tape. "Did he ask you a lot of leading questions?"

"Yeah, like he asked me, 'Do you think one of the kids was hurt worse than the rest of them?' So, I said, 'Yeah, I guess.'"

In effect, Damien said he tricked the police when he told them, "I'll tell you everything I know if you'll let me talk to my mother." After he talked to her, "I said, 'I don't know nothin'.' And he (the detective, Durham) got mad."

There were more explanations of issues that were of obvious concern to Price. Damien testified he didn't remember saying he was afraid of the electric chair; he admitted to owning a lot of knives at one time but said he'd left his collection behind in Oregon; and he denied the incident at the girls' softball game, saying he never discussed the murders.

Then Price asked him what Griffis said he had asked, about water and its connection with the killings. He replied:

"I've never heard of it like a demonic force, like he said. I've heard of it being, like, a giver of life, because all things need water to survive. Nothing can live without water." But he said he probably agreed with Ridge if the officer suggested it was a demonic force.

"How have you felt being charged with these three murders?" Price asked.

The prosecution objected. Fogleman and Davis said that question wasn't relevant. "His feelings two years ahead of time are relevant," Fogleman said. "Two years ahead of time is when he wrote that stuff." But the judge allowed it. And Damien said in his slow, sleepy voice, "Different ways on different days, I guess. Sometimes angry, when I see stuff on TV. Sometimes sad. Sometimes scared."

And that led into the follow-up Price had planned, his attempt to explain away one of the most damning Damien stories, the one where he blew kisses at the victims' families during a pretrial hearing.

"That was when I went to court in one of the other places, I can't remember the place it was. I do stuff like that sometimes, I just lost my temper. When I went outside, everybody was out there standing there, calling me names, screaming at me, things like that. I guess it just made me upset. And I did that."

There was a long pause.

"Did you kill any of these three boys?"

"No, I did not."

"No further questions."

His performance was solid. His manner had been controlled. Many believed that he had helped himself. But his testimony wasn't over. He faced cross-examination.

Davis stood, ready for a fight. And he had some good ammunition. He asked Echols if he was testifying under the influence of any drugs, and Echols acknowledged he was taking his prescription antidepressant. He said it made him sleepy. This, Davis was implying, explained Damien's languidness, his detachment on the witness stand. The jury could only imagine the way Damien might behave when he wasn't on his medication.

He then went over Narlene's testimony, establishing that it was unlikely she could have mistaken Damien—with his distinctive look—for someone else.

In a curious exchange, perhaps showing Damien's lack of mental acuity, he told Davis that at first when he was questioned about when he went to the Sanderses' home on the day of the murders, he probably told police he was there at about three to five P.M. But Damien's mother told police it was around five to 6:30 P.M.

"Then as time moves on, and the time period that's in question becomes later that evening, the visit to the Sanderses' becomes later that evening, correct?"

"Yes, sir."

"And so the story kind of changes to fit the facts we need to cover, right?"

"Yes, sir."

Damien's readiness to admit what seemed like a

falsification of his alibi threw Davis. There was a long pause before he moved on to the next series of questions.

Echols had said he was not a Satanist, Davis noted. Now Davis wanted to know what he knew of Aleister Crowley, the magician and a devotee of black magic and sexual perversion.

"Aleister Crowley is a guy who, based on his writings, believes in human sacrifice, doesn't he?" Davis asked.

"He also believed he was God," Echols countered.

"He also had writings that indicated that children were the best type of human sacrifice, correct?"

"Yes."

"Now, Aleister Crowley doesn't have any particular significance for you?"

"I know who he is. I've read a little about him, but I've never read anything by him."

Echols didn't see the ambush coming. Someone in jail had copied some doodlings from Echols's cell and passed them on to prosecutors. Davis, armed with fresh evidence, wanted to know about the significance of some lines Echols had jotted in a cryptic alphabet, that, when deciphered, appeared to list four names: his own, Baldwin's, his newborn son's, and Aleister Crowley's.

Before his lawyers could object, he acknowledged he'd written the list in jail. Both Baldwin's and Echols's lawyers objected to the list itself being placed in evidence, and Burnett agreed. However, he refused to instruct the jury to disregard the testimony.

An angry Price moved for a mistrial, and demanded a special prosecutor to examine how the state had obtained its evidence from jail. Price tossed in a renewed oral motion for prosecutorial misconduct.

All were denied.

Davis went back to Echols's comment that he'd had good days and bad days after his arrest.

"Was it a bad day, the day after you were arrested, when you blew a kiss to the victims' families? Was that a bad day when you did that?"

"That was one of the times I lost my temper."

His voice sarcastic and bitter, Davis replied, "Oh, so you lost your temper, is why you blew a kiss to the victims' families?"

"Yes," Damien said flatly.

Davis asked him if he told the officers, "I'll tell you all about it if you'll let me talk to my mother."

Damien replied, "I said, 'I'll tell you everything I know.'"

"And if he says in his report, 'I'll tell you all about it if you'll let me talk to my mother,' that's inaccurate, too?"

His calm voice intoned, "That's another of his lies."

Damien then testified that he compiled his writings when he was bored.

"Do you do any satanic incantations out there while you're bored?"

"No, I do not."

The Echols cross-examination extended into the trial's eighth day.

Early that morning, Davis presented the records about Damien's supposed attempt to pull someone's eyes out during a fight.

The defense objected.

"Your Honor," Davis complained, "they put on

evidence yesterday about him being a quiet, peace-loving Wiccan." Now, the state thought it was fair to ask him about his tendency toward violence.

Davis also asked Damien whether his statement that he would "eat your father alive" during the outburst while living in Oregon had anything to do with his medication being "out of whack."

Echols said he had been drinking the night he made the threat to his father.

Next, Davis wanted to explore some of what police had heard during their May 10 interview with Damien. The crime lab had found a spot of something that looked like candle wax; Echols, in his interrogation on May 10, had suggested that that was what they'd find at a ritual murder site.

Davis also asked about Echols's apparently flippant answers to police during the interrogation. Did he really say the killer might have considered the murders "funny" and probably wouldn't care about getting caught?

Echols answered coolly. It was clear— "common sense," he called it— that the killer killed for pleasure.

"So did you also tell (Detective Ridge) that the killer would want to hear the kids scream?"

"If he got off on killing people," Echols answered, "he'd probably want to hear them scream."

"And is it part of the common sense," Davis demanded, "that whoever kills eight-year-olds would feel good and whoever kills eight-year-olds would like to hear them scream? Is that part of your 'common sense' philosophy?"

"I figure they must have, if they did it," Echols replied.

Closing, Davis suddenly dropped his voice, almost

to a whisper. "How do you think that candle wax got there?"

Damien, his voice on edge, replied, "I don't know. Maybe whoever killed them put it there or maybe it was there before they left home."

Following Damien's testimony, several girls who amounted to trial groupies said they found him believable, intelligent, and innocent. The attractive young girls, students at local high schools or at Arkansas State University, said Damien was the victim of persecution.

"My favorite novelist is Stephen King," said one of the girls. "I read Stephen King's books. I wear black, that's my favorite color, and that has nothing to do with it. I've listened to Metallica for the last three to four years, and that has nothing to do with it. And they're digging for evidence. They haven't found anything, no fingerprints, nothing. . . . And the Harley-Davidson, it's nothing satanic . . . That's the new style now. Wearing black, wearing big jeans, dyeing your hair different colors, I mean that's just the style."

It was obvious that Echols's testimony thrilled his growing circle of fans. About fifteen young women cheered as Echols, falling into his out-of-courtroom swagger, was led to a waiting police car at the end of the day.

"I think he was very convincing. I believe his testimony," said a seventeen-year-old Jonesboro highschool student. "I thought they were guilty (before). The news media makes it out like they're Satanists."

And in the media swirl outside the courtroom, there was another spectator with still a different perspective on the proceedings. John Mark Byers said he didn't appreciate the defense's attempts to link him to the murders through innuendo.

When one reporter asked him about rumors of his drug involvement, Byers responded in his low drawl, "Rumors are rumors. . . . They're just looking for a scapegoat."

Twenty-four

Cult Cops and a Bloody Thumb

Echols's lawyers went for the jugular with their charges of police oversights and missed clues. Attacking the police investigation was their best hope.

They called Gary Gitchell as a hostile defense witness and went over the minutiae of the investigation. But Gitchell wasn't shaken. His testimony, like all his testimony, was straightforward. He wasn't perfect, he seemed to be saying. He was just a cop doing his job. He said that yes, police had lost the evidence of the Bojangles incident and made light of it. He was then asked about Vicki Hutcheson, who had not testified for the state in the second trial.

Gitchell said that, in the course of his investigation, Hutcheson's trailer had been wired so that police could overhear Echols's conversations with her. Had she signed any document giving police this right? Gitchell was sure she had but would need a brief break to find it.

After a search of available files, he couldn't produce it.

It didn't really matter anyway, said Gitchell. "With

THE BLOOD OF INNOCENTS

the music in the background, you couldn't hear any of the voices."

Echols's defense lawyers also believed they needed more witnesses about Echols's alibi for the night of the murders. A twelve-year-old girl testified that her parents were gambling at Splash Casino in Tunica, Mississippi, on May 5, when Damien, his sister, and his parents showed up at her house. The first of what is now a concentration of legal gambling casinos within an easy commute of Memphis, the permanently moored Splash barge had been open less than a year in May 1993 and drew people from throughout the region.

Echols's sister and mother had testified previously that they'd dropped in on the girl about seven P.M. on the night of the murders. The girls were sure of the hour and date because one of their favorite television shows, *Beverly Hills 90210,* had been on at the time.

But the girl also said she remembered that the episode of the popular show was just before her boyfriend's big band concert.

Fogleman, sitting at the prosecutors' table, got up and walked over to Davis, whispered something in his ear, then sat down. Davis asked if the band concert her boyfriend had played in was the big springtime concert. She said yes. Fogleman would make good use of that admission when he called a rebuttal witness.

Echols's lawyers then called Gail Sharp, who had won $10,000 on May 5, and who recalled seeing the same twelve-year-old girl's parents at Splash just prior to winning the slot-machine jackpot.

"I played twenty dollars and won ten thousand. And yes, I filed it on my taxes," she testified to laughter in the courtroom. Since she'd seen the girl's parents at the casino, the girl's recollection of the date that Damien came by her house might be accurate. And it solidified his alibi.

The eighth day of the Jonesboro trial ended with Burnett making a ruling in the Corning case. Misskelley's request for a new trial, based in part on the new time-of-death evidence, was denied.

Robert D. Hicks wrote the 1991 study *In Pursuit of Satan: The Police and The Occult*, after attending police seminars on Satanism and occult crime, and questioning the scholarship and the constitutionality of what was being taught in them. Talking to so-called experts, he came away with the conclusion that "the most alarming claims appear to have no validity in fact."

Hicks, called to Jonesboro by the defense, said that calling the West Memphis murders a crime with "occult trappings," without overt signs of Satanism, was meaningless but usefully inflammatory for the prosecution. The term "occult" lent an atmosphere of evil to a crime without a sound, scientific explanation. In essence, he said, a murder is a murder.

Hicks, who was a police policy analyst for the State of Virginia, sported long hair drawn into a ponytail. He derided the state's expert, Dale Griffis, as a "cult cop."

"We have no evidence at all," Hicks testified, "to support the idea that there is this big, underground cult that kills upwards of fifty thousand people a year— which is a figure, by the way, that Dale Griffis has frequently claimed in his teaching."

Hicks said some police officers believe they must be "spiritually armed" to investigate certain abhorrent crimes, a belief he said that "gets outside what law enforcement is here to do."

That Friday's main event was the questioning of John Mark Byers. Once Gitchell had acknowledged two days earlier that Byers had been a suspect in the first trial, it was obvious one of the defense teams would call the victim's stepfather.

Prior to Byers's testimony, Burnett held a hearing in chambers that dealt with Byers's work as an undercover informant and his suggestion that two people he'd dealt with could have killed his stepson in retaliation. Burnett ruled that information could not be given to the jury.

Val Price had asked Gitchell to verify that he'd asked certain questions of Byers during the interrogation in Corning. Now, he'd get the answers on the record.

Byers moved slowly to the witness stand. He spoke carefully as he described how he had given the folding knife to a member of the Creative Thinking crew as a gift in the weeks before Christmas. He knew the knife had been sent to the West Memphis police by Federal Express in early January. During his February session with Gitchell, Byers said he had "no idea how it could have any human blood on it."

But on the stand, his memory was restored. "Yes, I have an idea," he told Price. "I cut my thumb" preparing venison just before Thanksgiving.

"I might not have remembered it at the time when he was questioning me, but I could have remembered later on in the day."

Price also asked him about being called down to the police station on May 19—just two weeks after the murders. There, Detective Ridge tried to get Byers to own up to a role in the killings.

"Okay, what I want to say right now, what I'm going to say is that I may have information. This information suggests strongly that you have something to do with the disappearance of the boys and, ultimately, the murders," Ridge said.

Price asked Byers if he recalled his reaction to Ridge's statement.

"It seems to me that when he asked me that I got very upset and distraught and then he told me he just had to ask that to get my reaction."

After Byers testified, reporters asked him to confirm rumors that he had a brain tumor. His slow speech and movements, and the slightly misshapen side of his head, had betrayed a serious medical problem. Byers said the rumors were true.

Both defense teams rested their cases on Monday morning, March 14. Baldwin's lawyers told the court their client would not be taking the stand. Baldwin's lawyers called just one witness in his defense, a fiber-and-trace-evidence expert from the Southwestern Institute of Forensic Sciences in Dallas.

Charles Linch testified that the red rayon fiber found at the crime scene was not microscopically similar to fibers from a red woman's robe found in Baldwin's trailer the night of his arrest.

Davis and Fogleman were evidently surprised at the brevity of Baldwin's defense and dispatched police officers to locate and bring to Jonesboro several rebuttal witnesses. One of them was an amiable, very nervous assistant band director for the Marion schools. George W. Pokorski testified that the band played its big spring concert at the West Memphis Civic Auditorium on May 17. The testimony was critical because it effectively nullified the testimony of the twelve-year-old television-watcher. She may have been watching *Beverly Hills 90210,* but if it was just before the big band concert, Echols and his family had shown up at her house a week after the murders.

Paul Ford tried to elicit some sympathy for his client by asking about Pokorski's experience with Baldwin, who'd played a borrowed trumpet in the seventh grade. Pokorski said he'd shown some talent but never bought an instrument. By the end of the year, he was playing the school's drum set. Then he dropped out.

Burnett sent the jury home in the early afternoon with his usual admonition not to watch, listen to, or read news about the case, or talk to anyone about it. He warned them to tell their families that Wednesday was likely to be a long one, with closing arguments and their own deliberations.

But after the jury departed and the news media left to prepare for the evening's stories, prosecutors asked Burnett to delay the closing arguments and give them leave to introduce some new evidence that had come to light only after they'd rested their case.

The request required the circuit clerk to call jurors at home and tell them to take Wednesday off.

It would later turn out that on March 10, as Fogleman and the detectives were doing a last-minute review of physical evidence they might introduce, someone noticed tiny red spots on a pendant seized from Echols the night he was arrested. Thinking it could be blood, they sent it to the North Carolina genetics experts who'd been working on the case.

When court reconvened Thursday, the jury was sent back to the deliberating room as a hushed crowd waited to hear the state's argument for admitting the blood-spattered pendant. Test results showed the red dots were in fact blood, prosecutors told Burnett, and the blood turned up two sources of DNA—one consistent with Echols, and one consistent with both Baldwin and Steve Branch.

Burnett acknowledged that clearly, the two defendants' interpretation of this evidence would be antagonistic, especially since there was some suggestion the pendant had been worn at times by both of them.

Burnett told prosecutors that, if they insisted upon introducing the pendant, he would grant a mistrial for Baldwin, and Echols would face the jury's verdict alone.

Prosecutors asked for time to consult with the victims' families in a basement conference room. When they emerged, Fogleman told Burnett they'd forego the new evidence and move on to closing arguments.

It was up to the steady, now weary, Fogleman to stand before the jury and make his case. His voice was authoritative, folksy yet commanding.

To prove its case, he said, the prosecution had to show several elements.

"First, premeditation. All you have to do, ladies and gentlemen, is look at the nature of the injuries that these eight-year-old children suffered to conclude that there was premeditation and deliberation . . . Now you might say, 'Wait a minute. They had head injuries, they were beat up bad, drowned.'

"Think about it. You've got a kid whose got head injuries that are enough to be fatal in and of themselves.

"The left side of [one boy's] face—is practically gone. The other boy has his genital area removed. Now you say, 'Well, what if they just meant to hurt 'em bad or mutilate 'em.' Well, once they take one of those boys, and they beat him and give him injuries that would be fatal, and then they put him in that water, tied, where he can't do anything but go to the bottom, and he aspirates water, what do you think he's gonna do, no matter what the head injuries are? Use your common knowledge. What do you think he's gonna do? You think he's just going to sink to the bottom? Don't you think he'd be struggling, and thrashing to get some air? And once they've done one, when they see that they know, that he's still alive. And they know that puttin' them in that water is gonna kill 'em. And they've got the conscious object to cause these boys' deaths."

He paused. He turned to Narlene Hollingsworth, who said she saw him on the service road the night of the murders.

"We laughed, we all laughed. . . . They were dead serious. You don't pick your witnesses, and because they're simple, and they're not highly educated, that should be no reason to discount anything they said." And he asked the jury to consider that Damien could have been with Jason Baldwin instead of Domini that night, and he asked them to think about the night that Damien supposedly confessed to the softball crowd.

"You might ask yourself, 'Well, now wait a minute. We've got a crime scene that's clean. The killers were very meticulous about removing any evidence, hiding the bicycles, hiding the clothes, hiding the bodies. Why would he stand out there and tell everybody?' Well number one, who was he telling? He was telling the group of six or seven of his little groupies that followed him around.

"Remember, he said he dresses that way and everything to keep people away from him. But everywhere you look he's got little groupies hangin' around him. . . . You say, 'Still, why would he say that?' Remember when Mr. Davis was examining him about this manic-depressive situation? And in the manic phase you feel invincible? Nobody can touch you? Well, I submit, ladies and gentlemen, that in that manic phase, feeling invincible, he didn't care what you said. Why, he'd already been questioned by the police. Two or three times. They couldn't touch him, they couldn't touch him and he didn't care. Just like he told the police the killer didn't care."

Fogleman told the jury that the knife found behind Baldwin's trailer in the lake was similar to the knife that caused some of the injuries to Chris Byers. By innuendo, he called it the murder weapon. He asked the jury to closely examine the photos to make the judgment for themselves—to examine the knife to see if it matched the boys' wounds.

Deliberately, with the skill of a veteran prosecutor, Fogleman went over the fiber evidence, pointing out that fibers on one victim were consistent with fibers of a small shirt found in Damien's closet. He said of all the other clothing examined—retrieved from the victims' families, from the other suspects—that was the only shirt that matched the fibers on the boy's clothing. And he told the jury that the little fiber that matched the robe in Jason's closet was a critical piece of evidence—another link to the accused. And he refreshed the jury's memory about Michael Carson, quoting Jason as telling him about "sucking the blood from the kid's penis," and repeating Jason's supposed threat to get Misskelley because he "messed everything up."

Although the prosecution did not have to prove motive, it had little choice in a crime so heinous. To anyone with a conscience, Fogleman said, the motive was "inconceivable." And so he addressed it. He went into the "satanic" materials, which he said had nothing to do with Wicca.

"The reason to present it, is that to try to inflame you all, and make you all so angry, because it's something different, because it's something different and something we don't understand? Is that why we would present it? No, not at all.

"When you looked at those pictures of what was done to those three little boys, could you understand it? Could you have any reason to understand why someone would do that to three eight-year-old boys? Well, you've got three eight-year-old boys done that way, and you've got the defendants lookin' like choirboys during the trial . . . Well, think how hard it would be for you to conceive of typical teens doing what was done to these three eight-year-old boys. Now, I think you'll understand the need to put on this evidence.

"It's not something made up, it's not something dreamed up, it's not a figment of our imagination. It doesn't matter whether I believe it, whether the defense attorneys believe it, or you even believe in these concepts. The only thing that matters is what these defendants believe. . . .

"The testimony in this case was that these murders— when you take the crime scene, the injuries to these kids, the testimony about sucking of blood, and you remember there was testimony about that in the satanic areas, that blood is a life force, there is a transference of power from drinking of blood— when you take all of that together, the evidence was that this murder had the trappings of an occult murder. A satanic murder."

Fogleman talked about the history of religious killings in world history. He said religious motivations have often given people a reason to kill, in their own minds.

As he had done earlier, Fogleman then read to the jury "In the Middle," Damien's poem. He said Damien doesn't want to be on the good side, he "wants to be both." He "can go to the good side or bad side, however it fits his purpose."

"If he wants to be bad, he goes to the satanic side. If he wants to be good, he goes to the Wiccan side.

"Remember Mr. Price asking, probably Mr. Griffis, about is there anything that would motivate somebody to kill, about a spell about 'improving the memory' or about a 'love charm,' to 'stop bleeding,' to 'improve your chance of success', a 'cure for worms'? Are those evil? 'Well, no.' A cure for cramps— evil? 'Nah.' But he left out one, for some reason. 'Sacrifice addressed to Hecate.'

"I don't know why he left that out. Says in here, about, 'a friend and companion of darkness . . . you who rejoice to see the blood flow . . . wander among the tombs and hours of darkness thirsty for blood, and the terror of mortal men . . . look favorably on my sacrifice.' I don't know why he didn't read that to y'all."

His voice was soft and shaking slightly now. "You look at it together and you begin to see inside Damien Echols. You see inside that person. And you look inside there and there's *not a soul in there*.

"Not somebody that could commit this murder. And you see what is really there by his own writings— by *his own hand*.

"Now what shows all this? Anything wrong with wearing black, in and of itself? No. Anything wrong with the heavy-metal stuff in and of itself? No . . . But when you take the all-black, sucking blood, the tattoos— interesting thing about the tattoos. He testified he used a razor blade dipped in ink and tattooed a pentagram on his chest, an Egyptian ankh on his chest, and there was a cross on his hand, upside down depending on how you hold your hand. I submit to you it takes a certain degree of skill, and something else, to be able to take a razor blade and dip it in ink and do that to yourself."

Fogleman went to the issue of the police investigation.

"Were there mistakes made? Sure . . . There's never been anything done in this world where there haven't been mistakes made."

The real question, he said, is whether the mistakes really mattered.

Fogleman said police worked hundreds of hours, sending divers, draining water, walking shoulder to shoulder at the crime scene, but finding very little.

He said at least three different weapons were used. And, to poke a hole in the defense's theory of a serial killer at work, he said the knots were tied differently on the boys, suggesting multiple perpetrators.

Fogleman also ridiculed the defense notion that the murders could have been committed somewhere else. Aside from the logistics of kidnapping the boys— why hadn't anyone seen them abducted, why were there no vehicle tracks in the woods? (In the absence of tracks, he said, that meant someone had to carry the boys out of there without being seen, a virtual impossibility.)— he asked the jury to use its common sense about the idea that somebody would kidnap the boys, kill them, and bring them back to where people were looking for them. He talked about the portion of the bank that appeared sanitized— the mud was smooth and "shiny," he said, there were swirls on the ground. He mentioned the clothes stuck into the bayou bottom with sticks. Someone, he said, was covering up the crime—at the *scene* of the crime.

Then, the prosecutor had to address Dr. Peretti's conclusion that the time of death was between one and 5 A.M. The doctor, Fogleman said, was going by a single factor, "lividity"—or paleness of the bodies. That, Fogleman said, was the worst possible factor on which to base an opinion, and even the doctor admitted it was shaky.

Then Fogleman used a prop. Holding a grapefruit, he demonstrated the cutting action of the two crucial knives introduced into evidence. He apologized to the jury, saying they were again going to have to examine the photos of the boys' injuries. He showed that one knife—the state's, found in the lake behind Baldwin's trailer—would cut the grapefruit with a jagged pattern. First a cut, then a space, then a cut, then another space. That, he said, was the way Chris Byers was cut. But the defense's knife—the one tied to Mark Byers—was a straight edge and would have cut the grapefruit, and Chris Byers, in a straight line.

It was a brilliant tactical ploy. It didn't matter at that moment that there was no evidence to prove that the prosecution's knife was used in the cutting of Chris Byers—it seemed a better match than the defense's knife. And that made the prosecution's scenario more probable than the defense's.

Tired and wan, his voice faltering, Fogleman concluded simply. He asked the jury to go over all the evidence and to return a verdict against Jason Baldwin and Damien Echols.

THE BLOOD OF INNOCENTS

* * *

At the break observers could only imagine what the families were going through. After Fogleman's closing Jackie Hicks stood outside the courtroom and talked about the dead little boy, the family, and the case that had torn them apart.

In their closing remarks both defense teams would focus on their own lingering doubts, the inconclusive evidence and the police department's major miscues.

Val Price was a tall, solid, dark-suited figure before the jury. His face was pale and serious. He said the case showed four things: "Damien Echols tunnel vision; Damien Echols is kinda weird; third, police ineptitude; and fourth, no proof beyond a reasonable doubt."

Price said that despite Fogleman's comments, Peretti had said some of the injuries to Chris Byers were consistent with the Byers knife.

He would spend a lot of time on John Mark Byers.

In addition to Ridge's questioning of Byers, Price said, "We have the testimony of Mr. Byers's whereabouts that evening. He testified he left at one time to try to find Christopher, came back, then he left about eight-thirty. Of course he testified it was dark at eight-thirty. So what's he do when he leaves the house at eight-thirty? He leaves, still wearing shorts, still wearing flip-flops, still without a flashlight. Of course he leaves and it's dark, and then he says later on he went back. I think the questionable whereabouts of John Mark Byers is important."

Price's voice, unlike the consummate Arkansas drawl of Fogleman, was hurried. He seemed not as conscious as Fogleman was of making a connection with the jury.

Still, he made his points. In a scattershot closing, hitting on all the highlights of the defense's frustrations, Price told the jury that police had fingered the wrong people. He said the evidence suggested that a black male could have been involved in the killings. He cited the lost blood at Bojangles, the Negroid hair fragment found on the sheet used to transport Chris Byers to the crime lab. "Perhaps that hair matched up with the man at Bojangles. And that is certainly a reasonable doubt." And he also cited Gary Gitchell's own words, in the letter to the crime lab: "Is there any evidence of a black male involvement" in the crime?

Throwing out all the possibilities for the jury to consider, he said there were four types of knots used to tie the boys up. Could they have been truckers' knots? he asked. And there was a tennis-shoe print found at the scene. It didn't match Damien's boots. The crime scene was cleaned up—maybe—but maybe nothing happened there. There had to have been quite a struggle, yet there was no evidence of it, he said.

"Is there anything here at this crime scene, indicating an occult killing? Do you see any pentagrams out here? Do you see any nine-foot circles? Is there any indication whatsoever? Is there any indication the boys were killed out here?

"We have Dr. Peretti's testimony. He was asked about three possibilities. One, that the boys were killed in the water. That could explain why no blood was on this ground. He also testified that the injuries, particularly the injury to the penis, was very, very difficult even for him to do. He testified it would take him about ten or twelve minutes to do if you have somebody who's very familiar with surgical instruments, and he was in his lab doing that.

"Also, perhaps it took place on the ground. But there's no blood on the ground.

"The third possibility is that these murders took place someplace else. And that is not an imaginary doubt, that is a reasonable possibility of what took place in this crime."

Peretti's testimony concerning time of death, he said, hurt the state's case.

Next, he talked about the condition of the clothing. Though the pants were turned inside out, he noted, there were no tears or pulls on the clothing.

"Does that mean that the clothes were taken off in the presence of someone who knew the boys? That certainly is a reasonable possibility. . . .

"We had one pair of underwear that was found, two pair of underwear that was not."

He noted Griffis's testimony that sometimes a serial killer will take a souvenir.

Then he hammered the police again, pointing out that police left the stick, which had been used to stuff the clothes into the mud, at the crime scene.

"When the police went to the crime scene and found that particular stick that was wrapped around the clothing, what did they do with that stick?" His voice rose to a pitch of incredulity. "They left it at the crime scene. And it wasn't until not one, but two months later Detective Ridge went back out there and found that stick and I think found another one." And furthermore, he said, there was no proof that either stick, the sticks brought into the courtroom, was used in the killings.

Continuing the scattershot approach, Price said Damien's writings were strange, but had nothing to do with the murders.

"The whole part of a teenager, when you're growing up, in the teen years, is questioning things, questioning your religious beliefs, questioning your parental values. But just because you do that is not any kind of evidence of murder."

Picking up the picture of the goat-headed figure holding torches above its head, he admitted it was "weird."

"(It's a) strange-looking picture, but so what?" he said, sweating in the overheated courtroom and bright television lights. "It's still all right in America to have weird things in your room and it doesn't mean you're guilty of murder and it doesn't give any kind of motivation.

"It's not our job to prove what happened May fifth. It's the state's job, and they haven't done it."

Paul Ford, his blond hair shining before the documentary cameras, launched into an impassioned defense of Jason Baldwin. Though Ford had, perhaps, erred by not presenting much of a defense for Baldwin, he tried to make up for it by alternately preaching to and pleading with the jury to give his client justice. He told jurors to concentrate on all the evidence, particularly Peretti's testimony about the time of death and the statements of Anthony and Narlene Hollingsworth, who essentially placed Domini Teer in Baldwin's shoes outside the Blue Beacon truck wash. And, more than anyone else, Ford attacked the police investigation as inept, incompetent, and incomplete.

Addressing a point that Fogleman had made— that defense attorneys challenged every little thing about the case, even the paper bags that the boys' clothes were put in by investigators— Ford said the defense made a big deal out of the paper bags simply because the bags didn't have water or mud stains on them. Yet, he said, the boys' wet pants were dumped in them and kept there by police.

"That bottom's gonna fall out. There's gonna be dirt inside of it. There's gonna be water stains inside of it. And really, it's a worthless issue, it's not a point that really matters— *until they won't tell you the truth.* . . . Everybody has dealt with paper sacks that get wet, and the bottom falls out of them. You go to the grocery store and you buy hamburger meat and they put it in that sack and it drips out and before you get home it falls out. But these super bags, they don't take on water stains, they don't take on mud stains, and the bottom doesn't fall out of them. If they'll tell you something that silly on such a minor point, you begin to question their credibility. . . . The same officer whose paper bags are indestructible is the same officer who loses evidence."

His voice hinting outrage, Ford also questioned the existence of photographs supposedly made while Allen was searching for the boys. An officer testified that the pictures were made as a joke, taken as Allen was searching, in case Allen fell into the water. But Ford said officers searching for three missing boys in the woods shouldn't have much sense of humor. He suggested the photos were staged.

Ford charged that police didn't search the most obvious areas of Robin Hood for tire tracks— a crucial omission if the boys were kidnapped.

Making fun of police, he said, "Then, Officer Ridge hit the jackpot. 'I'll go back in July and find the murder weapon!' Take this stick," he told the jury, holding one of the clubs, "Take this stick. It's evidence. The bark just crumbles. Was there any of this on any of the injuries? . . . Yet that's what they want you to believe (that) this was the murder weapon."

And, he added, why were there no mosquito bites on the boys' bodies?

Then Ford gave his analysis of the murder. They were naked before they were tied up, he said; otherwise the tyings would have prevented them from being undressed.

"Are they injured at the time they're tied up? Makes no sense there either. Because there's . . . not a drop of blood on those clothes. So those boys are tied up, naked, and uninjured. And so all of this stuff that happens to them happens when they're naked."

His voice dropped a notch, as if suggesting a crucial truth. "And there's not a mosquito bite, not a one. And they were down there in that mosquito-infested woods, in that ditch, without a mosquito bite? That doesn't make any sense whatsoever."

Ford said the boys had no trauma inside the anus or inside their mouths, so there was no evidence of oral or anal sex.

He scoffed the most damning evidence presented against his client, saying Michael Carson's statement that he came forward about Jason's jailhouse "confession" because he had a "soft heart" was nonsense. "Where was his soft heart when he was stealing guns?" he wanted to know. And how could Jason, he wondered, have "spilled his guts" to Carson shortly after meeting him?

Then Ford went back to the police. "Inspector Gary Gitchell. He's in charge. But he's a nonexistent factor in this trial. He didn't tell you anything.

"One thing he told you was, 'The only reason we went to look for this knife was because the prosecutor told us to.'" And then, quoting Gitchell himself, " 'We're blindfolded. Help. We're blindfolded. *Help.*'

"It's very obvious why he didn't come in here and tell you anything. Because he doesn't know anything. And he's in *charge*. It was his investigation! We're walking through this case 'blindfolded'! He was under pressure. And when you are under pressure, you are going to make mistakes. . . . That's when you make mistakes, is when you let emotion, and sympathy, and pressure—the national attention was getting to him. And he's blindfolded. And this is a *week* before Jason's arrest."

He said that Narlene saw Domini on the service road, not Jason. And the reason he made fun of the prosecutions fiber evidence concerning the robe found in Jason's house—it was so small it could have floated in the air.

Griffis he dismissed with a single witty line: "He didn't go to college, he went to the post office."

And yet, he told the jury, even if they believed Griffis, there was absolutely nothing linking his client to the "occult trappings" of the murders.

Finally, appearing barely able to contain his anger, Ford questioned the prosecution's basic theory of the killings.

"It doesn't fit for a kid to bleed to death and not leave a drop behind," he said.

And that enigma, he said, led to this: "We can't figure it out. *It's a cult.* That's a scapegoat. They can't figure it out. There's no facts, there's no evidence. It's gotta be a cult, because they don't leave anything behind. I thought they left behind signs and pentagrams and crosses. That's talking out of both sides of your mouth."

He asked the jury to imagine criminals who would clean the bank of blood and debris, yet left behind a footprint. He said prosecutors concluded: "Let's call it a cult killing, and find somebody weird. Find somebody who wears black."

To Ford it didn't make sense. "Where's the other crime scene? Where's the blood? Where were they tied up away from mosquitos to do this delicate procedure that was done?"

Now finishing, he said, "When you play pin the tail on the donkey, you're blindfolded. And they turn you around and they give you the tail, and they say, 'Put it on the donkey.' And while you go up there and you try to find the right spot, everybody who's watching you is laughing at you. 'Cause you're sticking it on the nose, or on the foot."

He paused.

"They pinned this crime on the wrong boy because they were blindfolded and their evidence showed it."

Jason was guilty of nothing more than guilt by association, he said, his voice soft now. "Take the blindfolds off, and look at it for what it really is, and send Jason Baldwin home."

The jury retired at 4:59 P.M. Bailiffs ordered chicken dinners brought in.

As his future was being determined fifty feet away, Echols appeared nonchalant, rocking in his chair at the defense table. Each day, he had arrived at court with a sheriff's deputy on each side carrying a folder on which he'd written Pink Floyd in large letters. As the jury went away to decide his fate that Thursday evening, he granted an informal interview to reporters from *The Commercial Appeal*, *The Arkansas Democrat-Gazette* and *The Jonesboro Sun*.

For a man on trial for his life, Echols was relaxed.

And he retained his sarcastic streak. He said that, as soon as he was acquitted and released, he planned to move to Redding, California. When he got there, he said, he was considering getting a "mail-order PhD, and become an expert on cults."

Echols also joked that he didn't want the mother of his newborn son aware of the volume of letters he was receiving from young women interested in his case because "she'd kill me."

The jury worked until 10:35 P.M., then Burnett let them go home for rest. They'd return Friday morning, March 18.

Twenty-five

Where the Monsters Go

Anticipation had been building for hours. Gitchell, who threw his suit jacket off, exposing a leather side holster and 9-millimeter pistol, nervously smoked cigarettes on the sidewalk outside the courthouse. "The defense is using you guys," he muttered to a reporter, upset with the news coverage.

It was a bright balmy day, and reporters broke the monotony by tossing a football around the courthouse lawn. Others sat in lawn chairs lining a long row of television trucks topped with satellite dishes ready to transmit live coverage of the verdict.

Domini Teer, dressed in a black Harley-Davidson sweatshirt, black jeans, black nylons, and black pumps, stood among a circle of Echols's friends and family, all smoking, some drinking coffee. Joe Hutchison, wearing the same gray dress pants and blue button-down shirt he'd worn throughout the trial, hugged his little grandson, Seth, and kissed him. "No matter what happens, our lives will never be the same," he said.

Upstairs, Terry Hobbs leaned against a wall and talked about how tough the trials had been on the

THE BLOOD OF INNOCENTS 373

victims' families. Infighting had been a problem since the funerals.

For Pam and Terry Hobbs, little Steve's death triggered friction in their marriage. Pam left for a time to stay with her parents, but the pair would get back together and split a couple of times before settling down to put on a unified face at the trials.

Then troubles began with Steve Branch, little Steve's natural father.

First there was the pretrial fight between Branch and Pam's brother, Jackie Hicks, Jr. Now, in Jonesboro, Jackie Hicks, Sr., was telling reporters about Branch's past: He was convicted in 1981 of aggravated robbery with a firearm. A jury found him guilty that year for driving the getaway car on November 27, 1980, after two accomplices in ski masks held up the old Knight's Lodge restaurant in Marion. He served a year in prison.

The Hobbses claimed Branch never cared a lick for his son, and then began parading around like a concerned father after he died. Terry Hobbs claimed Branch was motivated, at least in part, by money. Donations raised by local churches helped pay for the funerals and the families' expensive trips to attend the trials. Branch said he didn't get any of the money.

But Hobbs said he was upset because Branch had made a play to get part of the Hobbs family's share.

"A lot of people are thriving on money in this. We have never asked for a penny," he said.

Branch denied the Hobbses' many charges. He was not after any money, he said, claiming it was the Hobbses who were the problem.

"I'm not the one jetting off to New York, *Geraldo* and *Inside Edition* for fame and fortune," said the broad-shouldered Branch. "They seem to have set aside what we're doing here. We're supposed to be here to see that justice is done for little Stevie and his two friends. But instead, for them at least, it seems that little Stevie has taken a back door to fame and fortune. Which I think is pathetic."

Waiting for a jury verdict can be a cathartic exercise. People found themselves pouring out their life stories to total strangers. Jackie Hicks, Sr., told how since the arrests, Hicks had returned to his fundamentalist Christian roots in the Assembly of God church.

"This Satanism business is real, it's very real," he said. "We're living proof of it."

The jury reached its verdict at 3:33 P.M., an omen, some said, that God himself was watching.

They'd deliberated for eleven and a half hours over two days. In the end, their verdicts came down to a few basic decisions. The jury weighed the evidence on large sheets of poster board paper.

First, they listed key witnesses. On a separate sheet of paper, they listed pros and cons. They had nothing negative to say about Sgt. Mike Allen, who discovered the first body. Bryn Ridge, who pulled the bodies from the water, was "honest," they noted, but he also had "left the stick" behind at the crime scene and "lost blood," the evidence at the Bojangles restaurant.

Michael Carson, who testified to Baldwin's jailhouse confession, was a burglar but he had "nothing to gain" and exhibited "courage," they noted. Occult-crime consultant Dale Griffis appeared "knowledgeable," they wrote, but also exhibited a "poor delivery" and "low self-esteem." The jury had only one thing to say about Anthony and Narlene Hollingsworth: "Honest."

On another sheet, the jury analyzed Baldwin. Pro: He was in school the day of the murders. He stuck to his story. He exhibited remorse. Con: "Damien's best friend, jailhouse confession, low self-esteem, fiber match . . ."

The jury's notes about Damien were even worse. His "pro" characteristics included his intelligence and his loyal family. His "manic depression" was also a characteristic listed in his favor. But under "con," the jury wrote that he was dishonest, manipulative, weird, and a "satanik (sic) follower." They said he had lied under oath and had "inappropriate thought patterns." In the same list, the jury wrote "blew kisses to parents" and "eat father alive." On a separate piece of paper, one of the jurors wrote, "You Are What You Think About!"

Echols and Baldwin were ordered to stand to hear the verdicts. When the jury announced them, no one was really surprised.

Echols and Baldwin were found guilty of three counts of capital murder.

The jury foreman signaled to Burnett that the panel was prepared to get on with the punishment phase right away and dispense with the case by the weekend. Burnett said that wouldn't be possible since both sides had a right to present evidence. The state would be arguing for the death penalty; the defense lawyers would be trying to save their clients' lives.

The jury had decided that the defendants had killed with premeditation and deliberation. Only death or the less serious sentence of life without possibility of parole were available to them. Burnett told the jury to reconvene in the jury box on Saturday morning.

Outside the courtroom, the victims' relatives and

both defendants' family members held impromptu press conferences, reporters scurrying between them.

"God did get His vengeance," said Pam Hobbs, facing the cameras. "I've gotta take a trip to a little boy's grave and tell him, 'We won.' Our God didn't let us down."

John Mark Byers, who'd had his share of courtroom torment, said he hoped Echols would die soon and meet the Devil. "If he wants to worship the Devil, and that's who his leader is, I hope he meets him soon."

Echols's mother said she'd been a witness to a horrible injustice. "The lives of three little innocent boys were taken and the West Memphis Police Department botched it up and they had to find somebody. So they take the lives of three more innocent boys."

Domini Teer ran sobbing to a waiting car.

"My son's been framed," screamed Baldwin's mother, Angela Grinnell. "I know Jason is innocent." Framed by whom? a reporter asked. She had no comment.

Gitchell and Ridge embraced in a bear hug, both in tears.

Nine months earlier, Gitchell had confidently said the case against Echols, Baldwin and Misskelley was solid. On a scale of one to ten, it was an eleven, he said. Then over the past couple weeks he'd seen that confident prediction shattered.

Everyone kept waiting for the eleven, the physical evidence that would shore up his prediction. It never came.

The best evidence involved about five fibers on the victims' bodies and clothing linked to Echols and Baldwin. The fibers were microscopically similar to fibers in clothing found in the defendants' homes but not exclusive to other clothing, a trace-evidence expert testified. In other words, the fibers could have come from any of a number of people who bought clothing produced from a single textile plant.

The prosecution linked one fiber to Echols through a child's size 6 Garanimals' T-shirt found in the search of Echols's trailer home. The shirt apparently belonged to Echols's eight-year-old half brother, but police contended the fiber could have transferred in a clothes dryer onto clothing Echols wore to the crime scene the day of the murder.

A single red rayon fiber was similar to fibers in a red bathrobe in Baldwin's house, but also was similar to fibers in an article of clothing in the Moore house.

Police also found a head hair that was microscopically similar to hair from Echols, but not exclusive to Caucasoid race. The hair also was similar to a resident in the nearby Mayfair Apartments, crime lab reports show.

The prosecution had no fingerprints, no blood, no semen, or any items that could corroborate Misskelley's statement. The sticks found at the crime scene and placed in evidence were consistent with the injuries the boys had suffered, but a Louisville Slugger would have been, too. The major reason for the lack of evidence, prosecution witnesses explained, involved the water the bodies lay in for hours. Water washes away semen and blood and dissolves fingerprints, which are nearly one hundred percent water.

Despite the struggle over the case, Gitchell said he was proud of his investigation and its results. "We knew our case. We felt it was strong. We knew our evidence was going to be not everything we wanted . . . They had time to get rid of a lot of items, and we knew that."

That night, Gitchell, Ridge, and other officers gathered at the Mallard Lounge, a $5-a-year members-only watering hole at the Jonesboro Holiday Inn, to celebrate over beers. They let their hair down. Ridge showed up wearing a Mickey Mouse T-shirt.

Gitchell made a special request of the disc jockey, joyfully singing along with the record and bobbing his head. "I fought the law and the law won," Gitchell sang. "I fought the law and the law won."

Echols's lawyers presented three witnesses during the unusual Saturday session of court held to determine the punishment for the now-convicted suspects. Echols's father, Eddie Joe Hutchison, and his stepfather, Jack Echols, both testified he'd had a troubled childhood. Hutchison said of his son: "I love him more than he'll ever realize."

They also called a psychologist to talk about his mental health. That strategic decision resulted in a windfall for prosecutors: It gave them an opportunity they otherwise wouldn't have had to present what amounted to the most damning evidence against Echols—his longtime practice of drinking blood.

The psychologist was James R. Moneypenny, who received an undergraduate degree in psychology and sociology in 1972 from the University of Northern Iowa, a master's degree in counseling in 1975 from the same school, and a doctorate in psychology from the University of Missouri in 1982. Moneypenny had a private practice in Little Rock and had interviewed Damien earlier in the year. The doctor also brought to court a packet of information about

Damien consisting of mental health, education, and medical records, including reports from other clinicians, which amounted to a profile of the youth.

"All right," Price asked him, "you have been able to form an opinion as to Damien Echols's mental state of diagnosis and also his overall psychological makeup?"

Yes, Moneypenny answered, he had.

"Okay, and would you explain that opinion to the jury and also elaborate on it?"

Moneypenny, in the calm, commanding style of a professional counselor, then launched into a lengthy examination of Echols and his basic motivations.

"Damien," he began, "suffers from a severe mental disturbance that's characterized by first depression and a history of alcohol abuse, and importantly, underlying that is a pretty disordered personality structure. And there is some unique— there is some unique aspects of his personality structure that I believe started back very early on in his upbringing.

"The particular characteristics— or I think the particular features of his personality have to do with what I call a pervasive or all-encompassing sense of alienation between himself and the world. In essence a sense of profound emotional restriction— a holding in of feeling and an inhibition of being able to express a lot of feelings that he has.

"And a related thing is, I think, a very painful sensitivity to things like betrayal, hypocrisy, lies, all things that might be hurtful or harmful to a person who's extremely sensitive as a result of what has happened to him.

"I think all of this goes back to what we refer to in my profession as a failure to bond as an infant. Ordinarily an infant will form an attachment or a bond with the care-giver, and as a result the infant will feel a sense of reassurance, a feeling of safety, a sense that his needs or her needs are going to be met. In the absence of that kind of bond or attachment developing, there's almost always a pretty significant disturbance in the functioning.

"What's unique in his case is how he reacted to that. I want to also say that the failure to bond or a failure to develop this attachment doesn't necessarily imply or mean that there was some kind of overt abuse or some kind of deliberate neglect. Sometimes this just happens and we don't know why. . . .

"A typical response to some of this when a child doesn't get these basic needs met is that they act out. They protest loudly. They become disruptive, sometimes unmanageable, sometimes out of control, together with a lot of emotional distress within themselves. It might be anxiety. It might be confused thinking. It might be depression. But there tends to be an acting out or disruptive nature.

"In contrast . . . what happened with him is he went inward. He withdrew and as he grew up, he withdrew and created in his own mind sort of a fantasy world.

"This withdrawal, I think, was an effort to pull away from what I think he perceived as a very dangerous, unnurturing, unsupportive world out there— not just within the family, but everyone else. He had a very transient lifestyle. They moved a lot. There were very few opportunities to develop close friendships, any kinds of bonds or relationships with people who could be supportive, who could identify and relate to him. Of course, this hurt him very deeply.

"But he was bright enough and he's very thoughtful and in his own mind he started answering— or attempting to answer a lot of the kinds of questions that all children ask. You know, who am I, why am I here, what am I going to do, where are we going, and asking the questions such as, you know, why is there unfairness? How come things don't always work the way they're supposed to? How come people get disappointed?

"Ordinarily children get— what we call corrective messagery. You know, you explain things to your children and you tell them how it can be okay, and you tell them how to survive and get along despite the world's imperfections.

"I think Damien missed a lot of that kind of thing. He was dealing with his own mind and he came up with his own value system where he attempted to come up with explanations. . . .

"But part and parcel of this coming up with solutions was a rejection of everything else out there. There was a rejection of other individuals' values— other people's ideas of how you ought to live life, of how to succeed and get along. He rejected that because he said that doesn't work. 'It didn't work for me. It doesn't relate to me. I'm not getting any of this.' So he just . . . kind of categorically rejected it and created a sense of deep alienation between himself and everyone else. And, of course, there is a lot of depression there as well along with this, I suspect, a lot of hurt and feelings that were never expressed built up, and I think he's full to the brim. I think he's very full of emotion so much so that it's overwhelming, and I think at times it was so overwhelming that he couldn't manage it, and I think at those times was when his depression was the worst and when he would feel alienated, or when he would feel enraged."

Though some on the jury might have viewed Moneypenny's opinions as psychobabble, Price was scoring the points he wanted—that Damien's behavior wasn't all his fault.

Moneypenny told Price that Damien did not fit the profile of the "antisocial personality" because of his tendency to withdraw rather than to become enraged. He was not, the doctor said, "a classic psychopath who's a thrill seeker and athletic and interested in doing anything they can without regard to how anybody else feels." He was, however, irrational and delusional at times, Moneypenny said.

"At one level he was angry at the world, but at another level, I think he recognized it. He, too, is part of the world, and has to account for it for himself. And I think in order to protect himself from that self-hate or what would ordinarily be self-hate, he developed grandiose, unrealistically powerful ideas about himself—almost godlike kinds of things. And I think this represents part of his fall into fantasy. . . ."

Moneypenny then quoted the defendant's words from a report taken by another mental health clinician. " 'Until I was twelve, I thought I was an alien put here from another planet. I wasn't never a little boy.'

"He made a comment one time. He said, 'I felt like a giant cramped into a tiny body.' These are not the typical kinds of things that you hear from teenagers, and you'll hear some pretty weird things from teenagers sometimes. It's a difficult time for them. But these things really reflect some very serious disturbances of identity, a sense of reality that reflects this flight into fantasy and borderline delusional thinking."

Moneypenny also said Damien's interest in Wicca—he consistently denied involvement in Satanism, the doctor said—was a method of trying to get some of the answers he had been denied as a boy.

Price asked him whether Damien fit the profile of the kind of person who could commit such horrible murders.

Sometimes, the psychologist replied, he felt uncomfortable with people he was examining—realizing they were capable of the most heinous deeds imaginable. Not so with Damien. "He doesn't fit that stereotype and doesn't—doesn't look like that sort of person," he said.

Moneypenny also said his evaluation of the defendant showed no signs of the manic-depression Echols claimed he suffered with when he took the stand in his own defense—though he did say that Echols was, at times, no doubt depressed.

Asked if he had anything more to add, Moneypenny reflected on a conversation he'd had with Damien about how Damien would raise his own son, if he had the opportunity.

"What he told me was, 'I would teach him that he was special, and I would teach him that he may not be the same, but that don't mean you're wrong.' And that's a real reflection of his own needs as well."

Price, noting that the jury had the choice between life and death, asked Moneypenny if he thought Damien could respond to treatment.

"Yes," Moneypenny said, "I do."

But on cross-examination, Fogleman lowered the boom. He hadn't had much time with the three-inch-thick sheaf of records, but he had found what he wanted the jury to hear. He asked Moneypenny to read other reports taken during Echols's stints with other mental health counselors.

But then Ford interrupted the questioning, fear-ing that the testimony he knew was coming might hurt Jason Baldwin. At a sidebar conference out of earshot of the jury, Ford told Judge Burnett, "We are totally and completely handcuffed and they are going to bring out statements about Damien making statements that he gets power from drinking blood, that there are sheep and wolves, and that the wolves eat the sheep, and that he is a wolf, and they are going to bring out statements about, I think a lot about, 'what happens after I'm dead because I want to go where the monsters go.'"

Burnett then told the jury to consider the testimony only as it concerned Echols, not Baldwin.

Fogleman then referred Moneypenny to Damien's commitment after telling his father he wanted to "eat him alive."

"You're familiar with the statement in the record where . . . it says the parents are concerned that he is also into Satanism or Devil worship?" Fogleman asked.

Moneypenny said he was. It wasn't lost on the jury that this meant Damien's parents had in effect contradicted his own claims that he was a Wiccan, not a Satanist.

The defense efforts to spare Echols's life fell apart. All doubts that police had the wrong man began to evaporate. Under Fogleman's guidance, Moneypenny read from an interview conducted by a health official with Damien just five months before the murders. There was the following exchange:

Moneypenny (reading): "'Reports that he thinks a lot about life after death. "I want to go where the monsters go." Describes himself as "pretty much hates the human race." Relates that he feels people are in two classes, sheeps and wolves. Wolves eat the sheep.'"

THE BLOOD OF INNOCENTS

Fogleman: "Thank you, Doctor. That would be he thinks a lot about life after death and he wants to go where the monsters go?"

Moneypenny: "That's what it says."

Fogleman: "And then are you familiar with the report from January twenty-fifth, 1993?"

Moneypenny: "Do you want me to read this?"

Fogleman: "Yes, sir, if you would read the part in pink."

Moneypenny (reading): " 'Damien explains that he obtains his powers by drinking blood of others. He typically drinks the blood of a sexual partner or of a ruling partner. This is achieved by biting or cutting. He said, "It makes me feel like a god." ' "

Fogleman: "It makes him feel like what?"

Moneypenny: "A god."

Fogleman: "A god. Okay. Go ahead."

Moneypenny (reading): " 'Damien describes drinking blood as giving him more power and strength. . . . He has also agreed to continue to discuss his issues with power and control as related to his practice of rituals.' "

Fogleman: "And then, finally, Doctor, are you familiar with the report where he was seen on January nineteenth, 1993? . . . If you would read this part."

Moneypenny (reading): " ' "I just put it all inside." Describes this as more than just anger like rage. Sometimes he does "blow up." Relates that when this happens, "the only solution is to hurt someone." Damien reports being told in the hospital that he could be another Charles Manson or Ted Bundy. When questioned on his feelings he states, "I know I'm going to influence the world. People will remember me." ' "

That was enough. Fogleman introduced the medical records as state's exhibit 500. He had turned

Price's attempt to save his client into a likely death sentence. On redirect, Price tried to undo the damage. Moneypenny cautioned jurors not to take these threats literally, to view the records as a whole. But most in the courtroom realized that Damien Echols's fate was sealed.

In his argument to spare his client's life, Ford said the state's own theory pointed to Baldwin being less involved in the killings. "Damien was the leader, Jason was the follower," he said.

But Davis told jurors that the case demanded the ultimate punishment.

"You're the conscience of this community," he said. "If there's ever an appropriate case for the death penalty, you've got it in your hands right now."

Fogleman, looking sad, said there was little more he could add. But he wanted them to go into the jury room thinking about Echols's own words: "I know I'm going to influence the world. People will remember me," he deadpanned. Then he dropped the heavy exhibition book on the prosecution table, and sat down.

The jury began its final deliberations at 2:04 P.M. and emerged two hours and twenty minutes later.

The courtroom was quiet. The decision was read.

The jury recommended Echols be put to death. Baldwin got life without parole.

Outside, a single protester picketed with a sign, Thou Shalt Not Kill.

Burnett turned to Echols and Baldwin. He first asked Baldwin whether he could give any reason not to carry out the sentences.

Baldwin said, "Because I'm innocent." They were

the only words he had spoken publicly during the trial. Burnett told him that twelve people had decided he was guilty.

In reply to Burnett's question, Echols, wearing a black T-shirt with a picture of a stallion and the inscription Running Free, replied, "No, sir."

As he was led away through the packed courtroom, Damien shouted to the crowd, "I'll be home soon." Someone in the second row of the victims' family members replied, "To your final resting place."

Domini Teer rocked in her seat, overcome with tears. There would be no wedding. No honeymoon in Redding.

Epilogue

A large billboard appeared along the interstate at the edge of Robin Hood Hills after the trials. Splashed in bright red and blue, it advertised the campaign of a rising star: Elect John N. Fogleman, Circuit Court Judge. By August, fresh from his victories in court, he was elected. His campaign advertisements urged voters to Elect a Circuit Court Judge You Know Can Make Tough Decisions in Tough Cases.

The end of the trials also brought change to the police department. Gitchell had put off retiring to work on the case. Now he announced he was leaving after twenty years on the force. Mayor Keith M. Ingram declared a Gary Gitchell Day. The forty-one-year-old detective took a job across the river as an executive with Pinkerton Investigation Services in Memphis.

By summer, all three convictions had been appealed to the Arkansas Supreme Court. All three defendants remained incarcerated in the complex of prisons south and east of Pine Bluff.

At last, local parents felt free again to let their children outside to play.

Yet the trials that terminated West Memphis Police case No. 93-05-0666 left many across the Mid-South unsatisfied. The fear that still grips West Memphis is that there has been no true closure, that the case was the beginning of something terrible that hasn't ended, and may never end. The bizarre twists and turns of the case, the shadowy cults, the police bungling, the dearth of physical evidence, the career-building pretensions, Mr. Bojangles, Lucifer, drug trafficking and undercover informants, and "nobody knows what happened but me"— plus dozens of still unanswered questions— produce a nagging sense that the case is still unresolved.

In May 1994 Judge Burnett lifted the seal on the police investigation files. It then became clear that, by itself, the tape recording in which Aaron says "nobody knows" simply wouldn't prompt any soul-searching. All Aaron Hutcheson said in his May 27, 1993, statement was that he knew more about the case than his friends, who knew nothing.

In context, nothing earth-shattering occurred. Ridge had asked: "Since this happened, and Chris and Michael were killed, okay, have you talked to any of your little friends that might know what happened?"

"Nobody knows what happened but me, out of all my friends," Aaron answered.

"But you know what happened?" Ridge inquired. The transcript of the interview shows whatever Aaron gave as an answer was inaudible. But he volunteered that his mother did not let him go down to the woods that day.

"Okay, what do you think happened to them?" Ridge asked.

"I think they was watching them men like . . .

like we always did, and they . . . they got caught and then they never told the men, and the men sorta killed them."

Aaron and his mother, Vicki, described a tree house where the boy and his friends often had played, but when Aaron took detectives back to the woods days before the arrests, "we discovered that the tree stand was no longer there," Ridge wrote in his report.

It remains curious why the "nobody knows" line would have so profound an effect on Misskelley. Vicki Hutcheson did tell the police on May 27, 1993 that Misskelley had written *FTW*— an abbreviation for Fuck The World— on her son as a tattoo. It suggested some ominous message. She testified she and Misskelley "became really close friends," but never clarified the relationship between herself, a thirty year-old former legal secretary, and Misskelley, seventeen and borderline retarded.

When the seal finally came off the police files, it became apparent Aaron had told police several things other than just "nobody knows." On May 10, 1993— four days after the bodies were found— Aaron told West Memphis police detective Diane Hester that when school let out the day of the murders, he last saw Michael Moore hopping into a maroon car driven by a black man with "yellow teeth" and "T-shirt with writing on it."

On June 2, 1993— a day before the arrests— Ridge conducted another tape-recorded interview with Aaron. He talked again about five men in Robin Hood who sat around a fire, did "nasty stuff," talked "in Spanish," and once cut a cat's head off and ate it. He said he didn't know any of the five men. Aaron said his tree house was a single board that he nailed to the tree.

On June 8, 1993—four days after Gitchell had announced the arrests to the entire Mid-South—Aaron gave another tape-recorded interview, in which he suddenly placed Echols, Baldwin, and Misskelley at the murder scene. Aaron told Don Bray that day in the Marion police station that he watched in the woods as the three defendants and two others he didn't know killed his pals. Aaron said Echols stabbed Steve Branch in the stomach, a wound not found on his body. Aaron also claimed that Misskelley told him, before the murders, "something" was going to happen to his friends.

Aaron told a similar story the next day in a recorded interview with Gitchell. Aaron said he, too, was tied up by the suspects.

"They didn't hurt you at all?" Gitchell asked.

"They couldn't hurt me, 'cause I kicked everyone . . . with foot, just like this." Aaron said his friends were tied up with a rope.

Case no. "666" amounted to a crescendo in America's satanic cult murder hysteria. In his confession that sent him to prison for life, Jessie Misskelley talked about a "cult," with seven to ten members, who he said passed around pictures of the three murdered boys at a meeting before the slayings. According to juvenile officer Jerry Driver, Damien Echols always maintained that an "older woman"—possibly in her twenties or thirties—had schooled him in the ways of witchcraft. And before his stories progressed into unbelievable horror tales, little Aaron Hutcheson maintained that the group of men with black-painted faces speaking Spanish in the woods consisted of five men, not just three.

If there is an occult component in these killings and the police just grazed its surface, there is still good reason to wonder if the crime was really solved. Legitimate leads raise disturbing questions and should demand a thorough examination of whether all involved were caught.

Unfortunately, the key police detectives—Gary Gitchell, Bryn Ridge, Mike Allen, and James Sudbury—all have declined to discuss details of the case pending disposition of the defendants' appeals. Making a few cursory remarks when the seal came off the investigation files after the trials, Gitchell said, "we looked and we looked and we looked" but couldn't link anyone else to the murders.

But not everyone accepts the official version. And for those who don't, two central questions remain: Did the police catch the right guys? Did they catch all of them?

Driving these musings is the scant physical evidence, the lack of convincing scientific explanations to neatly wrap up the case. The state never supported Gitchell's assertion that the strength of the case rated an eleven on a scale of one to ten. The evidence against Echols, Misskelley, and Baldwin yielded no fingerprints, no blood, no footprints, no saliva, no semen. In the end, four tiny fibers provided the weight of the physical evidence. The red rayon fiber taken from a boy's white polka-dot shirt found near Michael Moore's body was microscopically similar to fibers in a woman's red bathrobe in Jason Baldwin's trailer. A green polyester fiber taken from Michael's Cub Scout cap was similar to those in a blue cotton-polyester shirt in Damien's trailer. And two fibers—one cotton, one polyester—found on a pair of blue pants near Michael were similar to the shirt from Damien's trailer.

Neither the red bathrobe nor the shirt belonged to Jason or Damien. The bathrobe apparently belonged to Jason's mother. The shirt, a small boys

T-shirt, apparently belonged to one of Damien's relatives. Conceivably, the fibers could have been transferred onto the defendants when their clothes mixed with other clothing in a dryer. The fibers then would have been transferred onto the victims during the assault.

But there is nothing certain about this evidence. Fiber matches are not conclusive. Reviewing dyes and microscopic contours, the examiner can say— at best— that they are similar. But among people who buy clothing at Wal-Mart and other bulk retailers, it would not be uncommon to find matching fibers in many homes. A crime lab technician testified she examined three red cotton fibers at the crime scene that were similar to fibers from Damien's home, but they were also similar to fibers found in the Moore home. No fibers were linked to Misskelley.

In the absence of strong scientific evidence, speculation thrives. It goes something like this: The murders happened on the night of a full moon. Can it be mere coincidence also that the case number was 666 or that the bodies were found in a ditch that some kids called the Devil's Den? What of the West Memphis High School Blue Devils or Devil's Elbow in the old channel of the Mississippi? There were no overt occult symbols found at the crime scene, but an "occult crime" expert testified for the prosecution that the murders had the "trappings" of an occult killing. And the lack of evidence was, to some, *evidence* of a satanic cult obviously covering its tracks.

Caught in this void between intellectual dissatisfaction and wild speculation, Jerry Driver remains unsettled about the case. Nearly a year after the conclusion of the trials, Driver said he doesn't believe police caught all the killers; some got away.

"We always thought there were maybe five at the scene," Driver said. He thinks others were involved, in part, because several teens— perhaps as many as fourteen— seemed to know details of the murders within hours after the bodies were found. The reason three people were charged and convicted is because they were the ones Misskelley identified in his statement to police. But if there were others involved, why wouldn't Misskelley have named them? Driver suggested cult brainwashing could have played a role.

"I think they're still scared," he said. "Some of them are convinced these people had power over them, even after death."

Seventy miles up the road in the tidy city of Paragould, Arkansas, attorney Daniel T. Stidham remains deeply disturbed by the case. Despite the guilty verdicts, Stidham holds fast to his belief that his client, Misskelley, had been falsely accused.

"Every night when I go to sleep I think about my client sitting in the slammer for something he didn't do," Stidham said. "I'm haunted by it. I really believe it in my heart and soul. There's been nights when I wished he was guilty— so I could just let it rest."

Stidham says the case amounted to a major miscarriage of justice. But he does not expect the prosecution, or the police, to ever concede anything.

"To admit they screwed up would be a total and complete embarrassment," he said.

Misskelley made at least three documented admissions of guilt, two of them given with tape recorders running. Two of those statements also were made after he was found guilty and seemingly had nothing to gain or to lose. So why does Stidham hold onto his belief in Little Jessie's innocence?

"I believed Jessie was guilty in the beginning," Stidham said. For the first two to three months afte his arrest, Misskelley repeated the story he gave police. By midsummer of 1993, Stidham was working on a deal with prosecutors to give Little Jessie fifty years in prison in exchange for his testimony against Baldwin and Echols.

But, over time, Stidham noticed holes in Misskelley's story.

"He couldn't get it right. He got the boys mixed up. He kept insisting it was the blond-haired boy (Branch) who got castrated," Stidham said.

Misskelley's unsophisticated thinking apparently had prevented him from distinguishing between authority figures who were on his side and those who weren't. "He thought we were cops" at first, Stidham said. Because of that, Misskelley believed he needed to keep telling the story he had started, Stidham said.

Stidham is to argue on appeal that his defense was weakened when Burnett limited testimony from two expert witnesses. Dr. Richard Ofshe was allowed to testify about police interrogation techniques— but he was not allowed to discuss the exculpatory substance of an interview he had had with Misskelley.

Polygraph expert Warren D. Holmes had testified that Misskelley had gone along with police, but he was not allowed to discuss his analysis of Misskelley's lie-detector test. In Holmes's opinion, Misskelley did not fail the polygraph test that set up his confession.

Holmes said in a report to defense attorneys that false confessions often are triggered by invalid polygraph tests that cause investigators to become more assertive. People who falsely confess generally are of low IQ, like his client. Holmes's report cited the 1992 book, *In Spite of Innocence*, by Michael L. Radelet, Hugo Adam Bedau, and Constance E. Putnam, which purports to tell the stories of four hundred innocent people convicted of capital crimes in the United States.

Holmes also suggested that another factor was at play in the Misskelley case.

The reward offer, which exceeded $30,000, "adds a dimension not present in most suspected miscarriage of justice cases," Holmes's report said. "If Misskelley believed that his codefendants might be involved in the murders, based on their general reputation, he might have mentioned them as a gamble for the thirty thousand dollars. It's possible that when he started to play the duping game, he became an agent of his own victimization."

Stidham said Misskelley and his father both contend that West Memphis police sergeant Mike Allen had discussed the reward the morning he picked Misskelley up for questioning. According to Stidham, Allen told them, "You help us out, there's thirty thousand dollars in it for you."

During his testimony in Corning, Allen could not specifically recall discussing the reward with the Misskelleys, but he didn't rule it out, either. "If someone during that time period would have asked me, I would have told them whatever the reward was," Allen testified. "I would have told them 'Yeah, there's a reward available.'"

Stidham said police scared Misskelley "beyond belief" through tactics such as showing him a photo of one of the dead boys and playing the taped voice of Aaron Hutcheson. Short of any future explanations, the snippet "nobody knows what happened but me" appears to be a trick to provoke a response. Why it provoked the response it did also remains a mystery.

Misskelley never testified against his two codefendants, even after he was convicted, because the confession simply was not true, Stidham said.

"Jessie said, 'I just can't get up there and lie.'"

Stidham offers one other item to support his contentions. Police found only one pair of underwear that day at the crime scene, meaning that two pairs disappeared. That is evidence of classic "trophy taking" by a serial killer, he said.

"I'm convinced there's a killer running loose," he said. Most times, criminal defendants are guilty, Stidham said, which makes this case harder to swallow. "That's the nature of the game," he said. "It's been said a defense lawyer's worst nightmare is to have an innocent client."

Despite Stidham's impassioned assertions, there is evidence Misskelley told others his tale of murder before the police supposedly coerced him into a false confession. A fifteen-year-old Marion girl told *The Commercial Appeal* two days before Misskelley's confession was made public that she overheard Misskelley describing his participation in the murders a day or two before he was arrested.

"He was saying he hit the little boy and the little boy ran off and he was taking him back to where Damien and the other boy were," the girl told a reporter on June 5, 1993, the day after the arrests were announced. Two days later, *The Commercial Appeal* ran the first account of Misskelley's statement. Her comments appeared briefly in a companion story.

Spring came to Robin Hood Hills after the trials as it always had, lush and green. But now, two years after the murders, children often avoid the woods.

The owner's effort to clear and grade the land for some commercial venture was withdrawn. The woods remain. Wild lilies grow a few feet from the creek bed where the boys were found. A year after they were discovered, the tattered crime-scene tape warned all but the fearless or foolhardy from trespassing there.

And since the trials ended, two of the victims' families have had brushes with the law, and Echols's parents were questioned in connection with a murder case. Damien, too, even behind bars, had his run-in with authorities.

Damien was cited for having a shank, a contraband sharpened piece of metal, on Arkansas's Death Row on September 6, 1994, less than six months after his conviction, and he spent thirty days in isolation.

Since he's been on Death Row, Arkansas has held its first triple execution. Three men were put to death on the same night, one after another, for the same murder of a businessman who was killed before his wife and daughter. Echols later said he spent the night before the execution talking to one of the condemned men, trying to let him know he wasn't alone.

"It's strange," Echols said. "You can't believe they're dead. One minute you're standing there talking to them, the next minute you see them on TV saying he's dead."

Misskelley is in Pine Bluff, Baldwin at Varner. They have so far declined requests for interviews. The three complexes are close to one another, south and east of Little Rock.

John Mark Byers has had his own posttrial troubles. Along with his wife, he moved to Ash Flat, Arkansas, after the Jonesboro trial. He was charged in Sharp County in August 1994 when police found him in possession of stolen goods, including Oriental rugs and a life-sized cigar-store Indian. A hearing is scheduled for the summer of 1995. He was also later fined $161 for carrying a loaded weapon in Fulton County, Arkansas.

Things got worse for Byers. On January 13, 1995, he was convicted of contributing to the delinquency of a minor. Byers was accused of standing by while two juveniles engaged in a fist fight; one reportedly was beaten into unconsciousness. Byers was sentenced to a year in jail, with nine months suspended. He's appealing the judgment.

Pam Hobbs, her husband, and her father appeared on an August 2, 1994, tape-delayed edition of *The Maury Povich Show* with Byers and Vicki Hutcheson, where they traded accusations and insults. Vicki insisted that Aaron had told the truth about the murders. Byers, in his last national television appearance before his arrest, said Aaron was lying when he said he saw Byers at the scene. Povich asked Byers if Vicki was entitled to any reward money.

"If she's entitled to the reward money, what are the victims entitled to whose sons they can't hold and talk to anymore? I can't love and see my child and hold him. In two days, he would have been ten years old. On the twenty-third of this month, my son would have been ten. He'll have a birthday, but it'll be in heaven, not here on earth. I can't make him a birthday cake. I can't buy him another bicycle. I can't take him fishing. So she's entitled to a reward for whatever she helped do, whatever part it might be. What are the victims entitled to? Because we found out we didn't have any rights."

Vicki told Povich she never sought any reward money.

Terry Hobbs, Steve Branch's stepfather, was accused of shooting and seriously wounding his brother-in-law, Jackie Hicks, Jr., in early November 1994. Hicks was the brother-in-law who took after Pam Hobbs's first husband in a pretrial courthouse confrontation. Terry Hobbs was charged with aggravated assault.

Following his conviction, in an interview with WMC-TV reporter Rod Starns, Echols described his life on Death Row as tolerable. He had his books and his correspondence, he said. When Starns asked him about the blood-drinking, Echols replied, "I can't say I drank blood. I licked it." And he stuck out his tongue to demonstrate.

Echols told Starns that he had always wanted to be famous.

"At one time in my life, I wanted to be remembered. I wanted people to know who I was. Ever since I was really small, I always had this feeling that one day, people are going to know me. I never expected it to be like this."

Echols said his troubles had forced him to lose faith in God and in Satan, in heaven and in hell. "During my appeals, I am requesting that my death sentence not be converted to life without parole. I would rather be executed than spend my entire life here. What are they going to say when they found they killed an innocent man? Because 'oops' ain't gonna be enough."

When the execution comes, he said, "Sometimes I want it to be painless. But then sometimes I would want it to be painful, just to represent my life. My life has been very long, drawn out, and painful. Why should my death be any different?"

Trouble has continued to follow Echols's family.

On a cool September night in 1994, Joe, Pam, and Michelle joined a party of revelers drinking beer around a bonfire on the sandy west bank of the Mississippi River. Two shots rang out, and a man collapsed into a willow thicket. When authorities arrived on the scene, it didn't look good for the Hutchisons: The murder weapon was Pam's .22-caliber revolver. A deputy found the gun where Michelle had tossed it into bushes near the crest of the bank.

The drums of hysteria were beating once more. A newspaper reporter was told the shooting was a cult killing executed while a circle of Satan's minions chanted and danced devilish jigs around the fire. "Do it, and do it now!" a cult leader supposedly commanded. One of Satan's supposed foot soldiers then pumped two bullets into thirty-five-year-old Richard B. Ellison of West Memphis. The satanic clues of the crime were not lost on one tipster who noted the date, September 9, 1994— 9-9-94 in shorthand. Turn that upside down and the first three digits read 666. And the four? Victim four?

But police say the occult angle doesn't pan out.

Still, law-enforcement officers responding to the shooting call that night had their suspicions. Under the dim light of a slivered early moon, sheriff's investigator John L. Murray did a double take. There stood the familiar, slouched figure of Joe Hutchison, his robust ex-wife, Pam, and young Michelle. Officers began scanning the riverbank, searching for circles of stones, graffiti— anything that might suggest a cult connection. They found a couple of ice chests filled with beer.

Testimony at a probable cause hearing three weeks later indicated Ellison was killed as he and another man battled for Pam's affections. Joe, Pam, Michelle, and two other witnesses told Judge Rainey in West Memphis Municipal Court how Ellison and his accused murderer, Bryan J. McFadden, twenty-seven, had feuded that night. Pam, thirty-five, testified she had had amorous relations with both men—and at the time of the murder was living with both of them at Lakeshore Trailer Park.

"Both these men were living with you in your trailer?" Judge Rainey asked somewhat incredulously, leaning toward Pam in the witness chair.

"Yes, sir," she answered, her large dark eyes meeting Rainey's with a coolness characteristic of her clan. Pam explained that she and Joe had divorced again, ending their second marriage. She had been seeing Ellison, but in the weeks before the murder, had turned her affections to McFadden. McFadden moved in, but Ellison also rented a room from her, she said. Joe was friendly with Pam and her beaus.

Bryan McFadden later pleaded guilty to manslaughter and received a sentence of ten years in prison.

In rural Shelby County, east of Memphis, what's left of Christopher Byers lies beneath a pink granite slab—A Little Lamb of God, the marker reads. Michael Moore is buried west of the courthouse in Marion, the only victim who remains in Crittenden County, or in Arkansas. Steve Branch lies beneath a large gray tombstone marker in Steele, Missouri, just about as far from Interstate 55 as he was when police found his body in Robin Hood. A Rosebud In The Flower Garden Of Heaven, his epitaph reads.

In the month of May, shortly after the trials, near the noisy playground of Weaver Elementary School, a reading grove was dedicated to the memory of Michael Moore, Steve Branch, and Christopher Byers. A memorial stone was placed where three seedlings had been planted by the little boys before they died. Their Cub Scout troop dedicated the area in a solemn ceremony.

The plaque says simply, Do Your Best.

On the day before Halloween in 1994, Pam Hobbs went out to the monument for a few moments of quiet time. She had just picked up five-year-old Amanda from her grandparents' house in Blytheville, Arkansas, and stopped by the reading grove on her way home. There on the stone someone had scrawled a sideways cross and the numbers 666. She broke down.

Terry Hobbs's sad incredulity was in the next day's paper. "It's still going on. Believe it or not, there's a satanic group in West Memphis . . ."

Postscript

The maximum security prison at Tucker, Arkansas, sits in a wide, open field in rural Jefferson County, rising like a giant monolith from the flat countryside. A block of nearly windowless brown brick, the dreary structure is surrounded by a tall chain-link fence, razor wire and miles of nothing. Escape is rare. The prison lacks the notoriety of better-known southern rural prisons like Parchman in Mississippi or Louisiana's Angola, but Tucker is every bit as daunting.

Here, after a year on death row, Damien Wayne Echols claimed he had been repeatedly raped and beaten over several months. Echols pointed a finger at fellow death-row inmate Mark Edward Gardner, a 34-year-old ex-drifter convicted in 1986 for strangling three people to death in Fort Smith, Arkansas.

Echols pleaded for help in letters to Governor Jim Guy Tucker and others, claiming Gardner was receiving drugs and favors from prison officials.

"I was raped repeatedly, forced to perform oral sex, beaten repeatedly with leather belts, shoes, closed fist, open hands, and kicked in various parts of the body, including chest, stomach and genital area," Echols said in a March 15, 1995, letter to anyone who would listen.

"The same inmate also has taken pictures of me in states of nudity and semi-nudity, and on one instance made a tape recording. The pictures and tape recording were given to someone on the outside who's (sic) name I do not know. I could tell no one, because severeal (sic) high ranking officers were already aware of the fact, and would do nothing to prevent it. On a regular basis, Mark Gardner would be taken to the front offices of people of authority, and would come back to the barracks drunk or under the influence of drugs, and inform me that if I were to ever attempt to tell anyone, he would end my life, and often made the statement that, 'You won't have to worry about an execution date, because I'll kill you first.'"

By April, Echols' allegations were being investigated by the state Department of Correction and the Arkansas State Police.

And, suddenly, Echols was granting media interviews.

It started with an April 11 interview with *The Commercial Appeal*. Looking haggard and pale as ever, Echols elaborated on his allegations. He described Gardner as an inmate above the law. Echols claimed Gardner planted the shank in his cell the previous fall, conspiring to put Echols in isolation for 30 days.

"He comes talking about, 'I can have anything done in here I want done. There's nothing you can do about it. I'm in charge here.' All this kind of shit. 'I can have anything done I want to and I put that knife in your cell and you ain't going to do nothing about it.'"

Echols sipped a can of diet Dr. Pepper, cupping the drink with both hands, his wrists confined by handcuffs. His fingernails were long and white. The letters E-V-I-L were tattooed on the knuckles of his left hand, the second coming of a homemade tattoo that mysteriously had disappeared at his trial.

Now twenty years old, Echols wore his hair long and ratty. The cocky sneer he had flashed to spectators throughout much of his trial seemed in check now, yet, when it came, it was still intimidating on that hollow face.

His moods alternated between boyish enthusiasm, bitter sarcasm and morbid self-destruction, depending on the subject. He no longer was on medication, he said. He claimed he's leveled out emotionally. Still, suicide remains tempting, he said.

"Every once in a while, you know, you'll look up here and think about maybe breaking a light bulb and swallowing the pieces or something," he said with a snicker. "Anything to get the hell out of here. Basically I'd say I feel better (without the medication) . . . I don't have near as many depressed days. I have more energy."

Echols said he spends his days here in solitude, rarely venturing outside for daily two-hour yard privileges.

He reads a lot, often re-exploring the works of his favorite authors, horror writers Stephen King and Anne Rice. He says he's writing a book, but he won't say what it's about.

He watches TV (his favorite shows are *The X-Files* and *Tales From The Crypt*), listens to an alternative rock music station out of Little Rock and opens mail that still comes in volumes— at least 100 to 150 letters a week, he said.

And every week or so, he said, he gets a letter from

Paul Morrison, the former Memphis TV reporter who lost his job covering the West Memphis murder case.

Throughout most of the interview, Echols spoke in a soft, flat voice, so low at times a visitor had to press an ear up to a grid in the thick protective glass that separates inmates and guests in the prison visitor center.

Yet Echols' voice raised a notch as he described his abuse, accusing prison officials of complicity in the crimes against him.

"I can't wait for what these stupid son of a bitches done to catch up with them," he said, his dark eyes flashing anger. "The prosecutors, they were just doing their job, you know. They get paid to try to convict, using whatever means possible to do it. These idiots don't get paid to do what they do."

After he returned from solitary confinement, Echols said, he was moved into a cell adjacent to Gardner's. A cement block in the wall had been loosened free. That gave Gardner access to Arkansas' youngest and most infamous death-row inmate.

"When they put me in there, part of the wall was missing— they knew that. That's why they put me in there," he said. Echols pointed toward a nearby cinder-block wall to illustrate his point. A concrete block had been removed, he said, the hole enlarged by chipping at the blocks around it.

So, Gardner squeezed through the hole and entered your cell? the visitor inquired.

No, Echols said, "I went over there."

Why?

"Because he told me to. He's already set one guy on fire and threw boiling water on another guy. Chased one guy down the stairs and tried to butcher him."

Echols estimated he had been beaten and raped

in this manner at least forty times over the past several months.

Department of Correction spokesman Alan Ables declined to discuss specifics of the investigation, but confirmed there was a hole in the wall between the cells. An 8½-by-14-inch cinder block had been removed, Ables said.

"We're looking at a lot of things back there right now . . . throughout the unit, not just in (death row)," he said.

But Echols, troubled as he was over his loss of prison innocence, feared even greater indignities. Like the loss of his life, for starters.

As he has done from the start, Echols said he was innocent of the murders of Steve Branch, Christopher Byers and Michael Moore.

Echols blamed his death sentence and conviction on mass hysteria and a mad rush to judgment. There's nothing unusual here— claims of innocence by convicts are standard. But given the great void of evidence in this case— and developments since the trials— Echols' contentions may merit another look.

In perhaps the most startling development, one of the prosecution's star witnesses now was beginning to look either totally confused, a liar— or both.

Six months after she had thrilled jurors at Jessie Misskelley's trial with her tale of visiting an outdoors witches' meeting with Echols and Misskelley, Victoria M. Hutcheson told an entirely different story to attorney Dan Stidham and a private investigator working for Misskelley's defense.

In a tape-recorded interview on August 17, 1994, with Stidham and Memphis investigator Ronald L. Lax, Hutcheson said she wasn't sure whether the witches' meeting in a Crittenden County woods actually happened or whether she imagined it. Hutcheson had testified that, while "playing detective," she went to a "satanic esbat" one night between the May 5 murders and the June 5 arrests with Misskelley and Echols.

But in an interview at Lax's office in downtown Memphis, Hutcheson seemed sure of just one thing: On the night of the supposed satanic esbat, she was performing a disappearing act with a couple bottles of Wild Turkey bourbon.

Hutcheson stopped short of admitting she had committed perjury— she just wasn't sure anymore, she said. She said she had just broken up with a boyfriend that night, so she drowned her sorrows in two bottles of Wild Turkey 101. Straight.

She woke up the next morning with a hangover, flat on her back in her yard, she said.

"I had one fifth that had already went down me and I was drinking a fifth," she said.

"I was falling down drunk and laying out in the next morning in the grass with the— with a, um, Wild Turkey bottle," according to a transcript of the interview made public this year. ". . . I'm not sure where I— I'm not sure what happened that night, period."

In the interview, Hutcheson hinted that her use of the anti-depressant Prozac may have really skewed her sense of reality that night.

"I can't handle my liquor at all because I'm on Prozac and you can't combine the two," she said. Hutcheson said she also takes Xanax, a central nervous system depressant.

Hutcheson said she had begged her therapist before the Misskelley trial to ask the prosecutors not to put her on the witness stand.

Sobbing frequently, Hutcheson wondered out loud whether she might bear responsibility for three false convictions, saying at one point, "I'm upset. I'm, because, by God, if I, if it's my fault, we'll get it straightened out."

Hutcheson's importance to the investigation and case against Echols, Baldwin and Misskelley should not be underestimated. The police investigation had sputtered aimlessly for 3½ weeks before Hutcheson told them about attending the cult meeting in the woods. At last, they had a link supporting the Echols/Satanism theory.

When asked to name Echols' associates, Hutcheson told them about Misskelley, who had become a close friend of hers since she had moved into Highland Trailer Park. When police picked Misskelley up for questioning six days later, he told the story that sent him to prison.

In the interview with Lax and Stidham, Hutcheson said Misskelley had joked before his arrest that he would tell police he committed the murders if he was ever questioned. Hutcheson said she's sure this happened because "I was in my right set of mind that day."

"I about died" when Misskelley made his joke, Hutcheson said. "Because he goes, 'I'll just tell them I did it.' And I said, 'No you wouldn't. You stupid? what's wrong with you, boy?' And he started busting out laughing and he was like, 'It was a joke.'"

And Hutcheson apparently had more riding on the murder investigation than just finding the killers. She told Stidham and Lax the police had offered to help her with hot check charges she faced in northwest Arkansas.

In short, she indicated she might simply have been swept up in the hysteria surrounding the murders.

"I was trying to catch Damien. I was trying real

hard. And that—and they (the police)—had me so convinced that they were guilty."

As for Echols, he insisted he attended no witches' meeting with Hutcheson.

"It's a lie," he said. "A flat lie."

Echols bristled at Hutcheson's early accounts, including her suggestion to police that Echols was romantically interested in her.

"She lied about everything. I mean, why would I want anything to do with her?" he said with a hearty laugh.

Echols agreed that Hutcheson seemed to be conducting her own personal investigation in the weeks between the murders and the arrests. He said he received a phone call from Misskelley one day at Baldwin's trailer asking him to come over and meet someone. Echols said he ignored the call.

But then Misskelley and Hutcheson showed up at the door, he said, asking him to go with them to Hutcheson's trailer.

"And he kept saying, 'Come on, just for a few minutes.' 'Naw man, Domini will be looking for me. I'll get in trouble with that shit,'" Echols said he told Misskelley. But when Misskelley insisted, Echols went.

"We just sat around talking for a few minutes," Echols said. "I said probably no more than ten words to her in the whole time I was there."

Echols emphasized another point. Although he and Jason Baldwin were close friends, he had little patience for Jessie Misskelley. They seldom associated.

"Two things that I don't have time for is stupidity and ugliness. And Jessie Misskelley had both those qualities," he said coldly, then snickered.

So why did Misskelley tell this story to police?

"Well, he's mildly retarded anyway," Echols said. "If they put the kind of pressure on him that they did on me, I know that there's no way that he would stand up to it.

"I mean, I was wanting to confess and I didn't even do nothing. They would play these little games with you. One of them would come in and be real nice to ya, and the next one would come in all up in your face, screaming and yelling, 'You little bastard, we know you did it! You're going to fry for this!' I know if they were all over Misskelley like that, if he was even mildly retarded, he would have broke down and said yes no matter what."

New questions had arisen about the central piece of evidence against Jason Baldwin—his supposed jailhouse confession to the murders, which included the claim he'd sucked blood out of the penis of one of the victims.

That testimony by 16-year-old Michael Carson, a convicted burglar and LSD user, sealed Baldwin's fate.

But in January 1995 Baldwin received a letter from a counselor who worked with Carson. The counselor, Danny Williams, told Baldwin he believed Carson had made the whole thing up, simply parroting rumors he had heard from him.

Armed with news of the developments, Echols said the evidence pointed down an old trail—back to John Mark Byers, the stepfather of Chris Byers.

The persona of Damien Echols—defiant, arrogant, irreverent, dark, gloomy, boastful, manipulative—is the reason he now sits on death row, he and his supporters claim. It has nothing to do with guilt or innocence, they say.

With keen precision, Echols spelled out his theory. It all began in 1992 with juvenile officer Jerry Driver, he said. Driver was investigating "teen satanism." Echols boastfully sold himself as both a practitioner and local expert. When local graves were robbed or dead animals were found around the charred remnants of bonfires, Driver turned to Echols as an informant who could provide explanations.

Echols said he was more than happy to mess with Driver's mind.

"He would twist shit up," Echols said intently. "He goes, 'Well, say all these animals that we find dead are animal sacrifices. If that's true what would the next step be?' I said, 'Human, I guess,' you know. 'If they're going to kill animals now, they'll probably . . .' They twist it and make that out of it.

"Do you remember a few years ago, that girl that got murdered in Lonoke County?" he asked, referring to the 1991 knife slaying of fourteen-year-old Amy Childree. The girl was knifed to death in a rural cemetery in a murder that the local sheriff said was "carried out with ritualistic trappings."

Echols said Driver questioned him about the murder even though it occurred about one hundred miles west of West Memphis." 'We know you know something. Tell us now.' That's like, what, two or three counties over? How old was I then? 15, 16. I'm like a serial killer at the age of 14," he said sarcastically.

Contrary to Driver's claims, there was no "older woman" who led him into satanism, according to Echols. There was no cult, no animal sacrifices. Sure, there were kids dabbling with magic and witchcraft. And there were bonfires and late-night parties, he said.

But Crittenden County's underground satanic society and its would-be teen minions were purely a figment of Driver's active imagination, Echols contended.

"You know, they always say you should be careful when you do this kind of stuff because you don't want to see satanists behind every bush and rock. But that's exactly what they do," he said with a laugh. "It's pathetic."

Responding to Echols' assertions, Driver said he was flattered that the convicted killer thought so much of him.

"He thinks I'm the guy who put him in jail. I'm not. Damien put himself in jail," Driver said, dismissing Echols' claims.

"All I was doing was investigating the occult," Driver said. "He downplays it now, but when the stories were circulating, he promoted them. I know he drank human blood, or put it in his mouth. At the time, I had many people tell me about that.

"He thought he was smarter than the whole world, and would tell you so . . . He thought he was smart enough to deal with all these things and not be affected by them. That's why he called himself a gray witch."

Rehashing his "investigation of the occult" in the summer of 1992, Driver told again how he searched for the mysterious figure Lucifer.

"That's a name that just kept popping up," he said. "We heard Lucifer is behind this cult or that cult." Another name that kept popping up was Damien Echols. Driver paid particular attention following Echols' arrest in the trailer a year before the murders.

Driver said he continued to return to Echols, seeking explanations. Driver and fellow juvenile officer Steve Jones got an earful of strange tales from Echols.

"He claimed that he found this coffin floating down this bayou and that he took it home with him," Driver said, recalling a conversation Jones had had with Echols. "Everything weird that happened was attributed to Damien. I did not think he did all of it."

Sensing that Echols now may be turning the tables on him, making Driver seem the lunatic, the juvenile officer finds himself on the defensive.

"I don't think everyone that's not a hard-rocked Baptist is a satanist," said Driver, an Episcopalian by faith.

Driver agreed he once questioned Echols about the Lonoke murder, but said Echols misrepresented the nature of the visit.

"He was never a suspect . . . they knew who did it," Driver said. "We always figured the more we talked to him, the more we could figure out what he's up to."

Driver also said he initially could not get the West Memphis Police interested in considering Echols a suspect in the Robin Hood Hills murders— at least not for the first few days of the investigation.

"When it first started, we had a hard time getting them to look at them," Driver said. "They thought, 'Here's the juvenile officer, foaming at the mouth again.'"

But as time goes by, the juvenile officers' occult investigation becomes more and more interesting.

In interviews with *The Commercial Appeal* in the spring of 1995, authorities revealed for the first time that Steve Jones was present in Robin Hood Hills when the bodies were found. The official version about the discovery of the bodies had previously relied on West Memphis police Sgt. Mike Allen's account that he found the bodies when he fell into the creek as he reached for some clothing floating in the water.

"I was pointed out— observed what appeared to be two small tennis shoes floating in the creek," the Misskelley trial transcript quotes Allen's testimony.

There was no mention at the trials of Jones' presence at the crime scene, but Jones and Allen both said in later interviews that he was there.

Jones said he was in the woods assisting the search when he saw the clothing in the water. Most of the people searching that day missed the clothing because one had to stand right at the edge of the bank and look straight down, Jones said.

"I found the boy scout cap," Jones said, saying he then radioed Allen for help. "I felt like they had been out there swimming" and drowned.

In a brief interview, Allen said Jones and Denver Reed of the Crittenden County search and rescue squad were both present when he entered the woods. "I don't know that it was him (Jones) or Denver that actually saw the shoe," Allen said.

Numbed by the horror he'd witnessed in the woods, Jones took a police detective to Damien's trailer the next day. After investigating teen satanism the past year, Jones said he suspected Echols knew something about the murders.

Inside the trailer, Jones said he saw a pair of tennis shoes and Echols' black boots, all caked in mud— again, information that never came out at the trials.

"What am I, a dang fool?" Echols said, when told of Jones' contention. "The tennis shoes did have mud on them, the boots did not. I kept the boots in perfect condition because they were always what I wore when I went out. The tennis shoes I didn't care anything about, when it was raining or something like that I would wear them out to keep from messing my boots up."

By Echols' account, the entire case was a series of blunders, a big Catch-22.

He failed his lie detector test because he suffers heart palpitations and police got him excited, he said. An officer testified Echols said he'd tell him "all about" the murders if he could speak with his mother first—but that was just a clever trick that came back to haunt him, Echols said.

"He twisted my words. I said I'll tell you everything I know," which was nothing, Echols said. "You see, they kept me up there for hours and hours, wouldn't let me eat anything, drink anything. I said, 'All right, I'll tell you everything I know, but I want to talk to my mom first.'"

When his mother showed up, "They all ran in with their video cameras and tape recorders. 'All right, tell us everything you know,'" Echols recalled with a laugh.

The verdict was in even before the trial started, he said, explaining his odd behavior and defiant attitude. There is just no way to defend oneself from these types of attitudes and allegations, he insisted.

"What could you do? Jessie sits there with his head down on the floor. He's guilty. Jason sits there like he's in shock, you know. Won't make anybody's eye contact. He's guilty. I sat there and looked people straight in the face. I'm guilty. What the hell else is there left?"

And yet, for all his common sense analysis of the hysteria and bias leading to his death sentence, Echols still has a hard time accounting for his whereabouts the day of the murders.

"I can't remember everything, it's been so long ago," Echols said.

But whether he's eventually executed, or whether he's someday proven innocent, Echols said he has a plan.

When he dies, he doesn't want to leave this world—not immediately, anyway.

"I would like to stick around for a while, just sort of hang around after I was dead," he said. "Usually they say that most of those times when someone hangs around like that it's because they died like a violent death or when they weren't supposed to, or something.

"I guess I just want to hang around awhile."

HORRIFYING TRUE CRIME
FROM PINNACLE BOOKS

Body Count
by Burl Barer   0-7860-1405-9   **$6.50**US/**$8.50**CAN

The Babyface Killer
by Jon Bellini   0-7860-1202-1   **$6.50**US/**$8.50**CAN

Love Me to Death
by Steve Jackson   0-7860-1458-X   **$6.50**US/**$8.50**CAN

The Boston Stranglers
by Susan Kelly   0-7860-1466-0   **$6.50**US/**$8.50**CAN

Body Double
by Don Lasseter   0-7860-1474-1   **$6.50**US/**$8.50**CAN

The Killers Next Door
by Joel Norris   0-7860-1502-0   **$6.50**US/**$8.50**CAN

Available Wherever Books Are Sold!

Visit our website at **www.kensingtonbooks.com**.

MORE MUST-READ TRUE CRIME FROM PINNACLE

Under the Knife　　0-7860-1197-1　　**$6.50**US/**$8.50**CAN
By Karen Roebuck

Lobster Boy　　0-7860-1569-1　　**$6.50**US/**$8.50**CAN
By Fred Rosen

Body Dump　　0-7860-1133-5　　**$6.50**US/**$8.50**CAN
By Fred Rosen

Savage　　0-7860-1409-1　　**$6.50**US/**$8.50**CAN
By Robert Scott

Innocent Victims　　0-7860-1273-0　　**$6.50**US/**$8.50**CAN
By Brian J. Karem

The Boy Next Door　　0-7860-1459-8　　**$6.50**US/**$8.50**CAN
By Gretchen Brinck

Available Wherever Books Are Sold!

Visit our website at **www.kensingtonbooks.com**.